PEARSON CUSTOM
Education

EDUC 100
Issues in Education

Keene State College
School of Professional & Graduate Studies

Pearson Learning Solutions

New York   Boston   San Francisco
London   Toronto   Sydney   Tokyo   Singapore   Madrid
Mexico City   Munich   Paris   Cape Town   Hong Kong   Montreal

Senior Vice President, Editorial and Marketing: Patrick F. Boles
Senior Sponsoring Editor: Natalie Danner
Development Editor: Abbey Briggs
Assistant Editor: Jill Johnson
Operations Manager: Eric M. Kenney
Production Manager: Jennifer Berry
Art Director: Renée Sartell
Cover Designer: Kristen Kiley

Cover photograph: Appian Gateway, along Main Street in Keene,
By Chris Justice/KSC College and Media Relations Office.

Please visit our website at *www.pearsoncustom.com.*

Attention bookstores: For permission to return any unsold stock, contact us at *pe-uscustomreturns@pearson.com.*

Pearson Learning Solutions, 501 Boylston Street, Suite 900, Boston, MA 02116
A Pearson Education Company
www.pearsoned.com

ISBN 10: 1-256-03987-X
ISBN 13: 978-1-256-03987-7

Contents

Teachers and the Teaching Profession

In *Meet the Focus Teachers and Students* you were introduced to 10 focus teachers with whom you will interact throughout this text. Getting to know our focus teachers helps you explore how accomplished lifelong learners approach the classroom and the profession of teaching. Among the many questions to consider about teachers and teaching, here are some we address:

✦ Who teaches in the United States and why?

✦ How do we prepare to teach?

✦ Is teaching a profession?

✦ What is teacher professionalism?

✦ What are the characteristics of effective teachers?

No African tribe is considered to have warriors more fearsome or more intelligent than the Masai. It is perhaps surprising, then, to discover that the traditional greeting between Masai warriors is *Kasserian ingera*, which means "And how are the children?"

This traditional tribal greeting acknowledges the high value the Masai place on their children's well-being. Even warriors with no children of their own give the traditional answer, "All the children are well," meaning that peace and safety prevail, that the priority of protecting the young, the powerless, is in place, that Masai society has not forgotten its proper function and responsibility, its reason for being. "All the children are well" means that life is good.

If we greeted each other with this same daily question, "And how are the children?" how might it affect our awareness of children's welfare in the United States? If we asked this question of each other a dozen times a day, would it begin to make a difference in the reality of how children are thought of and cared for in the United States?

If everyone among us, teacher and nonteacher, parent and nonparent, comes to feel a shared sense of responsibility for the daily care and protection of all the children in our community, in our town, in our state, in our country, we might truly be able to answer without hesitation, "The children are well. Yes, all the children are well."

Sara Davis Powell

Shutterstock

Where
DO I Stand?

This inventory helps you explore your personal reasons for considering teaching as a career. Read each item and decide how meaningful it is to you. If an item resonates very strongly within you, then choose "4: I strongly agree." Reserve a choice of "4" for those items you genuinely care most about. If you agree with a statement, but are not overly enthusiastic about it, then choose "3: I agree." If you really don't care one way or the other about a statement, choose "2: I don't have an opinion." If you simply disagree with a statement, choose "1: I disagree." If you feel adamantly opposed to a statement, choose "0: I strongly disagree." There are no right or wrong answers, just differing experiences and viewpoints. Following the inventory are directions for how to organize your responses and what they may indicate in terms of where you stand.

4   I strongly agree
3   I agree
2   I don't have an opinion
1   I disagree
0   I strongly disagree

_____ **1.** Some of my fondest memories involve experiences working with children/teens.

_____ **2.** The health insurance and retirement benefits of teaching mean a lot to me.

_____ **3.** In K–12 school I enjoyed and excelled in a particular subject.

_____ **4.** As a teacher, I look forward to growing professionally.

_____ **5.** At least one member of my family is an educator.

_____ **6.** I am considering teaching because I believe education has necessary societal value.

_____ **7.** Teaching is most worthwhile because of the opportunity to influence students.

_____ **8.** Although I may be interested in other professions, the stability of a career in the public school system draws me to teaching.

_____ **9.** Both the daily work hours and the yearly schedule of a teacher appeal to me.

_____ **10.** Doing the same thing in the same way repeatedly does not appeal to me.

_____ **11.** My desire to teach is based on my love of a particular subject.

_____ **12.** There was a teacher in my K–12 experiences who had a profound impact on my life.

_____ **13.** My family is pleased with my decision to teach.

_____ **14.** A teacher's primary task is to help students become productive citizens.

_____ **15.** Being with children/adolescents is something I enjoy and look forward to.

_____ **16.** I am anxious to read whatever I can about the teaching profession.

_____ **17.** A major reason for choosing the teaching profession is the appeal of having holidays and spring break time off.

_____ **18.** Being a teacher means always having a job.

_____ **19.** Education is necessary for the continued success of our country.

_____ **20.** I have very fond memories of my relationship with one or more teachers in K–12 school.

_____ **21.** Having a long summer vacation means a lot to me.

_____ **22.** I have been drawn to a particular subject area for years.

_____ **23.** Professional self-growth motivates me.

_____ **24.** I am interested in teaching because I want to work with children and/or adolescents.

_____ **25.** I plan to teach because someone in my family is encouraging my choice.

_____ **26.** I want to teach because of the promise of job security.

_____ **27.** Being a camp counselor appeals to me.

_____ **28.** I want to teach to positively benefit society.

_____ **29.** Content knowledge is the primary goal of education.

_____ **30.** Someone in my family enjoys teaching and relays positive stories about the profession.

_____ **31.** I would like to be able to personally thank a former teacher for influencing me to be a teacher.

_____ **32.** I like the idea of having days off when my own children will also have time off.

_____ **33.** I have a passion for a content area.

_____ **34.** Even in difficult economic times, the fact that teachers will always be needed appeals to me.

_____ **35.** My family values education and emphasizes the worth of teachers.

_____ **36.** My career goal is to emulate a teacher I have known.

_____ **37.** Without quality public education our society suffers.

_____ **38.** I am still in touch with at least one of my K–12 teachers.

_____ **39.** Being home by about 4 P.M. is important to me.

_____ **40.** Teaching appeals to me most because I love to learn new things.

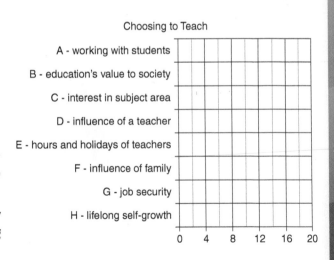

In the tables, record the number, 0 to 4, that you responded for each indicated item. Then find the sum for each table's responses.

ITEM #	MY #	ITEM #	MY #	ITEM #	MY #	ITEM #	MY #	ITEM #	MY #	ITEM #	MY #	ITEM #	MY #	ITEM #	MY #
1		6		3		12		9		5		2		4	
7		14		11		20		17		13		8		10	
15		19		22		31		21		25		18		16	
24		28		29		36		32		30		26		23	
27		37		33		38		39		35		34		40	
Sum A		Sum B		Sum C		Sum D		Sum E		Sum F		Sum G		Sum H	

Now it's time to graph your responses. Mark and then shade your sums on the Choosing to Teach _bar graph. The results show how much you value, relatively speaking, eight reasons for becoming a teacher that we discuss in this chapter. Your instructor may ask you to share your graph with others as part of the exploration of teachers and the teaching profession._

By the end of this book you will have explored many aspects of the teaching profession in very personal ways. As teachers, the better we know ourselves, the closer we come to understanding our students and finding ways to address their needs to help them grow. At the end of this chapter we revisit elements of Where Do I Stand? by responding to follow-up questions in Where Do I Stand Now?

Throughout this book you are asked to respond to ideas and questions. **Points of Reflection** features provide mental exercises that involve you in an extended conversation about teaching. **Reflection** requires us to honestly think about what we believe and do, why we believe it and how we do it, and the consequences of our beliefs and actions.

Are you surprised by your graph? Is this the first time you actually analyzed your reasons for choosing to teach or for at least considering being a teacher?

Choosing to Teach

A - working with students
B - education's value to society
C - interest in subject area
D - influence of a teacher
E - hours and holidays of teachers
F - influence of family
G - job security
H - lifelong self-growth

0   4   8   12   16   20

Teaching in Focus

Traci Peters teaches seventh grade math at Cario Middle School in South Carolina. By all accounts she's an excellent teacher— just ask her principal, her colleagues, and, most importantly, her students. Outside school Traci enjoys a very happy home life with husband Dwayne and young son Robert. The seventh graders in Traci's classes know all about these two very important people in her life, and that's the way Traci wants it. Although math is the subject she has chosen to teach, she is conscious of the fact that her responsibilities go well beyond fractions and equations. She views each student as an individual with relationships and often complex growing-up issues. Traci reveals herself to them, and they, in turn, feel comfortable enough to share with her.

In a prominent place in the classroom Traci has a "Mrs. Peters" bulletin board on which she displays, among other things, family photos (from her childhood to the present), her favorite poems and book titles, her own seventh grade report card, and her 5 x 7 middle school picture. Traci says her students spend lots of time examining the board's contents, laughing and asking questions.

Traci sees herself as a role model of a healthy, positive adult who makes good choices and tries to make a difference in other people's lives. When asked if she would just as freely share with students the not-so-positive aspects of her life, she replies yes. When she's not feeling well, she lets her students know. If her son Robert is sick and she needs to stay home to care for him, she tells her students.

Traci attends her students' basketball games, concerts, spelling bees, Odyssey of the Mind competitions—the typical year-long parade of events. She views this as a tangible way to show her students she is interested in them, their growth, and their lives.

Watch Traci's room tour, as well as her interview, in the Teaching in Focus section for Chapter 1 in MyEducationLab for this course.

Who Teaches in the United States and Why?

Teaching is the largest profession in the United States, with almost 4 million teachers in both public and private schools (National Center for Education Statistics [NCES], 2009). Examine Figure 1.1 to see who teaches in the United States.

Figure 1.1 U.S. teachers

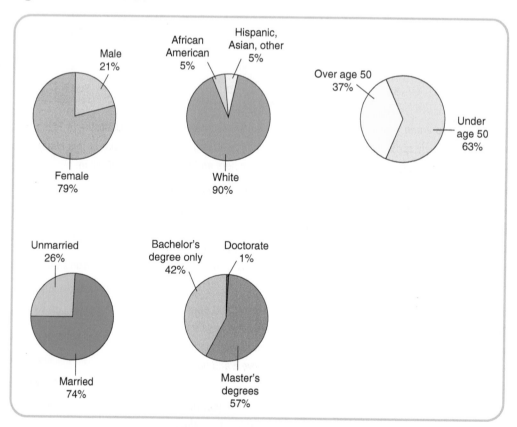

Source: National Education Association. (2003). Status of the American public school teacher 2000–2001. Retrieved May 15, 2005, from www.nea.org/edstats/images/status.pdf.

Teachers and the Teaching Profession

TEACHERS IN THE UNITED STATES

In Figure 1.1 you'll see that teachers are better educated than ever—more than 50% hold master's degrees. About 75% of U.S. teachers are married, 15% are single, and 11% are widowed, divorced, or separated. About a third of teachers have school-age children themselves (National Education Association [NEA], 2003). However, if you ask, they'll all likely tell you they "have" 20 or more children every year!

Also note that most teachers are white and female. There is considerable need for more diversity and gender balance in the teaching force. Do we want to discourage white women from becoming teachers? Absolutely not. Is there a need for more male teachers and teachers from minority population groups? Absolutely yes.

Most people join the teaching profession purposefully. In a large-scale survey of teachers with fewer than 5 years in the classroom, only about 12% said they "fell into teaching by chance." Some enter directly upon graduation from college, and some become teachers after pursuing one or more other careers. This same survey found that most teachers possess a strong inclination toward their career choice: 86% of the surveyed teachers believe that teaching requires a "sense of calling," and 96% say that teaching is work they love to do. The inference is that entering the teaching profession requires a commitment beyond that required by many other careers and, once in the profession, relatively new teachers overwhelmingly view teaching in positive ways (Public Agenda, 2003). But why did they choose to become teachers?

DECIDING TO TEACH

Helping you first make the decision to teach and then find your teaching identity is at the heart of this book. Exploring why other people choose to teach may help you clarify your own thoughts and desires. In 2001 the National Education Association (NEA) surveyed almost a thousand teachers, asking why they chose the teaching profession. The teachers were given a list of 21 possible reasons and asked to choose their top 3. Our discussion of the reasons for choosing to teach is organized around the eight reasons most often chosen by the teachers in the survey. As you read, think about your own reasons for considering teaching as your career.

DESIRE TO WORK WITH YOUNG PEOPLE.
Because 6 to 7 hours of a teacher's day are spent in direct contact with students, enjoying their company is a must. Getting to know the students we teach allows us to become familiar with their emotional and social needs as well as their cognitive needs. You may hear teachers talk about teaching the **whole child**. This simply means attending to all their developmental stages and needs, along with teaching them grade-level and subject-area content. When we view the whole child, we realize the depth of our responsibilities as classroom teachers.

VALUE OF EDUCATION TO SOCIETY.
Education is widely viewed as the great equalizer. This means that differences in opportunity and privilege diminish as children reach their potential through quality education. In other words, the achievement gap narrows with the

Traci Peters values young adolescents as individuals and develops strong positive relationships with them. Sara Davis Powell

increased educational success of the students who historically underachieve. An **achievement gap** is a disparity among students, as some excel while others languish with respect to learning and academic success. Through teaching you will make a difference in the lives of individuals and thereby benefit society as a whole.

INTEREST IN SUBJECT MATTER. According to the National Education Association (2003), high school teachers choose "interest in subject matter" more often than elementary teachers. An intense interest in a subject area is important if you are going to teach that subject all day. Middle school is a happy compromise for people who have both a strong desire to work with students and a passion for a specific subject. Most middle school teachers teach one or possibly two subjects all day to students whose development is challenging and intriguing.

INFLUENCE OF TEACHERS. Can you name the last five vice presidents of the United States? How about the current Miss America? Who represents your home district in the state legislature? Who was your fifth grade teacher? Who taught your favorite class when you were a freshman in high school? The last two questions are the easiest, aren't they? That's because teachers influence us. They are uniquely positioned to shape students' thoughts and interests during the formative years of childhood and adolescence.

LONG SUMMER VACATION. A joke that's been around for a long time goes like this: "What are the three best things about teaching?" Answer: "June, July, August." Here's another. "What's the best time to be a teacher?" Answer: "Friday at 4." Within our ranks we smile at these harmless jokes.

Those who have not taught, or don't understand the pressure of having 15 or 25 or even 100 students dependent on them for at least part of each day, may view the schedule of a teacher as excessively punctuated with days off. However, time away from school is well deserved, even if it is used to catch up on teaching-related tasks. The change of pace is refreshing, allowing opportunities for revitalization.

Aside from summer vacation and days off, other aspects of scheduling make teaching a desirable choice for many. During the school year most teachers do not have students after about 3:30 in the afternoon. To people who work 8 to 5 jobs, 3:30 seems like a luxury. However, most teachers spend additional time either at school or at home planning for the next day and completing necessary administrative tasks. The teaching schedule allows for this kind of flexibility. A teacher's schedule is also ideal for families with school-age children. Having a daily routine similar to that of other family members has definite benefits.

INFLUENCE OF FAMILY. Most of us who consider being teachers grew up in families that valued education and respected teachers. If there are teachers in your family who are energetic and enthusiastic about their careers, they may influence you to follow in their footsteps.

JOB SECURITY. We will always need teachers. Those who are competent are generally assured positions even in difficult economic times. Other benefits related to job security include the availability of group health insurance and a reasonable retirement plan. It's unlikely that a career in teaching is chosen because of salary, although some districts and states are making progress in raising teachers' pay to be competitive with other fields that require a bachelor's degree. Table 1.1 shows average teacher salaries by state.

In almost all states and school districts, teachers are paid for both longevity in the profession and levels of education completed. A beginning teacher with a master's degree will receive a higher salary than a beginning teacher with a bachelor's degree. Two teachers with bachelor's degrees will be paid differently if one has 3 years of teaching experience and the other has 15 years in the classroom. In most cases, the fact that the teacher with 3 years can point to contributing to outstanding verifiable improvement and student achievement whereas the more experienced teacher has little to show with regard to influencing measurable student learning makes no difference in compensation. Is this fair? No. Have we found ways to measure student growth and pay teachers accordingly? Some ideas exist. But for decades school systems have tried to pay teachers based on performance, or

Teachers and the Teaching Profession

TABLE 1.1 Average teacher salaries, 2006–2007

Rank	State	Salary	Rank	State	Salary
1	California	$63,640	26	Wisconsin	$46,707
2	Connecticut	$61,039	27	North Carolina	$46,137
3	New Jersey	$59,730	28	Colorado	$45,832
4	New York	$59,557	29	Texas	$45,392
5	Rhode Island	$58,420	30	Idaho	$45,094
6	Illinois	$58,275	31	Arizona	$44,700
7	Massachusetts	$58,178	32	Arkansas	$44,493
8	Maryland	$56,927	33	South Carolina	$44,355
9	Michigan	$55,541	34	Tennessee	$43,815
10	Pennsylvania	$54,977	35	Kentucky	$43,787
11	Alaska	$54,678	36	Alabama	$43,389
12	Delaware	$54,537	37	Kansas	$43,318
13	Ohio	$53,536	38	Iowa	$42,922
14	Hawaii	$51,916	39	Louisiana	$42,816
15	Oregon	$51,080	40	New Mexico	$42,780
16	Wyoming	$50,771	41	Oklahoma	$42,379
17	Georgia	$49,836	42	Maine	$42,103
18	Minnesota	$49,719	43	Nebraska	$42,044
19	Nevada	$49,426	44	Montana	$41,146
20	Virginia	$49,130	45	West Virginia	$40,534
21	Washington	$47,880	46	Missouri	$40,384
22	Indiana	$47,832	47	Mississippi	$40,182
23	Vermont	$47,645	48	North Dakota	$38,586
24	Florida	$47,219	49	Utah	$37,775
25	New Hampshire	$46,797	50	South Dakota	$35,378
	U.S. average	**$51,009**			

Source: American Federation of Teachers (2008).

merit, but without the kind of success that perpetuates merit pay to the satisfaction of those affected, the teachers themselves.

When considering salary, investigate the cost of living where you want to live. For example, in 2005, thousands of experienced teachers in the suburbs outside New York City made more than $100,000 a year (Fessenden & Barbanel, 2005). However, an examination of the cost of living in such places as Westchester County, New York, shows that $100,000 there is equivalent to a much lower salary in most of small-town America.

OPPORTUNITY FOR A LIFETIME OF SELF-GROWTH. This is exactly what teaching offers. Few careers are as exciting or as rewarding on a daily basis, including the satisfaction of positively impacting the future of children. Teachers experience growth, both personally and professionally, in many ways: through relationships, reading, attending conferences, and the wide variety of professional development opportunities available. Teaching is not a stagnant career; rather, it continually presents new experiences, all of which offer opportunities for self-growth.

Sonia Nieto (2009), a respected educator and writer, offers additional, and perhaps more intriguing, reasons for becoming and remaining a teacher in Figure 1.2. Nieto's reasons are somewhat more complex than the eight we just explored and require thoughtful consideration. All of the reasons for choosing to teach are positive of course. Yet only discussing all the benefits and rewards of teaching presents a picture that's out of balance. No career is without challenges; no career is without frustration.

Points of Reflection 1.1

We've looked at eight reasons for choosing teaching as a career. Which are your top three reasons for considering the teaching profession and why?

Figure 1.2 Additional reasons for choosing to teach

Desire to engage in intellectual work
Belief in the democratic potential of public education
Anger at the current conditions of education
Sense of mission
Empathy for students
Enjoyment of improvisation
Comfort with uncertainty
Passion for social justice

Source: From S. Nieto (2009). From surviving to thriving. *Educational Leadership, 66*(5), 8–13.

Brandi Wade, one of our focus teachers at Summit Primary School in Ohio, tells us that perhaps we don't choose teaching, but rather teaching *chooses us.* Read about her philosophy in **_Teaching in Focus_**.

TEACHER SATISFACTION

Regardless of why teachers choose their profession, few will remain if their choice is not satisfying. As in any life's work, there are good days and bad, successes and failures, questions with answers often difficult to find. Talking with real teachers who spend their days with real students yields stories and opinions as varied as the individuals themselves.

For over 25 years MetLife, Inc. has surveyed teachers, encouraging them to express their opinions about many aspects of teaching. Teacher responses concerning their satisfaction with the teaching profession in Figure 1.3 are revealing and encouraging. The graphic depicts a comparison between teacher views in 1984 and teacher views in 2008. In both years teachers said they love to teach at the same rate, 82%. That's where the similarities end. As you can see, in responses to every other statement, teachers were significantly more positive about their profession in 2008 than in 1984, with three quarters of the teachers in 2008 saying they would advise others to enter the profession.

Teaching in Focus

Brandi Wade, kindergarten, Summit Primary, Ohio. *In her own words. . . .*

It may not so much be that you choose teaching, but that teaching chooses you. It will be in your heart and on your mind constantly. Although it's never easy for more than 5 minutes at a time, teaching is the most important profession you can pursue. I am truly blessed to be a kindergarten teacher. I get to teach a different lesson, meet a different challenge, and see life from different perspectives every day in my classroom.

Laugh with the children, laugh at yourself, and never hold a grudge. Don't be afraid to say "I'm sorry" to a child when you have done something unprofessional or hurtful. If children do hurtful things, just hug them a little more tightly and make them feel safe. Children learn best when they feel safe and loved no matter what.

Sara Davis Powell

I don't teach to be remembered, although it's nice to think that you'll never be completely forgotten. I teach so that I can remember. I remember their personalities and how they grow. I remember the times we struggled with learning and succeeded, as well as those times when we fell short of our goals. I remember the laughter and the tears we shared.

Some people say, "Leave school at school." The best teachers I know often lose sleep thinking about and worrying about their students. It's worth every toss and turn!

Figure 1.3 25-year perspective on teacher satisfaction

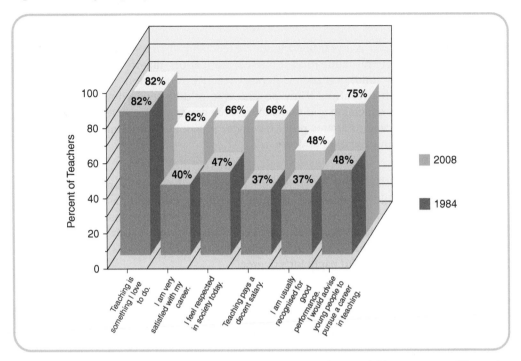

Source: MetLife. (2008). The MetLife survey of the American teacher. Available at: www.metlife.com/ assets/cao/contributions/foundation/american-teacher/ MetLife_Teacher_Survey_2009.pdf.

How Do We Prepare to Teach?

You may have heard it said of someone, "He's just a natural-born teacher." There's some truth in this statement. Teaching comes more naturally to some than to others. With varying degrees of natural talent and inclination for teaching, we all have much to do to prepare to effectively make the teaching and learning connection. Our nature-given attributes must be enhanced by the knowledge and skills gained through studying content, learning about theory and methods of teaching, being mentored, reading, observing, practicing, and reflecting.

Each state has its own preparation requirements for those who teach in public school classrooms. Most states require a prospective teacher to pass a test before they grant certification or licensure. The most widely used tests are part of the **Praxis Series** published by the Educational Testing Service (ETS). The state issues a teaching certificate or license when a teacher candidate is determined to be sufficiently qualified. Let's examine two broad paths to initial teacher preparation: traditional and alternative.

TRADITIONAL PATHS TO TEACHER PREPARATION

The traditional paths to initial teacher preparation come through a university department of education. National and state organizations carefully scrutinize university programs and evaluate how teacher candidates are prepared. About two thirds of states require university teacher education programs to be accredited (authorized to prepare teachers) through the **National Council for Accreditation of Teacher Education (NCATE)**.

All three of the following initial teacher preparation paths—bachelor's degree, fifth-year program, master's degree—include one or two semesters of **student teaching,** also called **clinical internship**. During this extended fieldwork, teacher candidates teach lessons and, for a designated time frame, take over all classroom duties. A classroom teacher

Teachers and the Teaching Profession

serves as the **cooperating teacher** (host and mentor) while a university instructor supervises the experience.

BACHELOR'S DEGREE. A 4-year undergraduate teacher preparation program consists of a combination of general education courses, education major courses, and field experiences. Most early childhood and elementary teacher preparation programs result in a degree with a major in education. Many programs in middle-level education result in a degree with a major in education and two subject area concentrations (15 to 24 hours). To teach in high school, most programs require a major in a content area and a minor, or the equivalent of a minor, in education coursework.

FIFTH-YEAR PROGRAM. Some universities offer a fifth-year teacher preparation program. Teacher candidates complete a major other than education and stay for a fifth year for more education coursework plus student teaching. For instance, a teacher candidate interested in science may major in biology and then stay a fifth year to become a certified, or licensed, teacher. Some of these programs include a master of arts in teaching degree rather than an extended bachelor's degree.

MASTER OF ARTS IN TEACHING. People who have a bachelor's degree in an area other than teacher education may pursue teacher preparation through a master of arts in teaching (MAT) degree. Most early childhood and elementary MAT programs consist of all teacher education courses and fieldwork, whereas middle-level MAT programs typically require 18 to 24 hours of subject area coursework in addition to education courses. High school MAT programs generally require a degree in a content area or the accumulation of enough content hours to be considered a concentration.

ALTERNATIVE PATHS TO TEACHER PREPARATION

There is a growing movement toward alternative paths to teacher preparation. In the 1980s alternative certification began as a way to address projected shortages of teachers. Since the first efforts, we have seen various models for recruiting, training, and certifying people who already have at least a bachelor's degree and want to become teachers.

Since 1983 the number of teachers entering the classroom through alternative means has rapidly increased. Now all 50 states offer one or more of over a hundred different programs offering alternative certification/licensure, with some estimates stating that as many as a third of new teachers are using alternative routes to the classroom. Adults who decide that teaching is for them after having other careers are likely to enter the profession through alternative paths (Feistritzer, 2009).

Many alternative programs grow out of specific needs and are developed and coordinated through partnerships among state departments of education, school districts, and university teacher education programs. Their structures vary widely, and they tend to be controversial. Some people doubt that teacher preparation is as effective outside the realm of university-based programs.

Perhaps the most widely known alternative path to the classroom is through the nonprofit organization **Teach for America** (TFA). Teach for America's goal is to increase the number of teachers willing to tackle the challenges of classrooms in low-income areas. TFA recruits individuals who are college seniors or recent graduates who agree to teach in high-needs rural or urban schools for at least 2 years in exchange for a salary plus reduction or elimination of college debt. In 2009 there were over 7,000 TFA teachers (Teach for America, 2010).

Diversity is an issue when hiring teachers, regardless of how they are prepared. Read about Mike Larsen's plans to hire a more diverse teaching force at Rees Elementary in *Diversity Dialogue.*

Mike Larsen, principal of Rees Elementary School, Utah

In this text you will read about teachers, students, principals, and schools as they struggle with issues involving diversity. All of the scenarios are based on our focus people and places introduced in *Meet the Focus Teachers and Students*. These *Diversity Dialogues* put what we are discussing in context so you can see how teachers, students, and principals address issues in schools and communities.

Sara Davis Powell

Mike Larsen of Rees Elementary School south of Salt lake City, Utah, is in his first year as principal of this K–5 school. Rees boasts a rich racial and ethnic diversity. The students are white, black, Hispanic, Native American, and Asian, all the broad racial distinctions recognized by the federal government. Their **ethnicities,** or where their families come from, represent an even greater spectrum of diversity.

Rees is a very good school as determined by multiple measures. The students achieve at levels above the state average, there are few real discipline issues, the facilities are more than adequate, and the teaching staff is both effective and stable. Mr. Larsen is quite pleased to have been appointed principal of such a school. If he simply maintained the status quo Rees would hum along just fine. But one thing bothers him. Although he considers every one of the Rees teachers to be good teachers, Mr. Larsen is concerned that the profile of the teaching staff closely mirrors the national average. Of the 45 teachers, 36 (80%) are female and 42 (92%) are white.

In March of his first year at Rees, Mr. Larsen finds out that three of his teachers are not returning to Rees in August. Two teachers plan to retire and one is marrying a Marine and moving to San Diego. All three are white. Mr. Larsen immediately recognizes an opportunity to introduce more diversity into the Rees teaching staff.

Respond to these items by writing one well-developed paragraph for each.

1. Mr. Larsen is aware that at Rees the tradition is for an entire grade level of teachers to spend time with candidates for teaching positions. The openings will be in second grade, fourth grade, and on one of the third/fourth/fifth grade multiage teams. Mr. Larsen plans to meet with each group of teachers to express his desire to hire teachers who are more diverse. What kinds of things might he say to the groups?

2. Mr. Larsen plans to do some recruiting at local colleges. Why might he find a more diverse pool of teacher candidates in alternative programs?

GETTING TO KNOW SCHOOLS, TEACHERS, AND STUDENTS

Regardless of the route you take to become a teacher, the more experiences you have in schools with teachers and students, the better prepared you will be to have a classroom of your own. The more experiences you have, the more certain your decision will be concerning whether teaching is for you. Experience in classrooms will also lead to more informed decision making about your teaching identity.

Most preparation programs require field experiences throughout. You may begin with observations in one course and then work with individual students and small groups in another, with whole group lessons before and during student teaching/clinical practice. These experiences may hold many surprises for you. Having a 5-year-old nephew you enjoy seeing several times a year is very different from working all day with 20 5-year-olds in a kindergarten classroom. Your memories of senior advanced placement literature that inspired you to want to teach high school English may be a romantic picture of students paying rapt attention as the sonnets of Elizabeth Barrett Browning are discussed. However, this may be a far cry from an actual freshman English class. If you fit the profile of most teachers and are a white woman from suburbia, chances are classrooms in urban America will expand your view of what it's like to be a teacher. You can read about differences in settings and students in this and other books and be somewhat informed. Seeing for yourself brings reality into view.

The Teaching in Focus videos aligned with this text allow you inside four real schools to get to know 10 real teachers and 12 real students. The videos may be accessed through MyEducationLab for this course.

Teachers and the Teaching Profession

Preparing to teach requires reflection on the many roles involved in the profession. Sara Davis Powell

There are other ways to gain insights into the classroom. Finding opportunities to have conversations with teachers is an excellent way to learn more about the realities of the classroom. Volunteering at schools, places of worship, and community organizations will present opportunities both to get to know kids and to observe adults interacting with them. Being a summer camp counselor, tutoring in an after-school program, and coaching in community recreation leagues all provide valuable experiences.

Is Teaching a Profession?

This text repeatedly refers to teaching as the *teaching profession*. Whether a particular job or career qualifies as a **profession** depends, in large measure, on who is making the determination. We hear references to the plumbing profession, the culinary profession, the cosmetology profession, but there are established guidelines for determining if a career or job is universally considered a profession. These characteristics of a profession will likely not affect common usage of the word, but examining teaching with regard to them helps spotlight aspects of what we do that may need to be strengthened.

CHARACTERISTICS OF A PROFESSION

For decades authors have delineated characteristics of a "full" profession. For equally as long, educators and others have debated whether teaching is indeed a profession. This debate is healthy because as we consider the characteristics of a profession and measure teaching by them, we see what teaching is and is not, what teachers have evolved into, and what teachers may still need to become. A summary of a full profession's characteristics, from both a historical perspective and a modern one, is presented in Figure 1.4. Let's look briefly at these 10 characteristics and think about whether each applies to teaching.

Considering that in the United States children ages 5 through 16 are required to receive a formal education, and that most do this through public schools, a dedicated teaching workforce can collectively deliver this *essential service* (1). Members of this teaching workforce agree that teaching requires *unique knowledge and skills* (2), whether acquired through traditional or alternative paths. On-the-job *training, ongoing study* (2), and development are encouraged, but not necessarily required, although most teachers must renew their teaching

Figure 1.4 Characteristics of a full profession

1. Provides an essential service no other group can provide.
2. Requires unique knowledge and skills acquired through extensive initial and ongoing study/training.
3. Involves intellectual work in the performance of duties.
4. Individual practitioners are committed to service and continual competence.
5. Identified performance standards guide practice.
6. Self-governance in admitting, policing, and excluding members.
7. Allows for a considerable amount of autonomy and decision-making authority.
8. Members accept individual responsibility for actions and decisions.
9. Enjoys prestige, public trust.
10. Granted higher-than-average financial rewards.

Sources: Howsam et al. (1976); Ingersoll (1997); Rowan (1994); Webb, Metha, and Jordan (2007).

Teachers and the Teaching Profession

certification/license every 5 years or so by completing graduate coursework or participating in other forms of professional development.

Teaching definitely *involves intellectual work* (3). Teachers pass along intellectual concepts and skills, which is the very heart of what teachers do. To enter and remain in a teaching career requires a *commitment to service* (4) and, hopefully, *continual competence* (4) as guided and measured by *performance standards* (5). The word "hopefully" is included because teachers rarely *police their own ranks* (6) to the point of excluding someone who does not live up to accepted teacher standards. If policing occurs, it is generally accomplished by administrators.

When the classroom door closes, teachers have a great deal of *autonomy* (7), sometimes approaching isolation. However, public school teachers must accept any student placed in their classrooms and must teach a set curriculum over which they have little or no control. Even with certain constraints, we are *decision makers* (7), and we must *accept individual responsibility* (8) for the decisions we make.

A great level of *trust* (9) is placed in teachers. After all, for 7 to 10 hours a day families allow teachers to have almost exclusive control over their children. In most communities, teachers enjoy a degree of positional *prestige* (9), but they are rarely *granted higher-than-average financial rewards* (10).

As you can see, not all 10 characteristics of a full profession apply to teaching. We still have few mechanisms for policing our own ranks (6), and the financial rewards of teaching are not higher than average (10). Teachers should continue to work together to perpetuate each of the eight characteristics we exemplify while exploring ways to incorporate the other two. Many associations and organizations are helping teaching to be a profession by allowing teachers through collaborative efforts to set common goals, speak with a collective voice, and build research-based foundations to support what we do and how we do it.

PROFESSIONAL ASSOCIATIONS

National and regional professional associations provide leadership and support for teachers. Some serve the general teacher population; others are specific to a grade span or subject area. Most associations solicit members, hold annual conferences, publish materials, provide information, and advocate for those who teach and those who learn. Participating in professional organizations is a positive step toward growing as a professional.

The **National Education Association (NEA)** and the **American Federation of Teachers (AFT)** are the largest professional education associations in the United States, with a total of more than 5 million members, including teachers, administrators, professors, counselors, and other educators. Both organizations are unions and represent their members in **collective bargaining,** or negotiating with employers and states to gain additional benefits for their members. Large nonunion professional organizations such as ASCD Learn. Teach. Lead., Kappa Delta Pi (KDP), and the Council for Exceptional Children (CEC) serve a wide spectrum of educators. Most national organizations have regional and state affiliate associations. These more local groups provide easily accessible face-to-face opportunities for interaction among members.

An organization that specifically deals with the needs of, and standards for, beginning teachers is the **Interstate New Teacher Assessment and Support Consortium** (INTASC, 1992). The standards endorsed by INTASC address what beginning teachers should know and be able to do. They provide the framework for beginning teacher performance.

Each subject area has a professional organization that provides guidelines for what to teach, sponsors annual conferences, publishes relevant books and journals, represents subject areas in educational and political arenas, and both encourages and disseminates research on teaching and learning. Table 1.2 lists some of the professional associations available to teachers to assist with their professionalism. Visiting their Web sites will give you valuable insight into just how important these, and other professional organizations, are and can be.

TABLE 1.2 Professional Organizations

Teacher Unions

AFT	American Federation of Teachers	www.aft.org
NEA	National Education Association	www.nea.org

Subject-Area Organizations

AAHPERD	American Alliance for Health, Physical Education, Recreation and Dance	www.aahperd.org
ACTFL	American Council on the Teaching of Foreign Languages	www.actfl.org
IRA	International Reading Association	www.reading.org
MTNA	Music Teachers National Association	www.mtna.org
NAEA	National Art Education Association	www.naea-reston.org
NATIE	National Association for Trade and Industrial Education	www.skillsusa.org/NATIE/
NBEA	National Business Education Association	www.nbea.org
NCSS	National Council for the Social Studies	www.ncss.org
NCTE	National Council of Teachers of English	www.ncte.org
NCTM	National Council of Teachers of Mathematics	www.nctm.org
NSTA	National Science Teachers Association	www.nsta.org/
RIF	Reading Is Fundamental	www.rif.org

Level-Specific Organizations

ACEI	Association for Childhood Education International	www.acei.org
NAEYC	National Association for the Education of Young Children	www.naeyc.org
NMSA	National Middle School Association	www.nmsa.org

Need-Specific Organizations

INTASC	Interstate New Teacher Assessment and Support Consortium	www.intasc.org
CEC	Council for Exceptional Children	www.cec.sped.org
NAGC	National Association for Gifted Children	www.nagc.org
SCA	Speech Communication Association	www.isca-speech.org
TESOL	Teachers of English to Speakers of Other Languages	www.tesol.org

General Associations

ASCD	ASCD Learn. Teach. Lead.	www.ascd.org
KDP	Kappa Delta Pi	www.kdp.org
PDK	Phi Delta Kappa	www.pdkintl.org

What Is Teacher Professionalism?

Professionalism is a way of being. It involves attitudes and actions that convey respect, uphold high standards, and demonstrate commitment to those served. Fulfilling responsibilities and making the most of growth opportunities are core aspects of teacher professionalism. Patricia Phelps, former academic editor of the *Kappa Delta Pi Record* (a publication of KDP), presents a philosophical framework within which characteristics of teacher professionalism may be placed. Phelps (2003) states that teachers achieve greater levels of professionalism when they are willing to do what it takes, to do what must be done. In other words, professionalism involves hard work. This hard work requires commitment in three broad areas.

COMMITMENT TO MAKE STUDENTS OUR FIRST PRIORITY

Student welfare and learning must be paramount. Ask yourself, as a Masai might, "And how are the children? Are they all well?" Putting students first requires that we become advocates for their welfare.

ADVOCATING FOR STUDENTS. To be an **advocate for students** is to support and defend them, always putting their needs first. How do we become advocates for our students? Here are some components of advocacy to consider.

- Understand that advocacy takes multiple forms with individuals, groups, or causes, in both large endeavors and small actions.
- In all conversations, with educators and noneducators alike, keep the focus on what's best for students.
- Take an informed stance on issues that affect children. Actively promote that stance to have widespread impact.
- Support families in every way possible.

Advocacy guides our efforts and decisions directly toward our goal—improving students' learning, which, ultimately, improves students' lives.

MAKING WISE DECISIONS. As teachers we continually make decisions. Some of the decisions are made on autopilot, especially those that have to do with routines in the classroom. The quality of other decisions often rests on common sense and maturity, characteristics that are enhanced by preparation and experience. It's important to remember that our decisions have consequences and require thoughtful consideration to make sure we are advocating for our students and maintaining a classroom climate that is conducive to learning.

DETERMINING CLASSROOM CLIMATE. Our classrooms can be respectful environments that promote learning, or not. The sobering words of Haim Ginott (1993), a respected teacher and psychologist, should occupy a prominent position in both your classroom and your consciousness.

I've come to a frightening conclusion. I am the decisive element in the classroom. It's my personal approach that creates the climate. It's my daily mood that makes the weather. As a teacher, I possess a tremendous power to make a child's life miserable or joyous. I can be a tool of torture or an instrument of inspiration. I can humiliate or humor, hurt or heal. In all situations, it is my response that decides whether a crisis will be escalated or de-escalated, a child humanized or de-humanized.

Points of Reflection 1.2

Does the commitment to put students first sound like something you are willing to do? Explain the reason(s) for your answer.

Advocating for students is important at all grade levels. Renee, a second grade teacher, and her twin sister, Tara, a high school physics teacher, both advocate for their students in developmentally appropriate ways.
Sara Davis Powell

Teachers and the Teaching Profession

COMMITMENT TO QUALITY

Quality should characterize our knowledge of content and our relationships and interactions with students, colleagues, administrators and families. Phelps (2003) tells us that "modeling quality is the most significant way to motivate others to put forth the same effort" (p. 10). Modeling quality requires that we have positive and productive values leading to teaching that facilitates learning.

FACILITATING LEARNING. Making the teaching and learning connection is the primary role of a teacher. Learning is why students are in school, and teaching is how we guide and facilitate learning. Our effectiveness as teachers should be measured by how much and how thoroughly students learn.

We can categorize the responsibilities involved in facilitating learning in a number of valid ways. Perhaps none is more important than evaluating each of our actions in terms of its contribution to academic rigor and developmental appropriateness. **Academic rigor** refers both to teaching meaningful content and to having high expectations for student learning. **Developmental appropriateness** means that our teaching addresses students' physical, cognitive, social, emotional, and character development. Academic rigor without developmental appropriateness will result in frustration for teachers and foster discouragement and defeatism in students. Developmental appropriateness without academic rigor will accomplish little in terms of student learning. Neither concept is mutually exclusive. In fact, they shouldn't be exclusive at all but rather should interact in supportive ways and balance one another as they guide our decision making.

Points of Reflection 1.3

Are these dispositions part of your personal beliefs? What other dispositions do you think contribute to being a teacher who promotes academic rigor and development appropriateness?

DEVELOPING DISPOSITIONS. **Dispositions** are composed of our attitudes, values, and beliefs. They powerfully influence our teaching approaches and actions. Dispositions that are favorable to effective teaching include, among many others:

- I believe all students can learn.
- I value student diversity.
- I respect individual students and their families.
- I am enthusiastic about the subjects I teach.
- I value other teachers as colleagues and partners in teaching and learning.
- I believe families are important in making the teaching and learning connection.

COMMITMENT TO CONTINUAL GROWTH

Teacher effectiveness is enhanced when a lifelong learning orientation is in place. A commitment to continual growth provides a powerful model for students.

BECOMING A REFLECTIVE PRACTITIONER. We grow when we reflect on our teaching practices. As discussed earlier in this chapter, reflection with regard to teaching is thinking about what we do, how we do it, and the consequences of our actions or inactions, all with the goal of being better teachers. To be **reflective practitioners** means that we deliberately think about our practice, that is, what we do as teachers. We do this with the purpose of analysis and improvement. Sounds pretty automatic and unavoidable, doesn't it? But it's not. A teacher can repeatedly go through the motions of planning, teaching, and assessing throughout a career yet seldom engage in reflection that results in improved practice.

John Dewey (1933), one of the great American educators, described reflection using words such as *active, persistent*, and *careful*. So how do we become reflective practitioners who actively, persistently, and carefully think about how we teach? Here are some concepts to consider:

- Reflective practice requires conscious effort.
- Self-knowledge is vital and can be aided by thoughtfully completing the *Points of Reflection* throughout this text.

- Reading about and researching aspects of teaching will ground our practice and provide subject matter on which to reflect.
- Talking with other educators will both inform and strengthen what we do and how we do it.
- Being deliberate—doing what we do for a reason—will result in better decisions based on reflection.

21ST-CENTURY KNOWLEDGE AND SKILLS. Teachers committed to continual growth are determined to increase their knowledge and skills to keep up with current research and thought concerning teaching practices. During the first decade of the 21st century some major forces both inside of, and external to, the education community recognized and espoused the need for knowledge and skills that reflect the realities of the 21st-century world. Perhaps the most influential source of information about teacher and learner characteristics for the new century is the **Partnership for 21st Century Skills (P21)**.

In 2009 there were 14 states officially and voluntarily aligned with the Partnership for 21st Century Skills: Arizona, Illinois, Iowa, Kansas, Louisiana, Maine, Massachusetts, Nevada, New Jersey, North Carolina, Ohio, South Dakota, Wisconsin, and West Virginia. On the P21 Web site we find the organization's self-description. "The Partnership for 21st Century Skills has emerged as the leading advocacy organization focused on infusing 21st century skills into education. Bringing together the business community, education leaders, and policymakers, we have defined a powerful vision for 21st century education to ensure every child's success as citizens and workers in the 21st century" (Partnership for 21st Century Skills, 2009).

The Partnership for 21st Century Skills outlines characteristics of teachers that help them teach students in ways that lead to success, including

- Critical thinker
- Problem solver
- Innovator
- Effective communicator
- Effective collaborator
- Self-directed learner
- Information and media literate
- Globally aware
- Civically engaged
- Health conscious
- Financially and economically literate

These are characteristics for teachers to spend their careers developing and improving. A commitment to continual growth requires it.

DELAWARE VISION 2015

Teacher professionalism is required for any large-scale education initiative to succeed. Vision 2015 is Delaware's plan to transform its public education system, focusing on student achievement, fairness, and accountability. To accomplish this transformation, teachers who exemplify Phelps's three areas of professional commitment—putting students first, quality, continual growth—are absolutely necessary.

Delaware's stated goal is to create the best schools for every student, no exceptions and no excuses. In other words, Vision 2015 calls for professional educators to respect the uniqueness of each student and provide the schools necessary for all students to succeed. Delaware proposes to make the changes necessary closest to the students—in the

Points of Reflection 1.4

Do you have a desire to continually grow professionally and personally? If so, how do you know? If you are hesitant to answer this question, what areas of your own motivation do you think you need to consider?

schools and in the classrooms—and sets high expectations for every child and every educator. The initiative revolves around six major areas of reform: setting high sights, investing in early childhood education, developing and supporting great teachers, empowering principals to be great school leaders, encouraging innovation and requiring accountability, and establishing a simple and fair funding system (Delaware Department of Education, 2006).

This chapter's *Letter to the Editor* covers a lot of ground, with topics related to Delaware's Vision 2015. The writer suggests that the lofty goals of Vision 2015 will not be accomplished without eliminating ineffective teachers.

Letter to the Editor

This letter appeared in the Wilmington, Delaware, newspaper, the *Wilmington News Journal*.

NOVEMBER 12, 2009 SAME TEACHERS, ADMINISTRATORS WILL NOT GET REFORM JOB DONE

I applaud Marvin "Skip" Schoenhals and his team at Vision 2015 for trying to turn around our public school system here in Delaware and for giving us a report on the current status of education in Delaware.

Unfortunately, his report of some progress contained no quantitative assessments. The only numbers were those related to possible additional federal funding—throwing more money at the problem. Again, unfortunately, the Vision 2015 team is trying to produce a winning team with the same old players (teachers and administrators). Some of these players may well respond favorably to their new coaches.

However, many will probably not, and, at best, will do so grudgingly as new strategies and plays are being developed and attempted to be implemented—these teachers simply carry too much old baggage. In turnaround situations, even the best of coaches will need substantially new players. Players with more talent should be recruited; old players should be given five years to demonstrate new talent or find themselves alternate occupations—they won't make the cut.

Existing players should be given five years to obtain degrees in the subject matter they are teaching—subject matter degrees, not degrees in education or pseudo-subject matter degrees such as physics for non-scientists. All new teachers should be required to have such substantive degrees.

James R. Thomen

Montchanin

Now it's your turn. Write a letter to the editor from the perspective of a future teacher expressing your views concerning the letter writer's concerns. You may comment on any, or all, of the writer's expressed opinions.

The following information and questions may help you frame your thinking but should not limit nor determine what you write.

1. The writer expresses apparent disgust at what he calls "throwing more money at the problem." As a future teacher, how would you answer this common criticism?
2. Does the sports metaphor work in this case? Are there problems with the analogy you want to point out?
3. Is characterizing experienced teachers as "carrying too much baggage" a generalization that's fair? Do you think it likely applies to some teachers?
4. What do you think about the 5-year time frame to demonstrate new talent?
5. Should all teachers, regardless of the grade level they teach, be required to have subject-area degrees as opposed to maybe a degree in elementary education or early childhood education? What about middle and high school teachers?
6. How does what you know about what's considered a full profession relate to the writer's view of getting rid of teachers who are judged to be ineffective?

Write your letter in understandable terminology, remembering that readers of newspaper letters to the editor are citizens who may have limited knowledge of school practices and policies.

Figure 1.5 is a scoring guide that may be used to assess your letter to the editor. It is the same guide that the Educational Testing Service uses to assess the writing portion of the Praxis II *Principles of Learning and Teaching* exam many states require for either initial teacher licensure/certification or at the completion of the first year of teaching. You will refer to Figure 1.5 in subsequent chapters as you write additional letters to the editor.

Figure 1.5 General scoring guide for *Letter to the Editor* features

A response that receives a score of 3:

- Demonstrates a thorough understanding of the aspects of the case that are relevant to the question
- Responds appropriately to all parts of the question
- If an explanation is required, provides a strong explanation that is well supported by relevant evidence
- Demonstrates a strong knowledge of pedagogical concepts, theories, facts, procedures, or methodologies relevant to the question

A response that receives a score of 2:

- Demonstrates a basic understanding of the aspects of the case that are relevant to the question
- Responds appropriately to one portion of the question
- If an explanation is required, provides a weak explanation that is supported by relevant evidence
- Demonstrates some knowledge of pedagogical concepts, theories, facts, procedures, or methodologies relevant to the question

A response that receives a score of 1:

- Demonstrates misunderstanding of the aspects of the case that are relevant to the question
- Fails to respond appropriately to the question
- Is not supported by relevant evidence
- Demonstrates little knowledge of pedagogical concepts, theories, facts, procedures, or methodologies relevant to the question

No credit is given for blank or off-topic responses.

Deirdre Huger-McGrew expresses her views about continual professional growth in the *Teaching in Focus*.

This text will continue to refer to a career in teaching as the *teaching profession* and to teachers as *professionals.* Commitment to students, quality, and growth—everything a professional teacher does can be placed within this framework. Remember these three commitments as we examine what it means to be an effective teacher.

Teaching in Focus

Sara Davis Powell

Deirdre Huger-McGrew, language arts/social studies, Cario Middle School, South Carolina. *In her own words. . . .*

Throughout my 12 years as a teacher, I've taken many courses beyond my initial teacher training. I have been involved in teaching-related projects, most by choice and others as directed by my principal to achieve school and district goals. I have taken my professional development personally because I feel it is a part of my responsibility to nurture my growth as a teacher. It is my identity. It is who I am as a teacher. Seeking to enhance my skills makes a difference in my classroom. I take delight in embracing changing views and trying strategies that have the potential to improve my teaching.

What makes athletes, doctors, or lawyers the best in their fields? I believe it is their desire and ability to seek ways to improve what they do as professionals. This gives them an edge. Teachers should want the same. I want to continually accomplish growth-enhancing professional goals.

What Are the Characteristics of Effective Teachers?

"From the moment students enter a school, the most important factor in their success is not the color of the skin or the income of their parents, it's the person standing at the front of the classroom." This powerful statement was made in a speech to the Hispanic Chamber of Commerce in 2009 by President Barack Obama. Sobering, isn't it? The president of the United States is stating what recent research corroborates. Teachers make the most difference when it comes to student learning. Our effectiveness, or lack of it, matters.

The search for a neatly packaged description of an effective teacher dates back for centuries, even millennia. The best we can come up with are lists of characteristics based on observation and available data, along with narrative anecdotal descriptions. There's a lot to be learned from considering a number of perspectives.

Standards for teachers are expectations for what they should know and be able to do. All teacher education standards address teacher effectiveness. School-level organizations such as the National Middle School Association (NMSA) and the Association for Childhood Education International (ACEI) prescribe standards for new teachers. The 10 standards of the Interstate New Teacher Assessment and Support Consortium (INTASC) describe what effective teachers should know and be able to do regardless of the level they teach (Figure 1.6).

The **No Child Left Behind Act of 2001 (NCLB),** the 2001 to 2010 reauthorization of the Elementary and Secondary Education Act, was the most sweeping school legislation in decades. One of the major aspects of NCLB was the requirement that teachers be **highly qualified,** meaning that they have a standard of content knowledge and specialized

Figure 1.6 INTASC standards

1. The teacher understands the central concepts, tools of inquiry, and structures of the discipline(s) he or she teaches and can create learning experiences that make these aspects of subject matter meaningful for students.
2. The teacher understands how children learn and develop and can provide learning opportunities that support their intellectual, social, and personal development.
3. The teacher understands how students differ in their approaches to learning and creates instructional opportunities that are adapted to diverse learners.
4. The teacher understands and uses a variety of instructional strategies to encourage students' development of critical thinking, problem solving, and performance skills.
5. The teacher uses an understanding of individual and group motivation and behavior to create a learning environment that encourages positive social interaction, active engagement in learning, and self-motivation.
6. The teacher uses knowledge of effective verbal, nonverbal, and media communication techniques to foster active inquiry, collaboration, and supportive interaction in the classroom.
7. The teacher plans instruction based upon knowledge of subject matter, students, the community, and curriculum goals.
8. The teacher understands and uses formal and informal assessment strategies to evaluate and ensure the continuous intellectual and social development of the learner.
9. The teacher is a reflective practitioner who continually evaluates the effects of his/her choices and actions on others (students, parents, and other professionals in the learning community) and who actively seeks out opportunities to grow professionally.
10. The teacher fosters relationships with school colleagues, parents, and agencies in the larger community to support students' learning and well-being.

Source: The Interstate New Teacher Assessment and Support Consortium (INTASC) standards were developed by the Council of Chief State School Officers and member states. Copies may be downloaded from the Council's Web site at www.ccsso.org. Council of Chief State School Officers. (1992). *Model standards for beginning teacher licensing, assessment, and development: A resource for state dialogue.* Washington, DC: Author.

preparation for their chosen level. The federal government set guidelines for the quality of teachers in public schools, but each state determines its own policy for what teachers must do to be considered highly qualified. Experienced teachers have options in terms of how to meet the highly qualified stipulations.

WHAT PARENTS SAY ABOUT TEACHER EFFECTIVENESS

In the 41st annual *Phi Delta Kappan/Gallup Poll of the Public's Attitudes Toward the Public Schools*, parents were asked to rank nine teacher traits. From most important to least, the parents polled chose the following:

1. Dedication to, and enthusiasm for, the teaching profession
2. Caring about students
3. Intelligence
4. Ability to communicate, to understand, to relate
5. High moral character
6. Friendliness, good personality, sense of humor
7. Ability to discipline, to be firm and fair
8. Patience
9. Ability to inspire, motivate students (Bushaw & McNee, 2009)

A surprising and welcome statistic to come from the 2009 poll is that 7 of 10 parents report that they would like their children to become public school teachers. This whopping 70% is the highest percentage to respond favorably concerning their own children becoming teachers in over 30 years.

WHAT TEACH FOR AMERICA HAS DISCOVERED ABOUT EFFECTIVE TEACHERS

While attempting to determine why some teachers are significantly more effective than others in facilitating student learning, Teach for America has systematically observed and analyzed the results achieved by TFA teachers. They found some intriguing characteristics linked to teachers who facilitate student learning beyond what might be predicted for the mostly poor, mostly minority, student population taught by TFA teachers. Effective teachers tend to . . .

1. set high, long-term goals for their students
2. perpetually look for ways to improve their effectiveness
3. constantly reevaluate what they are doing
4. recruit students and their families into the teaching and learning process
5. maintain focus, making sure everything they do contributes to student learning
6. plan exhaustively and purposefully
7. refuse to surrender to poverty, bureaucracy, and budgetary shortfalls
8. establish efficient classroom routines
9. possess a relentless mind-set of perseverance
10. reflect on their performance and adapt accordingly
11. show signs of contentment with their lives
12. have a history of personal goal achievement
13. know the content they teach (Ripley, 2010)

Although not necessarily a trait appropriate for this list, Teach for America tells us that a predictor of a TFA teacher's classroom success is grade point average (GPA) in the last 2 years

Effective teachers purposefully and collaboratively plan for instruction.
Sara Davis Powell

of college, rather than overall GPA. In other words, a GPA that starts out mediocre and then improves appears to be associated with greater teacher effectiveness than a 4.0 all 4 years. Another interesting point is that the more college extracurricular accomplishments, the better the teacher. These are areas you can work on *right now* that will help shape the teacher you will become. Encouraging, isn't it?

WHAT STUDENTS SAY ABOUT TEACHER EFFECTIVENESS

Emphasis has shifted recently from the teacher to the pupil as the focal point for defining teacher effectiveness. Very simply stated, the "ultimate proof of teacher effectiveness is student results" (Stronge, 2002, p. 65). But what results? What seems like a simple statement has complicated nuances because accurately assessing student learning is itself complex. Do we judge the effectiveness of a teacher solely by the standardized test scores of students? That would be easy if standardized test scores told the whole story.

In a survey of about 400 urban, low-income middle and high school students conducted by Corbett and Wilson (2002), all of them identified their teachers as the main factor in determining how much they learned. They listed a variety of characteristics of the diverse teachers most effective in helping them learn, all of which fit into the following six categories. Effective teachers . . .

1. push students to learn
2. maintain order
3. are willing to help
4. explain until everyone understands
5. vary classroom activities
6. try to understand students (pp. 19–20)

Points of Reflection 1.5

Think about the teachers you have had. What made some effective and others relatively ineffective?

EFFECTIVE TEACHERS MAKE A DIFFERENCE

"Substantial research evidence suggests that well-prepared, capable teachers have the largest impact on student learning" (Darling-Hammond, 2003, p. 7). This is not to say that other factors we discuss throughout this book do not significantly influence student learning. However, Linda Darling-Hammond, a noted expert on teacher quality, and others contend that an effective teacher can overcome many of the circumstances in students' lives and positively impact student learning. When the outside influences on student learning result in an achievement gap, Kati Haycock (2003), director of the Education Trust, tells us, "If we insist on quality teachers for every student, we can dramatically improve the achievement of poor and minority students and substantially narrow the achievement gap" (p. 11). Reiterating the need for effective teachers, James Stronge (2002), another respected educator, writes, "Teachers have a powerful, long-lasting influence on their students. They directly affect how students learn, what they learn, how much they learn, and the ways they interact with one another, and the world around them" (p. vii).

Teachers can be effective using very different approaches. You can probably name two teachers in your own experience who were effective but who had different traits. Stronge (2002) tells us "teaching effectiveness draws on a multitude of skills and attributes in different combinations and in different contexts to produce the results that define effectiveness" (p. 64).

Teachers and the Teaching Profession

An important factor to understand when it comes to the characteristics of effective teachers and teaching is that much of what makes teachers effective comes through experience in the classroom. This is not to say that new teachers can't be effective. Of course they can! But think about this. Teaching is a profession that expects a brand-new teacher to do the same job as an experienced veteran (Johnson & Kardos, 2005). Don't count on someone saying, "Hey, it's okay if only half your kids learn about half of what you attempt to teach. After all, you're new." David Berliner (2000), a noted leader in teacher education, estimates that it takes about 5 years to "get smart about teaching" (p. 360). Some of the characteristics of effectiveness take time to develop: It takes time to be able to make decisions with automaticity and to draw on experience to supplement formal training.

Throughout this text you are urged to ask repeatedly, as the Masai do, "And how are the children? Are they all well?" However, when you are a novice teacher, your primary question may often be "How am I doing?" In *Educating Esme: Diary of a Teacher's First Year*, Esme Codell (1999) reveals that her mentor told her that with experience the question "How am I doing?" increasingly becomes "How are the children doing?"

Effective teachers, regardless of whom or what they teach, share many common characteristics. Teacher professionalism is a thread that binds them all. But although there are many similarities, the day-to-day responsibilities may vary in many ways. Teachers of students with special needs; teachers who specialize in art, music, or physical education; teachers who teach all or most subjects to one group of students; and teachers who teach the same content area each day to several groups of students—all have specific preparation requirements and position responsibilities.

CONCLUDING THOUGHTS

Learning to be a teacher . . . teaching so others learn . . . learning to be a better teacher—this life-affirming cycle can be yours. Think of the cycle as a wheel that gathers momentum and takes you on a profound journey. You have begun to grow toward the profession. As a teacher you'll grow within the profession. Read what becoming a teacher meant to one young man, Jamie Sawatsky, a seventh grade history teacher in Chantilly, Virginia.

> I noticed the change in myself the first time I walked into my classroom. I was no longer Jamie. That was the name of the young man who had delivered pizzas or worked at the office. My newfound teaching life had metamorphosed me into "Mr. Sawatsky." My previous work experiences had taught me a variety of skills, but accepting the title of teacher has cast me into a world where I am charged with the awesome responsibility of sculpting young minds and preparing students for positive participation in their community. When asked why they entered the profession, many teachers respond, "I wanted a chance to make a positive change in the world." In my case, perhaps selfishly, I wanted to be in a profession that would make a positive change in me. With my first year of teaching about to conclude, I can say that I am happy to be a teacher and happy to be "Mr. Sawatsky." (Tell, 2001, p. 18)

After reading the ***Chapter in Review,*** interact with Traci Peters in this chapter's ***Developing Professional Competence.***

Chapter in Review

Who teaches in the United States and why?

- Teaching is the largest profession in the United States.
- Most teachers are white women, leading to a need for more men and people of color in teaching.
- Almost 90% of teachers believe teaching requires a "true sense of calling."

- The most common reasons for choosing to teach include the desire to work with young people, the value of education to society, interest in a subject, the influence of a teacher or of family, the teaching schedule, job security, and the opportunity for a lifetime of self-growth.
- Teacher satisfaction with the profession has grown over the last 25 years.

How do we prepare to teach?

- States issue a certificate or license to teach in public schools based on their own criteria.
- The traditional path to becoming a teacher is through a university-based teacher preparation program.
- Alternative paths to teacher preparation provide timely, but somewhat controversial, routes to teacher certification.
- There are many ways to get to know teachers, students, and schools, including field experiences through teacher preparation programs, volunteer opportunities, watching movies about teachers, and participating online through this and other texts.

Is teaching a profession?

- A profession is an occupation that includes extensive training before entering, a code of ethics, and service as the primary product.
- Teaching meets most of the criteria generally agreed upon for a full profession.
- Numerous professional organizations support teachers and teaching.

- Teachers can and should make contributions to the knowledge base of the teaching profession.

What is teacher professionalism?

- Teacher professionalism involves a commitment to make students the first priority.
- Teacher professionalism involves a commitment to quality in both our work and our relationships.
- Teacher professionalism involves a commitment to continual growth.

What are the characteristics of effective teachers?

- Effective teachers may have very different styles of teaching.
- The most important factor in determining teacher effectiveness is the extent of student learning.
- There are established standards for teacher effectiveness through organizations like the Interstate New Teacher Assessment and Support Consortium and the National Board of Professional Teaching Standards.
- Both individuals and organizations have opinions about what makes a teacher effective. There is much to learn from the differing viewpoints.

Developing Professional Competence

Visit the Developing Professional Competence section on Chapter 1 of the MyEducationLab for this text to answer the following questions and begin your preparation for licensure exams.

You met Traci Peters in *Meet the Focus Teachers and Students* and again in the beginning of this chapter in the *Teaching in Focus* section. She is the math teacher on her four-person interdisciplinary team at Cario Middle School. In March one of her teammates, Melanie Richardson, announced that her husband was being sent to Iraq and that without his help with their five children, she was going to have to move to another state where her parents live. Melanie teaches English-language arts and has been on Traci's team, the Dolphins, for 3 years. This is a big blow to Traci and her two other teammates. Melanie will leave Cario in mid-April. The Dolphin team teachers are very easy to work with and have enjoyed a collegial relationship with Melanie.

Carol Bartlett, principal of Cario, understands the importance of finding the right person to fill the position, but she is told that a teacher from another school will be

placed in Melanie's classroom for the remainder of the school year. Ms. Bartlett knows the teacher the district personnel office plans to place on the Dolphin team. Linda Merchant's reputation is that of a veteran teacher who does not collaborate, sits behind her desk during class, and consistently finds ways to undermine administrators. Ms. Bartlett suspects her position was purposefully eliminated at the other school and the district just needs to find a place for her. Ms. Bartlett is certain the Dolphin teachers will not be pleased with the district's choice.

1. Which of the following attributes of a full profession does this scenario directly violate?
   a. A full profession enjoys prestige and public trust.
   b. A full profession admits, polices, and excludes members.
   c. A full profession provides an essential service no other group can provide.
   d. A full profession involves intellectual work in the performance of duties.

Washington, DC: Author. Retrieved May 15, 2005, from http://www.nea.org/edstats/images/status.pdf

Nieto, S. (2009). From surviving to thriving. *Educational Leadership, 66*(5), 8-13.

Partnership for 21st Century Skills. (2009). About us. Retrieved November 17, 2009, from http://www.21stcenturyskills.org/index.php?option=com_content&task=view&id=42&Itemid=69

Phelps, P. H. (2003). Teacher professionalism. *Kappa Delta Pi Record, 40*(1), 10-11.

Public Agenda. (2003). Attitudes about teaching. New York: Author.

Public Education Network. (2003). *The voice of the new teacher.* Washington, DC: Author.

Ripley, A. (2010, January/February). What makes a great teacher? *The Atlantic.* Retrieved January 29, 2010, from http://www.theatlantic.com/doc/201001/good-teaching

Rowan, B. (1994). Comparing teachers' work with work in other occupations: Notes on the professional status of teaching. *Educational Researcher, 23*(6), 4-17, 21.

Stronge, J. H. (2002). *Qualities of effective teachers.* Alexandria, VA: Association for Supervision and Curriculum Development.

Teach for America. (2010). *Growth plan.* Retrieved January 24, 2010, from http://www.teachforamerica.org/about/our_growth_plan.htm

Tell, C. (2001). Who's in our classrooms: Teachers speak for themselves. *Educational Leadership, 58*(8), 18-23.

Webb, L., Metha, A., & Jordan, K. F. (2007). *Foundations of American education* (5th ed.). Upper Saddle River, NJ: Merrill/Prentice Hall.

17TH-CENTURY AMERICAN SCHOOLS

The early colonists recognized the need to provide schooling for their children, at least for their male children. They also knew that learning a trade was perhaps best accomplished by working with an expert artisan. Later, as colonies flourished in New England, the middle Atlantic area, and the South, more formal types of schools grew in both number and variety.

EARLY COLONIAL SCHOOLS. Having left England and suffered the hardships of the transatlantic voyage to the New World, the Puritans established an early type of schooling influenced both by European theorists, some of whom are listed in Table 7.1, and by Puritan religious beliefs and social customs. Although the first colonial schools were established for religious purposes, they helped the secular aspects of society develop and prosper as well by teaching students to read and write. These students, overwhelmingly white boys, then had the skills to participate in commerce.

The earliest Puritan settlers educated their children within their own homes, but **dame schools** soon became common. Dames were respected women who, usually without formal schooling, had learned to read and write, and who turned their homes into schools where parents paid to have their children educated. Some children went from a dame school, which was essentially the first American elementary school, or from no schooling at all, to an apprenticeship that required them (virtually all boys) to move into the home of a master. The master taught them a trade and often also taught them basic literacy skills. Girls usually stayed home and learned homemaking skills from their mothers.

As education moved from individual homes into schools throughout colonial America, notable differences in education emerged among colonies in different geographic areas. Figure 7.2 is a map of colonial America showing the three basic geographic areas we discuss next.

SCHOOLS IN THE NEW ENGLAND COLONIES. In 1630 the Massachusetts Bay Colony was established, followed by Rhode Island, Connecticut, and New Hampshire. These four colonies made up early New England. Their inhabitants tended to be very much alike, sharing the Puritan faith and English roots. They tended to settle in towns that made formal education a relatively easy endeavor. Dame schools were commonplace for New England children, who learned basic reading, writing, and arithmetic skills, all within a religious context. Girls in New England were allowed to attend the dame schools, although their curriculum was different and focused primarily on homemaking. The elementary education of a dame school was generally the extent of what girls received in terms of formal schooling for much of the colonial period.

In 1635 the first **Latin grammar school** was established in Boston for boys whose families could afford education beyond the dame school. The word *grammar* is associated with elementary school today but was a term for secondary schools in the 17th century. Students learned higher levels of reading, writing, and arithmetic, along with classical literature. The Latin grammar schools were considered the forerunners of modern high schools and specifically prepared boys to attend Harvard University, established in 1636 (Tehie, 2007).

Only the wealthiest New Englanders went beyond dame schools. Schooling opportunities and apprenticeships for white boys from poorer families were either less desirable or nonexistent. Girls, African Americans, and Native Americans had even fewer opportunities for educational advancement.

Some Puritan leaders recognized the benefits of educating all children, at least all white children. The **Massachusetts Act of 1642** was the first **compulsory education law** in the New World. Although the law required all white children to attend school, it did not specify how or where children would get an education. Nor did the law provide funding, making it the first **unfunded mandate,** a legally enforceable law without provision for monetary support. Five years later, the Massachusetts Act of 1647, also known as the **Old Deluder Satan Act** because education was considered the best way to fight the devil, established that every town of 50 or more households must provide a school. Again, no funding was attached, and either parents or the whole community contributed to supporting a

Figure 7.1 U.S. education in historical perspective

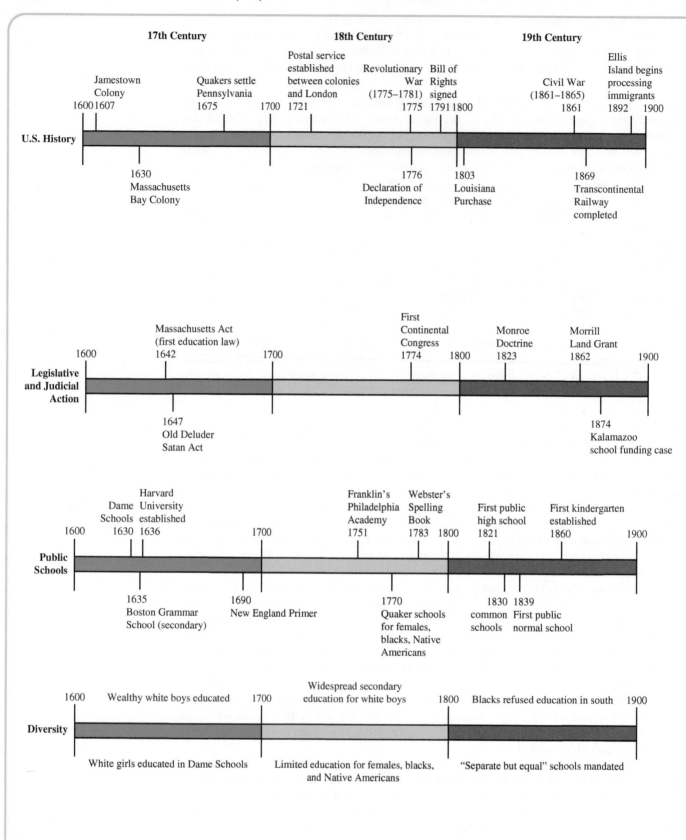

History of Education in the United States

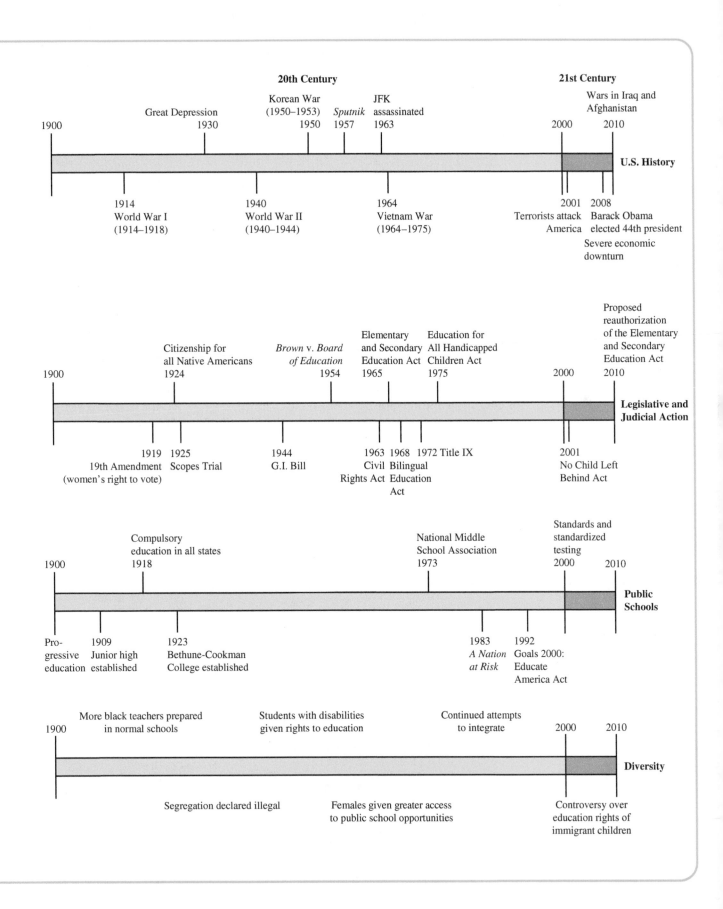

20th Century

1900

Great Depression
1930

Korean War
(1950–1953)
1950

Sputnik
1957

JFK
assassinated
1963

21st Century

Wars in Iraq and
Afghanistan

2000   2010

U.S. History

1914
World War I
(1914–1918)

1940
World War II
(1940–1944)

1964
Vietnam War
(1964–1975)

2001
Terrorists attack
America

2008
Barack Obama
elected 44th president

Severe economic
downturn

1900

Citizenship for
all Native Americans
1924

Brown v. *Board
of Education*
1954

Elementary
and Secondary
Education Act
1965

Education for
All Handicapped
Children Act
1975

Proposed
reauthorization
of the Elementary
and Secondary
Education Act

2000   2010

**Legislative and
Judicial Action**

1919
19th Amendment
(women's right to vote)

1925
Scopes Trial

1944
G.I. Bill

1963
Civil
Rights Act

1968
Bilingual
Education
Act

1972 Title IX

2001
No Child Left
Behind Act

1900

Compulsory
education in all states
1918

National Middle
School Association
1973

Standards and
standardized
testing
2000   2010

**Public
Schools**

Pro-
gressive
education

1909
Junior high
established

1923
Bethune-Cookman
College established

1983
*A Nation
at Risk*

1992
Goals 2000:
Educate
America Act

1900

More black teachers prepared
in normal schools

Students with disabilities
given rights to education

Continued attempts
to integrate

2000   2010

Diversity

Segregation declared illegal

Females given greater access
to public school opportunities

Controversy over
education rights of
immigrant children

History of Education in the United States

TABLE 7.1 Influence of major theorists on early American education

Theorist	Summary of Influence
Erasmus (1466–1536)	Need for systematic training of teachers; liberal arts education includes classics
Luther (1483–1546)	Education necessary for religious instruction; education should include vocational training; need for free and compulsory education
Calvin (1509–1564)	Education serves religious and political establishments; elementary education for all; secondary education for leaders; emphasis on literacy
Bacon (1561–1626)	Education should advance scientific inquiry; provide rationale for development of critical thinking skills
Comenius (1592–1670)	Learning must come through the senses; general body of knowledge (paideia) should be possessed by all
Locke (1632–1704)	Goal of education is to promote the development of reason and morality to enable men to participate in the governing process

Source: Webb, L. D., Metha, A., & Jordan, K. F. (2010). Foundations of American education (6th ed.). Upper Saddle River, NJ: Pearson/Merrill.

school and teacher. These two acts, along with Puritan determination, led to the New England colonies having about the same literacy rate as England by 1700 (Cohen, 1974).

The *New England Primer* was first published in 1690 for children in upper elementary and secondary levels. The book was a perfect example of the interrelatedness of education and religion in colonial New England. Published for over 150 years with few substantial changes over its lifetime, the *New England Primer* included a spelling

Figure 7.2 The 13 original colonies

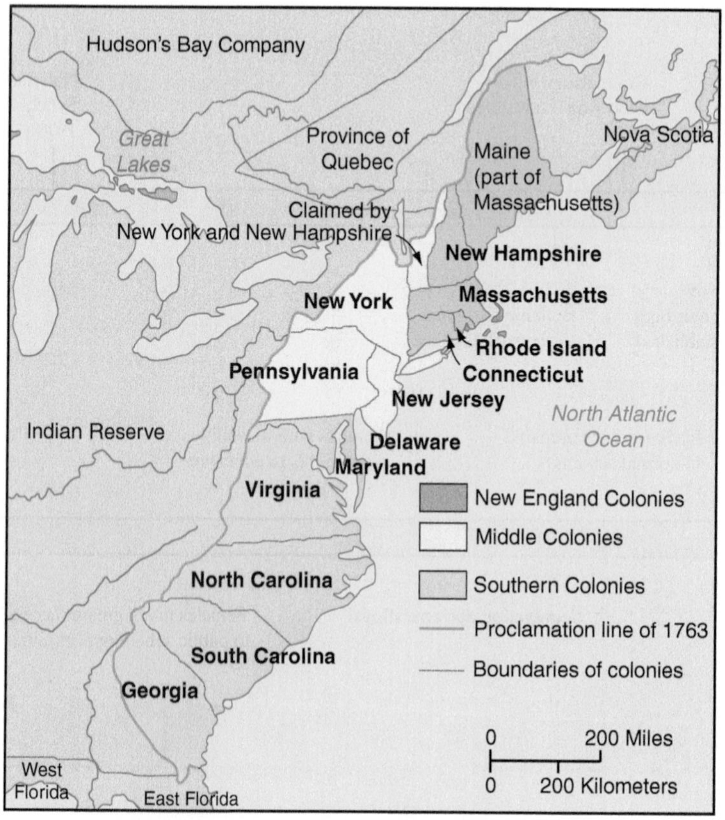

History of Education in the United States

Figure 7.3 New England Primer

In *Adam's* Fall
We Sinned all.

Thy Life to Mend
This *Book* Attend.

The *Cat* doth play
And after flay.

A *Dog* will bite
A Thief at night.

An *Eagles* flight
Is out of fight.

The Idle *Fool*
Is whipt at School.

Getty Images Inc.–
Hulton Archive Photos

guide based on the alphabet denoted in brief rhymes and pictures. The *New England Primer* also included the Lord's Prayer, the Apostles' Creed, the Ten Commandments, a list of the books of the Bible, and the numbers 1 to 100. Figure 7.3 contains a sample from the *New England Primer.*

SCHOOLS IN THE MIDDLE COLONIES. New York, New Jersey, Pennsylvania, and Delaware made up the middle colonies. Their population was much less homogeneous than that of New England. Settlers came from Sweden, the Netherlands, Germany, France, and other parts of Europe, along with people of the Quaker faith who primarily settled in Pennsylvania.

No one kind of school could satisfy the diversity of the middle colonists. Each religious sect established its own brand of schooling: Lutherans, Presbyterians, Jews, Mennonites, Catholics, Quakers, Baptists, Huguenots, and so on. The colonies attempted to license schools but did not provide financing. The middle colony schools were mostly private, or *parochial,* a term typically associated with religion. These parochial schools often taught a greater variety of subjects than the New England schools and included topics such as business, bookkeeping, and navigation.

SCHOOLS IN THE SOUTHERN COLONIES. Like the middle colonies, the southern colonies were settled by diverse groups, but the settlers were even more widespread geographically. In Virginia, Maryland, Georgia, and the Carolinas, more so than in New England or the middle colonies, opportunities for education were based almost exclusively on social class. Children of plantation owners and wealthy merchants either attended private schools or were taught at home by tutors. These privileged students went from elementary to secondary schools either in the South or in Europe. Children who lived on small farms or children of laborers experienced whatever education was available through charity schools run by people who believed education should be more widely available, apprentice programs, or church schools. The children of slaves received no formal education in the southern colonies during the 17th century.

TEACHERS IN COLONIAL AMERICA

During the 17th century there was no formal system of teacher preparation. The closest parallel would have been apprentices assigned to Quaker teachers, who themselves lacked formal training in the education of both children and teachers. In dame schools the teachers were widows or housewives who could read and write to some unspecified degree of

Points of Reflection 7.1

What evidence are you aware of that leads you to believe that where students live today affects their educational opportunities?

proficiency. Men who taught in the first elementary schools often did so for very short periods of time before beginning official training for the ministry or law.

Many teachers were indentured servants who taught in exchange for passage to the New World. Often people were teachers because they were not successful in other occupations; some were even of questionable character or conduct (Pulliam & Van Patten, 2007).

Teachers in the secondary schools (Latin grammar schools) enjoyed more status than those in elementary-level schools. They often had more education themselves, and many had college training (Ornstein & Levine, 2006).

Many teachers in both the 17th and 18th centuries participated in the curious custom of boarding 'round. To save lodging money, towns required teachers to live with the families of their students for 1 week at a time. This practice did nothing for the dignity of the teacher or the profession. Pay was low, about what farmhands made, and without permanent homes, teachers often thought of themselves as expendable part-time employees.

What Were the Major Influences, Issues, Ideologies, and Individuals in 18th-Century American Education?

The first half of the 18th century was one of geographic expansion on American soil and the maturation of economic and political climate. In perspective, it was relatively calm in terms of history and schools when compared to the second half.

CONTEXT FOR CHANGE

Representatives to the First Continental Congress (1774) in Philadelphia met originally to discuss how to claim their rights as British citizens in America. However, the Declaration of Independence soon followed, as did the writing of the Constitution, and then the Bill of Rights. The United States of America was rapidly taking shape (Boyer & Stuckey, 2005).

Future leaders, such as Benjamin Franklin (1706–1790) and Thomas Jefferson (1743–1826), were born and grew up not only to pave the way for the new nation, but also to influence the direction in which 18th-century education was heading.

18TH-CENTURY AMERICAN SCHOOLS

In 1751 Benjamin Franklin established the Franklin Academy, a school that was oriented toward real-world, useful learning. The Franklin Academy offered mathematics, astronomy, navigation, accounting, bookkeeping, French, and Spanish. One significant contribution of the Franklin Academy was its provision for students to choose some courses, the forerunner of today's electives.

Private **academies** sprang up across America. These schools were designed to teach content intended to prepare students to participate in business and trade. They met not only intellectual needs but also economic needs. In addition to these academies, **town schools** were established for whole communities. Although some schools still limited curriculum to reading, writing, and the classics, specialized schools in the form of academies became popular.

Thomas Jefferson had political, practical, and intellectual motives for his interest in and attention to education. He believed that education

Benjamin Franklin (1706–1790)

A pudgy, bookish man with long curly hair and little square glasses, flying a kite in the middle of a thunderstorm, is the image most have of Ben Franklin. Inventor and philosopher extraordinaire, Franklin contributed to American education in many valuable ways. In the mid-18th century he espoused educating America's youth in the practical and useful arts and trades. In addition to the traditional study of reading and math, he was the first to propose the study of history that included not just past politics and wars but also customs and commerce. He founded the Library Company of Philadelphia in 1731 to promote reading by subscription to help tradesmen and farmers become as intelligent as gentlemen of other countries. In his *Proposals Relating to the Youth of Pennsylvania* (1749), Franklin said that wise men view the education of youth as "the surest foundation of. . . happiness" (Franklin, 1931, p. 151).

Franklin (1749/1931); Good (1964). CORBIS–NY

was essential to the maintenance of a viable republic. Education, in Jefferson's view, would increase production and preserve health. In 1779 he proposed the Virginia Bill for the More General Diffusion of Knowledge that provided for broader availability of education for more children. Jefferson's bill did not pass the Virginia legislature, but it raised awareness of the need and potential value of education among both lawmakers and the public (Good, 1964).

In the 18th century many Quakers came to America. They believed that education should be all-inclusive. In Philadelphia in 1770 Quakers established a school for elementary students that included girls, African Americans, and Native Americans. In the South, however, formal education for African and Native Americans was nonexistent, despite a high literacy rate for white men and women. In Virginia, for example, 9 of 10 white men, and 2 of 3 white women were able to read (Button & Provenzo, 1989).

Noah Webster (1758–1843) had a profound influence on 18th-century American schools, particularly because of his writing. His most important work was the *American Spelling Book*, published in 1783. Some scholars say Webster had more influence on American education than anyone else in the 18th century and have referred to him as "Schoolmaster of the Republic" (Webb, Metha, & Jordan, 2010).

Several colleges were established in the colonies prior to the American Revolution, among them Yale University in 1701, the University of Pennsylvania in 1753, Brown University in 1764, and Dartmouth College in 1769. At first, theology was the most popular degree; later, other majors, such as law, medicine, and commerce, increased in popularity (Cohen, 1974).

Thomas Jefferson (1743–1826)

As author of the Declaration of Independence and the third president of the United States (1801-1809), Thomas Jefferson believed that only through education could people preserve freedom and promote their own happiness. Historian S. Alexander Rippa (1997) said of Jefferson that "none has so consistently viewed public education as the indispensable cornerstone of freedom" (p. 55). Jefferson believed that government must be by the consent of the governed, and he wanted those governed to read. In fact, he suggested to President John Adams that anyone who was given the opportunity to learn to read but didn't, should not be allowed to vote. President Adams disagreed with this idea.

Disappointed by the Virginia House of Burgess's refusal to pass his Bill for the More General Diffusion of Knowledge, Jefferson spent the years following his presidency establishing the University of Virginia (UVA). It was truly his university in the beginning. He designed both the curriculum and the buildings, bought the trees and designed the landscaping, purchased the library books, chose the faculty, and admitted the first class of students. Thomas Jefferson died on July 4, 1826, 1 year after UVA opened and exactly 50 years following the adoption of the Declaration of Independence.

Good (1964); Rippa (1997). Corbis RF

18TH-CENTURY TEACHERS

As was true in the 17th century, teachers in the 18th century continued to be undervalued in most of colonial America. Figure 7.4 contains a description of the life circumstances of an itinerant teacher who, while enjoying a stellar reputation, found that employment was both uncertain and difficult. The second excerpt is from the journal of a female teacher who lived with her students' families and found teaching to be a very exasperating job.

EDUCATION AS A PRIORITY

Education received a boost in priority with the passage of the **Northwest Land Ordinance of 1787,** which divided federally owned wilderness land into townships and required the building of schools. Article Three of the Ordinance proclaimed "Religion, morality, and knowledge being necessary to good government and the happiness of mankind, schools and the means of education shall be forever encouraged."

Education is not directly mentioned in the U.S. Constitution ratified in 1788. However, the Tenth Amendment in the Bill of Rights states, "The powers not delegated to the United States by the

Noah Webster (1758–1843)

More than any other education statesman of the late 18th and early 19th centuries, Noah Webster reshaped the English language and literature into America's own. He was intensely patriotic and believed that America needed not only political independence from Europe but also cultural independence. The enormous success of Webster's *American Spelling Book*, which included moral stories, lists of words, and a pronunciation guide, put an end to the importing of English books to be used as textbooks. Webster believed in free education for all American boys and girls. Interestingly, he saw the education of women as an absolute necessity because they are the first teachers of children. A Yale graduate, member of the Massachusetts legislature, lawyer, writer, scholar, and businessman, Noah Webster had a tremendous impact on American education.

Good (1964); Gutek (2005); Webb et al. (2010). CORBIS–NY

Figure 7.4 Teachers in the 18th century

About Silas Crocker.

Mr. Crocker is an itinerant schoolteacher, going from village to village in search of employment. During the summer months he earns a living plowing, mowing, and carting manure. In the winter, he teaches school. Having the reputation as the greatest 'arithmeticker' in the county, he is a respected schoolmaster. Most of the schoolrooms in the area are familiar with this tall, gaunt master.

From Mistress Robbins' Journal.

My name is Elizabeth Robbins, and I am in my seventeenth year. I have been engaged to teach at Litchfield. A committee of the subscribers examined me and asked that I read passages from the Old Testament. They seemed pleased when I did not stumble over the big words....I was hired for a period of five months, at four dollars a month.

I find a wretched schoolhouse, in the road, as it were, with a tiny fireplace. At first, it was easy, as the older scholars stayed away. When the school is full, however, it is very difficult to teach. The older boys make threats against me. They are generally lawless, and in the habit of using profane language. I have to resort to using severe corporal punishment to maintain order.

Source: Loeper, J. L. (1973). *Going to school in 1776.* New York: Macmillan.

Constitution, nor prohibited by it to the states, are reserved to the States respectively, or to the people." Thus, from the inception of the United States to the present, except for the occasional federal mandate, states have grappled independently with educational issues.

As the new nation of the United States of America approached the 19th century, a surge of energy was directed toward education. Leaders and policies emerged that would place American education squarely in the foreground of thought and action.

What Were the Major Influences, Issues, Ideologies, and Individuals in 19th-Century American Education?

The 19th century was one of unprecedented growth, both geographically and governmentally.

CONTEXT FOR CHANGE

In 1800 American geography lessons included maps showing 17 states. By the end of the century maps of America boasted 45 states. During this century the United States established a functioning and flourishing economy, endured a protracted test of the strength of its union (the Civil War), and matured into a stable, respected political entity.

With the election of President Andrew Jackson in 1828, the birth of the Democratic Party brought changes to American politics, turning a nation governed largely by an aristocratic society to one based in greater measure on government of, by, and for the people. Westward expansion propelled by the continuing desire for individual independence and opportunity took the growing nation all the way to the Pacific Ocean.

Cultural and economic differences between an increasingly industrialized North and an agrarian South grew and festered in the 19th century. The rift erupted into the Civil War in 1861 as southern states seceded from the Union and formed the Confederacy.

Although the most commonly perceived reason for the Civil War is slavery, other actual issues surrounding the onset of hostilities revolved around states' rights and economics. Over 600,000 Americans on both sides lost their lives before the North and South were reunited in 1865.

Of all the issues facing the American population as the 19th century drew to a close, the most significant were associated with the Industrial Revolution. Poverty-level wages, a workforce that would soon include too many children, unchecked immigration, and abysmal working conditions all reflected poorly on the country's ability to cope with the abuses actually brought about by its wonderful spirit of inventiveness. Each of these issues would have to be

History of Education in the United States

faced and solved, and the educational system revamped to meet the needs of the more commerce- and industry-based society that was on the horizon.

19TH-CENTURY AMERICAN SCHOOLS

The 19th century in the United States was characterized by a wide variety of schools. There were town schools, primarily in the northern states; charity schools, run by churches and philanthropic groups; and widely varying dame schools serving as small venues for local education. Religious schools grew as families banded together with others of the same denomination and country of origin. Academies of all descriptions, some prestigious and some humble, flourished in the first half of the 19th century. In the South most educational opportunities still belonged to the wealthy; in the West most frontier children did not attend school. The obvious lack of consistency and opportunity did not mirror the ideals of America's founders, who saw education as a means to accomplish the goal stated in the Preamble of the U.S. Constitution to "promote the general Welfare."

On the post–Civil War education front, one fact was crystal clear: Both the classical educational system popular in the Northeast and the one-room schoolhouse approach adopted during western frontier days were increasingly incapable of meeting the needs of the country. Let's look at some of the categories of schools developed in 19th-century America.

Horace Mann and the common school movement made it possible for some black children to be educated in public schools.
Provided by the author

COMMON SCHOOLS. The system of free public schools that exists today had its beginnings in the common schools movement, first established about 1830. **Common schools** were community-supported elementary schools for *all* children established in response to a variety of economic, social, and political factors. This was a radical departure from previous schooling that catered primarily to wealthy males. Think about it... *all* children. Because free public education for all children was a new concept, common schools were debated, with many citizens seeing their value and others remaining skeptical, as illustrated in Table 7.2. Horace Mann was the champion of common schools. In fact, he was widely regarded as a champion of children in general and of the basic American ideal of opportunity for all.

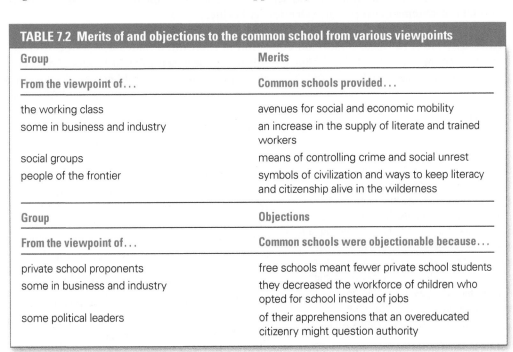

TABLE 7.2 Merits of and objections to the common school from various viewpoints

Group	Merits
From the viewpoint of...	Common schools provided...
the working class	avenues for social and economic mobility
some in business and industry	an increase in the supply of literate and trained workers
social groups	means of controlling crime and social unrest
people of the frontier	symbols of civilization and ways to keep literacy and citizenship alive in the wilderness
Group	**Objections**
From the viewpoint of...	Common schools were objectionable because...
private school proponents	free schools meant fewer private school students
some in business and industry	they decreased the workforce of children who opted for school instead of jobs
some political leaders	of their apprehensions that an overeducated citizenry might question authority

Points of Reflection 7.2

How would you compare the views of businesspeople and politicians today concerning public schools to the views held by businesspeople and politicians in the 19th century concerning common schools, the first public schools?

Horace Mann (1796–1859)

Widely known as the Father of American Education, Horace Mann had a profound influence not only on early American schools but also on modern schools. He believed that regular attendance in schools with quality teachers would serve to equalize opportunities for poor, African American, and disabled children. He vigorously advocated for common schools.

As attorney and state legislator turned education advocate, Mann established the first **normal school** in 1839 in Lexington, Massachusetts. Normal schools proved to be incredibly important as 2-year colleges specifically designed to prepare teachers. Mann was not afraid of controversy as he pushed for separation of church and schools, not a popular stance in 19th-century America. Even as an avowed religious man, he was often criticized from church pulpits. As the first secretary of education for the Massachusetts Board of Education, which he helped establish in 1837, and throughout his life, Horace Mann spoke eloquently and worked tirelessly as a champion of schools and students.

Not only was Horace Mann an advocate for free quality education, but he also worked for the abolition of slavery and the limiting of alcohol as a social problem and was a vocal supporter of women's rights.

Chartock (2004) North Wind Picture Archives

In common schools, and most other schools of the 19th century, the works of William Holmes McGuffey had the most significant impact on what children learned. McGuffey's books differed from the unimaginative literature of previous centuries and included stories that promoted truth, honesty, and hard work.

As common schools increased in number, their inconsistencies became more and more apparent. Some were housed in acceptable buildings with adequate supplies and appropriate heating and lighting. Other common schools were housed in dilapidated, poorly heated and lit, filthy surroundings.

SECONDARY SCHOOLS. When the English Classical School opened for young men in Boston in 1821, it marked the beginning of the public high school. In 1824 the school's name was changed to the Boston English High School. In 1838 a coeducational high school opened in Philadelphia. This school offered three tracks: a classical (Latin) curriculum (4 years), a modern language curriculum (4 years), and an English curriculum (2 years) (Webb et al., 2010).

Before the Civil War, high schools were almost exclusively found in the North and always in cities. Because children could learn to read in common schools, and reading was considered sufficient education by many citizens, high schools were slow to grow in number.

In the aftermath of the Civil War, with Reconstruction and rapidly growing industrialization, economic growth spurred the establishment of more schools—not just common schools, but also secondary schools. High schools began to flourish about 1850 and by 1870 had replaced academies as the dominant secondary school. In 1874 a case in the Michigan Supreme Court called the **Kalamazoo case** established that the legislature could tax for support of both common and secondary schools, propelling public high schools into school systems in every state (Ornstein & Levine, 2006).

KINDERGARTEN. Early childhood education in the United States developed after elementary (common schools) and high schools (secondary schools). In Europe, Swiss educator Johann Pestalozzi (1746–1827) developed the theory of child-centered education and the concept of individual differences among children. German educator Friedrich Froebel (1782–1852) agreed with Pestalozzi, but he took child-centered education further. Froebel was a proponent of an activity-based curriculum in an early childhood setting, where children are encouraged to be creative and expressive. This setting was called a kindergarten, or "children's garden." The first kindergarten in the United States was established in 1860 in Boston. By 1873 kindergartens had become part of many public school systems (Chartock, 2004).

With the establishment of kindergarten, common school, and high school, the need for specially prepared teachers grew.

W. H. McGuffey (1800–1873)

Far from the overly pious and drab books that painted a dreary picture of the worth of children and first appeared in American schools, W. H. McGuffey's six-volume set of *McGuffey's Readers* included stories and poetry that appealed to the interests of students. The volumes were geared to specific levels and paved the way to the separation of elementary school into grade levels. The volumes sold over 1 million copies between 1836 and 1906 and helped students learn to read and study while instilling in them virtues such as patriotism, morality, and a work ethic. McGuffey, as a minister, professor, and college president, indelibly left his mark on American education.

McNergney and McNergney (2009); Webb et al. (2010). © Bettmann/CORBIS All Rights Reserved.

TEACHER PREPARATION

Before Horace Mann's proposal that teachers receive special training, few completed any form of secondary education. Teachers were inadequately and inconsistently prepared. Notable exceptions were the teachers prepared at the Troy Female Seminary, the first institution of higher learning for women in the United States, established in Troy, New York, in 1821 by Emma Willard (1787-1870).

The first normal school, a publicly funded institution dedicated exclusively to preparing teachers, was established 18 years later, in 1839 in Lexington, Massachusetts. Catherine Beecher (1800-1878), along with Horace Mann, was instrumental in making teacher preparation a priority in normal schools.

As these first specially prepared teachers entered their classrooms, they seldom encountered children with disabilities, children of color, or children of poor immigrants. This situation would change with time.

19TH-CENTURY EDUCATION FOR CHILDREN WITH DISABILITIES, MINORITIES, AND IMMIGRANTS

The 19th century was marked by meager, yet important, advances in education for children with disabilities, children of color, and children of poor immigrants.

CHILDREN WITH DISABILITIES. Social mores of the day demanded that any educational opportunities for children with disabilities be separate from those for children without disabilities. A few innovative schools were established in the 19th century for students with certain disabilities. In 1817 Thomas Gallaudet established the first school for the deaf in Hartford, Connecticut. In the mid-19th century, physician Samuel Howe was influential in the establishment of the first school for blind children, the Perkins School for the Blind in Watertown, Massachusetts (Cubberly, 1934). Mental and behavioral disabilities were not addressed in 19th-century schools.

NATIVE AMERICAN CHILDREN. In 1824 the U.S. government established the Bureau of Indian Affairs and began placing whole tribes of Native Americans on reservations. Most of what little formal schooling Native American children received was provided by missionaries, whose efforts were fueled by a desire to convert the children to Christianity. The missionary schools were not consistently organized or maintained (Chartock, 2004).

A further goal of most efforts to educate Native American children in the 19th century was **assimilation,** that is, making the children more like white children, the dominant culture, or, in the terms of the time, "civilizing" them. The

Friedrich Froebel (1782–1852)

When the first English-speaking kindergarten in the United States opened in Boston in 1860, it was the direct result of the work of Friedrich Froebel, widely viewed as the father of the kindergarten or "children's garden." Froebel thought of young children as flowers that would blossom into healthy adults if given the opportunity to be creative in an active curriculum. His emphasis on self-development and self-expression is the theoretical basis for early childhood education.

Johnson, Musial, Hall, Golnick, and Dupuis (2005). Courtesy of the Library of Congress

Emma Willard (1787–1870)

While boarding schools were teaching girls how to be polite, proper wives who could serve tea and make gentile conversation, Emma Willard was formulating plans for a school to teach girls and women useful, solid skills in homemaking as well as content and pedagogy to enable them to be teachers or to enter other professions. In 1821 she established the Troy Female Seminary, the first institution of higher learning for girls. Before the first normal school was established in 1839 by Horace Mann and others, the Troy Seminary had prepared over 200 teachers. Emma Willard is also credited with the establishment of home economics as a legitimate subject area. Willard wrote textbooks, traveled extensively, and was a lifelong activist for women's rights.

Chartock (2004); Good (1964); Webb et al. (2010). © CORBIS All Rights Reserved.

Catherine Beecher (1800–1878)

Although Catherine Beecher's sister, Harriet Beecher Stowe, author of *Uncle Tom's Cabin*, may have more name recognition, Catherine had a great impact on the establishment of teacher training schools, or normal schools. In 1832 she established the Western Institute for Women, partially because she saw a need for better educated teachers. The institute was not publicly funded and did not prepare teachers exclusively, but it spawned other institutions of higher learning for women. In 1839 Beecher, along with Horace Mann and others, started the first publicly supported normal school for teacher preparation.

Holmes and Weiss (1995). The Schlesinger Library

Prudence Crandall (1803–1889)

Way ahead of her time, and incredibly courageous, Prudence Crandall believed strongly in the rights of African American students to an education. Her Quaker roots and her own education under a noted abolitionist, Moses Brown, helped shape her steadfast belief in equal opportunity. In 1830 Crandall founded a school for neighborhood girls in Canterbury, Connecticut. When she admitted an African American girl, Sarah Harris, Crandall and her school became the target for vandalism and ostracism. White parents withdrew their daughters. When Crandall established a school populated entirely by African American girls, it was destroyed by outraged whites. Sarah Harris went on to teach many years in Louisiana, thus carrying on Prudence Crandall's legacy.

Pulliam and Van Patten (2007). The Prudence Crandall Museum

American government built boarding schools in the latter part of the 19th century and forced thousands of Native American children to leave their homes and live in these boarding schools where attempts were made to diminish their culture in favor of English-speaking, white social norms of the time. The boarding schools proved to be complete failures with Native American students running away or returning to their reservations immediately after graduation (Webb et al., 2010).

MEXICAN AMERICAN CHILDREN. At the end of the Mexican American War in 1848, vast territories comprising what are now Arizona, California, Colorado, Nevada, New Mexico, and Utah came under U.S. control. The Mexican families who stayed in these territories after the United States took over suffered discrimination much like the Native Americans. Like Native Americans, Mexican Americans were targets of efforts at assimilation. For much of the 19th century most Mexican American children had few, if any, educational options. When they did attend school, teachers generally tried to Americanize them, or assimilate them into the dominant culture by insisting they learn and use English and give up some of their customs (Webb et al., 2010).

AFRICAN AMERICAN CHILDREN. Although the education of Native American and Mexican American children was far from ideal and was inconsistently implemented, at least it didn't face legal objection by state or federal governments. The education of African American children in the 19th century did. For example, when Prudence Crandall admitted an African American student, Sarah Harris, to the school she founded in Connecticut in 1830, the school was forced to close. Crandall reopened the school for girls and enrolled 15 African American students from other states. The Connecticut legislature subsequently passed the **Black Law,** a law that specifically forbade a school intended to educate African Americans from other states without the permission of local authorities.

Prior to the Civil War, **Black Codes** were enacted, predominantly in the South, prohibiting the education of slaves. Some white people feared that educating slaves would give the slaves a sense of self-importance and they might begin to think they were created equal and had certain inalienable rights as stated in the Declaration of Independence. In 1850, with increasing numbers of free African Americans in the North desiring education, the Massachusetts Supreme Court upheld the decision in *Roberts* v. *City of Boston* that separate-but-equal schools did not violate the rights of African American children. This ruling solidified the practice of separate but equal, meaning that separate schools for black and white children supposedly offered the same opportunities for children. This assumption proved to be false, with schools for black children receiving less funding and housed in inferior facilities (Kaplan & Owings, 2011). At the end of the 19th century, the practice was reinforced by the ruling in a similar case, *Plessy* v. *Ferguson.*

The doctrine of separate but equal was evident in schooling in the United States until well past the middle of the 20th century.
Courtesy of Millican Art and Photography

Following the Civil War, the Bureau of Refugees, Freedmen, and Abandoned Lands, more commonly referred to as the Freedmen Bureau, made efforts to help African Americans find ways of making a living and settle into a free lifestyle. The Freedman's Bureau opened 3,000 schools in the South to educate African American children. By 1869 about 114,000 African American students were being educated in these schools. Along with typical school subjects, these new schools added industrial training in an effort to prepare African American students for employment (Gutek, 2005). In addition, many ex-slaves formed their own education associations that sponsored schools exclusively for black children, staffed exclusively by African American teachers. By 1870 southern African Americans had established over 500 of these schools, resembling the earlier common schools movement (Kaplan & Owings, 2011). Hampton Institute, founded in 1868, was an institution of higher education that emphasized industrial skills and teacher preparation for African Americans.

The most famous graduate of the Hampton Institute was Booker T. Washington. Following graduation he became Hampton's first African American teacher. Washington was a major supporter of vocational education for African Americans. He viewed learning practical skills as a way of advancing socially and economically in the United States. In 1881 Washington founded the Tuskegee Institute in rural Alabama. By 1890 Tuskegee had 88 faculty members and more than 1,200 students, making it one of the larger colleges in the South (McNergney & McNergney, 2009).

Booker T. Washington (1856–1915)

As a steadfast believer that education was the way to advance socially and economically, Booker T. Washington spent his life furthering educational opportunities for African American students. First graduating from, and then teaching at, the Hampton Institute, Washington later founded the Tuskegee Institute in Alabama in 1881. Throughout his career, Washington promoted his message that African Americans needed vocational skills to get and keep good jobs. Washington led the Tuskegee Institute until his death in 1915.

Chartock (2004); McNergney and McNergney (2009). Getty Images Inc.–Hulton Archive Photos

ASIAN AMERICAN CHILDREN. Although their numbers were smaller than immigrants from Mexico, there were children of Asian parents in U.S. schools in the 19th century. Most were Chinese, who began to arrive midcentury and filled a need for laborers in an increasingly industrialized America. The Immigration Act of 1882 slowed the arrival of people from China. In the latter part of the century traders from India began arriving, mostly on the East Coast of the United States. Until 1886 people from Japan could not leave their country. Once the restriction was lifted, Japanese (mostly men) moved to the United States and began to fill the void for inexpensive labor created by the Chinese government's crackdown on emigration (Note that to *emigrate* means to leave one's country. When people emigrate, they become *immigrants* in their destination country.)

CHILDREN OF POOR IMMIGRANTS. The United States is a nation of immigrants. The country's motto, *E Pluribus Unum*, means "from many, one." The issue of how to educate the *many* and have a strong *one* is not new. From 1870 to 1900, the United States experienced an influx of almost 2 million immigrants, many from Mexico, Asia, and Eastern Europe, and many whose primary language was not English (Boyer & Stuckey, 2005).

Many immigrants were very poor, but their skills were needed in the rapid industrialization of the United States. As the economy grew, so did the tax base for supporting free elementary schools and high schools. The number of free public schools increased dramatically as the country attempted to cope with its industrial growth and with the many coming to its shores to become one nation (Gutek, 2005; Takaki, 1993).

Most poor immigrants in the 19th century had no means of providing for their families when they first arrived in the United States, generally in the already heavily populated cities of New York and Chicago. **Settlement houses**

Jane Addams (1860–1935)

Raised in a wealthy home with an abolitionist Quaker father, Jane Addams set her sights on becoming a doctor. However, because of back problems, she quit her studies and determined to dedicate her life to helping the urban poor. She founded Hull House in an old, rundown Chicago mansion. Located in the middle of an immigrant neighborhood, Hull House provided education for both children and adults.

Addams recruited college-educated young women to work at Hull House. Many later used what they learned there to propel them to make major contributions to social reform. For years Hull House served as a model for other successful settlement houses, which numbered almost 100 by 1900.

Addams tirelessly promoted women's suffrage (right to vote) and was president of the Women's International League for Peace and Freedom from 1919 until her death in 1935. In 1931 she received the Nobel Peace Prize.

Boyer and Stuckey (2005). Corbis RF

Letter to the Editor

This letter appeared in the Waco, Texas, newspaper, the *Waco Tribune Herald*. It was written by a citizen advocating for a way for immigrant children to achieve citizenship.

APRIL 30, 2010 PATH TO CITIZENSHIP

In 1982, the U.S. Supreme Court struck down a Texas state law prohibiting undocumented children from attending public school. Justice William Brennan, writing for the majority, said the law was unjust toward children who were "not accountable for their disabling status."

In 2005, there were roughly 1.8 million undocumented children attending U.S. schools from kindergarten through high school. About 65,000 undocumented students graduated from high school in 2009, and about 13,000 enrolled in college nationwide. However, these ambitious, bright students have no way to become taxpaying, legal residents after they graduate.

If passed, the DREAM Act—which stands for the Development, Relief and Education for Alien Minors Act—would allow undocumented students a pathway to citizenship after attending college.

Comprehensive immigration reform will be a slow and arduous process. In the meantime, we have an obligation to protect the rights of these children, many of whom had no choice in immigrating to the United States with their families.

Support the DREAM Act in 2011 by writing your state and national lawmakers. For more information, go to dreamact.info.

Elena Solano
Austin

Now it's your turn. Write a letter to the editor from the perspective of a future teacher expressing your views about children who come to America through little or no choice of their own. Consider if the DREAM Act would be good for America, for the children involved, or for U.S. public schools. The following questions may help you frame your thinking but should not limit nor determine what you write.

1. What is your response to Justice Brennan's characterization of immigrant children as "not accountable for their disabling status"? Do you consider children who are immigrants to be disabled in some way?

2. What do you believe the economic impact might be of college graduates who are not citizens? If employers can't legally hire them and, if they do, cannot take federal and state taxes from their pay, what effects might this have?

3. The DREAM Act has been in the works since 2009. Knowing what you do from this letter, does it sound like something you want to support?

4. Do you think the DREAM Act might encourage more families to come to America illegally because it provides hope to their children? In your opinion, would this be positive or negative?

Write your letter in understandable terminology, remembering that readers of newspaper Letters to the Editor are citizens who may have limited knowledge of school practices and policies.

were established by reformers to address the problems of urban poverty. These were community service centers that provided educational opportunities, skills training, and cultural events. Jane Addams (1860–1935), raised in a wealthy Quaker home, established the most famous of the settlement houses, Hull House, in Chicago in 1889.

In this chapter's ***Letter to the Editor*** we see that the United States remains a nation with many immigrants. The dilemmas involving immigration are complex and, for many in America, emotionally charged.

HIGHER EDUCATION

In 1862 President Lincoln signed a congressional bill called the **Morrill Act.** Through this act the government granted states 30,000 acres of land for every senator and representative it had in Congress in 1860. The income the states could generate from this land was to be used to support at least one college. The Second Morrill Act of 1890 further stipulated that no grants would be given to states where college admission was denied because of race unless the state provided a separate-but-equal institution. As a result of the Morrill legislation, 65 land-grant colleges were established, including the universities of Maine (1865), Illinois (1867), and California (1868); Purdue University (1869); and Texas A&M (1871) (Rippa, 1997).

As colleges flourished, more progressive ways of educating children and adolescents also began to grow. The discussion of 20th-century education begins with progressive education, first introduced at the close of the 19th century.

What Were the Major Influences, Issues, Ideologies, and Individuals in 20th-Century American Education?

Varying population patterns, American inventiveness, wars, and technology made the 20th century one of extremes.

CONTEXT FOR CHANGE

In the 20th century, America survived two world wars, numerous regional conflicts in Korea, Vietnam, and elsewhere, and a protracted period of dire economic stress. It also thrived in years of unprecedented economic prosperity. The populace of the United States grew increasingly aware of its own diversity. Periods of rampant racial tension necessitated healing and both legal and educational responses on a national level.

Technological advances took us to the moon and beyond, enhanced communication of all sorts, and brought about global awareness unimagined in other centuries. In schools, the beginning of the century ushered more of the components of John Dewey's progressive education into classrooms.

PROGRESSIVE EDUCATION

In 1896 John Dewey established the first laboratory school at the University of Chicago to test the principles of **progressive education.** The progressive method was very different from the traditional 19th-century approach to education. What started with students learn-ing in cooperative groups and letting their interests guide what they learned about traditional subjects grew into a major movement with far-reaching implications. The influence of John Dewey was tremendous as the United States moved from the 19th to the 20th century.

The progressive movement gained momentum during the first quarter of the 20th century and flourished until the end of World War II. The influences of progressivism are still evident in the 21st century. The basic principles of progressive education are summarized in Figure 7.5. These principles show the sharp contrast between the philosophy of progressivism and the established ways of doing school discussed earlier. John Dewey's primary focus was the implementation of schooling as a means of social reform and the improvement of life for Americans.

JUNIOR HIGH AND MIDDLE SCHOOL

The need for a bridge between elementary and high school became apparent as the high school developed into a 4-year institution and the courses taught there became more standardized in content. Educators began to delineate the kinds of preparation necessary for high school

John Dewey (1859–1952)

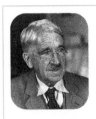

Think about all the things that happened in the United States during John Dewey's life, from the Civil War to the Korean War. He lived and wrote a very long time. In terms of education, many consider Dewey the most influential American of the 20th century. He was a professor of philosophy and pedagogy at the University of Chicago and at Columbia University. In Chicago, Dewey's son attended a school run by an ardent follower of Pestalozzi and Froebel. Dewey was so impressed with the approach of the school that he began researching, thinking, and writing about it. What we know today as progressive education was given an intellectual foundation by Dewey.

Dewey wrote more than 500 articles and 40 books, among which *The School and Society* (1900) and *The Child and the Curriculum* (1902) had perhaps the greatest impact on American education. In his laboratory school at the University of Chicago, he implemented progressive education and introduced projects such as carpentry, weaving, sewing, and cooking into the curriculum. Dewey believed that education should be experiential and child centered, rather than subject driven. He proposed that education is best served when the whole child is considered, including all the aspects of development.

John Dewey believed that democracy should be practiced not only in the governance of the United States but also in the day-to-day life of a school. Children should be free to question, investigate, and make changes in their environments. Learning the principles of democracy early in life would serve them well later as adults.

Dewey (1956); Rippa (1997). CORBIS–NY

Figure 7.5 Basic principles of progressive education

1. Education is life, not just preparation for life.
2. Learning should be directly related to the interests of the child.
3. Learning through problem solving should be emphasized more than rote memorization of subject matter.
4. The role of the teacher is to facilitate learning more so than to direct it.
5. Cooperation among students should be emphasized more than competition.
6. Democracy should be practiced to encourage the free interplay of ideas that leads to growth.

Source: Kneller, G. F. (1971). *Introduction to the philosophy of education.* New York: Wiley.

success. High school teachers and administrators asked for basic preparation in algebra and English before high school. Writers such as G. Stanley Hall began recognizing a period of life called adolescence and acknowledging that adolescence was different from childhood. This new viewpoint led to a change in the configuration of schools; elementary schools shifted from eight grades to five or six, and the remaining two or three grades became junior high schools. Later in the century, junior high most frequently encompassed grades 7 through 9.

In the 1960s, another concept of schooling was formed to meet the unique needs of young adolescents: the middle school. Rather than viewing grades 5 to 8 or 6 to 8 as merely a time of preparation for high school, middle school philosophy called for recognition of the unique developmental qualities of young adolescents and use of developmental appropriateness in the school, in both curriculum and instruction.

Maria Montessori (1870–1952)

A compassionate medical doctor, Maria Montessori established a children's house, a kind of school within a house, for poor children in early 20th-century Italy. As people recognized transformation in these children they began studying Montessori's methodology and opening other children's houses, later referred to as Montessori schools. As Maria Montessori herself said, "The task of the child is to construct a man [or woman] oriented to his environment, adapted to his time, place, and culture" (1967, p. xiv). She believed that children are capable of integrating aspects of the world around them through the use of their senses. Children ages 3 to 6 are the ideal participants in the Montessori method. Montessori insisted that children's environments be carefully constructed to allow them to sense their learning with materials, such as letters made of sandpaper and colored objects to count.

Chartock (2004); Good (1964); Montessori (1967). CORBIS–NY

MONTESSORI METHOD

Although Maria Montessori (1870–1952) was developing a philosophy of early childhood education in Italy and other parts of Europe in the beginning of the 20th century, the Montessori method was not widely implemented in the United States until the 1950s. Today many Montessori principles can be found in early childhood settings across the United States.

INFLUENTIAL AFRICAN AMERICAN LEADERS

W. E. B. Du Bois believed that African Americans should pursue higher education to become leaders in politics and education. He sharply disagreed with Booker T. Washington's philosophy that African Americans would best serve themselves and their race by pursuing vocational arts and skills to prepare them to compete in the workplace with white people.

Mary McLeod Bethune was influential in both education and government policy. Her long career as a teacher, as well as college instructor and founder, took her from her home in South Carolina to college experiences in Chicago, to Florida, where she founded Bethune-Cookman College, and all the way to Washington, D.C., where she served as an adviser to President Franklin D. Roosevelt in the 1930s (Chartock, 2004).

W. E. B. Du Bois (1868–1963)

As a champion for equality of Africans and African Americans, W. E. B. Du Bois spent his life as a scholar, a writer, and a reformer. In 1895 he was the first African American to earn a doctorate from Harvard. From 1895 through the 1950s he was a college professor and a civil rights activist. He organized worldwide conferences of black leaders. Du Bois considered Africa the homeland of all black people and wrote about the dual citizenry of black people who had left Africa in his 1903 book, *The Souls of Black Folks.* In 1907 he cofounded the National Association for the Advancement of Colored People (NAACP). Disillusioned by lack of progress for people of African descent in the United States, Du Bois embraced socialism. At age 93, he joined the Communist Party and moved to Ghana, where he died at age 95.

Boyer and Stuckey (2005). The New York Public Library/Art Resource, NY

History of Education in the United States

THE LAST FIVE DECADES OF THE 20TH CENTURY

Mary McLeod Bethune (1875–1955)

1950S. The *Leave It to Beaver* white-bread world of Ward and June Cleaver and their two sons was experienced by many families in the United States and was considered a desirable social paradigm during the period of unprecedented economic growth and prosperity following World War II. In 1957, however, the "all's right with the world" syndrome was shaken by the Soviet launch of *Sputnik*, the first satellite to venture into space. The **National Defense Education Act of 1958** called for strengthening of science, math, and foreign language programs. Teachers were given training in the use of new methods and materials in hopes of bringing American student learning up to, and beyond, the levels of learning in other countries.

Another major factor in the American schools of the 1950s was the increasing pressure to desegregate. After all the years of separate-but-equal schools, the Supreme Court upheld the complaints of the National Association for the Advancement of Colored People (NAACP) made on behalf of a Kansas family in the now famous ***Brown v. Board of Education*** ruling of 1954. Chief Justice Earl Warren declared that segregating children based solely on race was wrong and illegal. Some schools integrated peacefully, but others did not. Still other segregated schools made little or no attempt to change at all.

While the launching of *Sputnik* triggered immediate changes in American education, and desegregation came to the forefront as an ongoing issue with significant moral implications, another, quieter, yet very important change was also taking place in the 1950s. Educators began to examine curriculum more carefully as a result of the thinking of Ralph Tyler (1902-1994). Tyler proposed that data concerning the needs of the learner, the needs of society, and the needs of the subject area should all be considered in the process of developing curricula. Tyler believed that learning should have both specific objectives and appropriate assessments.

Another influential person in American education, Benjamin Bloom (1913-1999), headed a group that composed what has become known as Bloom's taxonomy of learning objectives. The taxonomy was introduced in 1956 and continues to influence how educators think about and write learning objectives today.

1960S. The 1960s were characterized by a more outspoken U.S. citizenry. The election of a young, vibrant president, John F. Kennedy, gave rise to a sense of idealism among younger voters. After the assassination of President Kennedy in 1963, Lyndon Johnson attempted to continue in this vein with what he called the War on Poverty and the creation of the Great Society. Both the Kennedy and Johnson administrations allocated large amounts of money to break the

Born in South Carolina of former slave parents, Mary McLeod Bethune was educated in a Presbyterian mission school and attended Moody Bible Institute in Chicago. The school in her hometown of Mayesville was for whites only. Although Bethune originally wanted to be a missionary to Africa and was often quoted as saying the drums of Africa still beat in her heart, she dedicated her life to educating African American students. She established a school in Florida that became a normal school to train female African American teachers. Later the school evolved into Bethune-Cookman College, a 4-year coeducational college with mostly African American students.

In the midst of her work with education, Bethune became good friends with Eleanor Roosevelt, who drew her into government service, specifically the National Youth Administration (NYA), a branch of the Works Progress Administration (WPA) created by President Franklin D. Roosevelt. In 1935 Bethune founded the National Council of Negro Women, an umbrella group for all organizations working on behalf of African American women.

Boyer and Stuckey (2005). Courtesy of the Library of Congress

Ralph Tyler (1902–1994)

Upon his death, a news release from the Stanford University News Service called Ralph Tyler "the grand old man of educational research." Ralph Tyler's contributions to education were many, with his impact on curriculum development perhaps the most meaningful. Of the 16 books and over 700 journal articles he wrote, the one with perhaps the most impact was among his first, *Basic Principles of Curriculum and Instruction*, published in 1949.

Tyler's commonsense approach to curriculum development involved

- determining the goals of the school
- selecting learning experiences useful in attaining the goals
- organizing instruction around the experiences
- and then deciding how best to evaluate the learning

Tyler conducted a groundbreaking longitudinal analysis of 30 schools and the careers of their students called the Eight-Year Study (1933-1941). This study focused on the opportunities students had who stayed in school rather than joining the workforce during the depression.

Tyler is also responsible for initiating the National Assessment of Educational Progress (NAEP) test in the 1960s, still the only test that evaluates the U.S. school system rather than the success of the students in it. Ralph Tyler was often heard to make two statements: "I never wanted to be anything but a teacher," and "I never met a child who couldn't learn."

McNeil (1995); Stanford News Service (1994); Tyler (1949). Ansel Adams/University of Chicago Library

Benjamin Bloom (1913–1999)

Following the 1948 convention of the American Psychological Association, Benjamin Bloom chaired a team that examined the cognitive, affective, and psychomotor domains of educational activity. From their work came what today is known as Bloom's taxonomy, discussed in Chapter 4. As part of his work at the University of Chicago, Bloom observed that about 95% of all classroom questions were at the knowledge (recall) level. The taxonomy provides a way to structure both activities and questions that run the gamut of intellectual processing.

Bloom also did extensive work in the area of assessment. He was influenced by Ralph Tyler and recognized that comparing students wasn't as important in terms of assessment as helping students master the learning.

Benjamin Bloom's work has been both condensed and expanded over the years by scholars and practitioners. His contributions to education are meaningful and enduring.

Bloom (1956); Eisner (2000). University of Chicago Library

cycle of poverty in the United States (Boyer & Stuckey, 2005). For example, the **Vocational Education Act of 1963** quadrupled the amount of money allocated for vocational education.

The following year, the **Civil Rights Act of 1964** stipulated that if schools discriminated based on race, color, or national origin, they would not be eligible for federal funding. Similarly, in a series of court battles, the Supreme Court continued to strike down school segregation.

In 1965 Congress passed the Elementary and Secondary Education Act (ESEA), which provided extra money for school districts with low-income families. Project Head Start was also established to boost the early learning of children ages 3 to 6 from low-income homes. The **Bilingual Education Act of 1968** (Title VII of the ESEA of 1965) validated children's native language and provided funds to assist non-English-speaking students who were dropping out of high school at a rate of about 70%. The dramatic increases in numbers of Mexican and Mexican American children in the schools as a result of both legal and illegal immigration have created an ongoing challenge for educators that the Bilingual Education Act only partially addresses.

1970S. During the first half of the decade, the country's attention was focused on the Vietnam conflict and the administration of President Richard Nixon. Public trust in establishment institutions was repeatedly shaken, resulting in a general lack of confidence in schools and teachers. The number of students in public schools decreased during the 1970s while private schools and homeschooling grew. Public school students' test scores dropped. Many perceived the need to implement a back-to-basics curriculum, and demands for accountability increased.

At the same time, some good things happened in 1970s education. Title IX of the Education Amendment Acts, which prohibited sexual discrimination in any education program receiving federal funding, took effect in 1972. Additionally, in 1979 President Carter elevated the federal office of education to a department, making its secretary a member of his cabinet.

PL 94–142, the Education for All Handicapped Children Act, passed in 1975. This important legislation granted children with disabilities the right to an education that meets their needs in the least restrictive environment.

It wasn't until the 1970s that the U.S. policy changed from one of assimilation to fostering self-determination, encouraging Native Americans to take charge of their own education, whether on reservations or in other public schools. Today, even though there are more Native Americans under age 20, proportionally speaking, than in the general white population, a smaller percentage of Native Americans participate in formal education (Ornstein & Levine, 2006). In other words, in the whole Native American population, there is a greater percentage of people under the age of 20 when compared to the white population. Yet there is a smaller percentage of these young people in school when compared to white young people.

1980S. During the 8 years of Ronald Reagan's presidency (1981–1989) federal funding for elementary and secondary education declined by 17%. Even so, the quality of education received renewed attention for two basic reasons. The first reason was concern over economic competition with Japan. Many Americans believed that the United States had begun to compare unfavorably with Japan, in part because of inferior schools.

The second reason for the renewed attention to education was the release in 1983 of a report commissioned by President Reagan called *A Nation at Risk: The Imperative for*

Educational Reform. The language of the report was strong, referring to public education in the United States as a "rising tide of mediocrity." In response, various proposals for reform and improvement surfaced. The *Paideia Proposal* (1982) by Mortimer Adler called for a core curriculum based on Great Books. The 1989 Carnegie Council on Adolescent Development report, *Turning Points: Preparing American Youth for the 21st Century,* validated the middle-level philosophy of the National Middle School Association, which called for small learning communities, the elimination of tracking, and careful guidance.

Restructuring became a buzzword in education. Some of the efforts included year-round schools, longer school days, longer school years, and more funding for technology.

1990S. The 1990s might be labeled as the era of standards. Along with the standards came tests designed to determine whether students had met the standards. The emphasis shifted from the input of education (what teachers do, funding, support) to the output of education (student learning). President Bill Clinton brought increased attention to education as he promised to be an effective "education president." He formalized Goals 2000, an initiative begun by his predecessor, George H. W. Bush (1988–1992). Although the goals were admirably lofty, they were also unrealistically high and have, for the most part, been unfulfilled.

In the 1990s, teachers began taking on leadership roles in schools and in school districts. There was more collaboration among parents, the community, students, administrators, and teachers. Record enrollments resulted in a teacher shortage. President Clinton, in addition to providing federal support for the recruitment of 100,000 new teachers, joined policy makers in asking states to raise teacher standards (Webb et al., 2010).

What Major Influences, Issues, Ideologies, and Individuals Are We Experiencing in 21st-Century American Education?

One full decade of this new century has passed. Our nation has experienced turbulence on every front.

CONTEXT FOR CHANGE

The new century was ushered in with fears that proved to be unfounded as we anticipated what was called Y2K, or Year 2000. Many gathered around televisions to watch as the year 2000 dawned in countries around the globe, complete with celebrations and massive displays of fireworks—and an eerie sense of anxiety about events such as worldwide computer blackouts and destruction of all sorts that were prophesized but never materialized.

Less than 2 years later, our worst fears did materialize in the form of the disastrous day now simply known as 9/11. When terrorists killed thousands of Americans on American soil, our way of life changed, both politically and practically. The subsequent conflicts and political unrest in Iraq and Afghanistan continued to take their toll. The administration of George W. Bush (2000–2008) was one of turmoil and strong disagreements in terms of war, economics, and governmental controls. The economic downturn that began during the Bush years strangled American prosperity and perpetuated a downward spiral of failed businesses and unemployment that made life very difficult for many in the first decade of the 21st century. Rampant mistrust and suspicion plagued America.

The election in 2008 of America's first African American president, Barack Obama, brought jubilation for some and a newly expressed animosity for others. The abrupt change from a conservative Republican administration to what many viewed as a liberal Democrat occupant in the White House put American's political tolerance for bipartisan decision making and action to the test.

NO CHILD LEFT BEHIND

The defining legislation of the first decade of the 21st century was the No Child Left Behind Act of 2001 (NCLB). The act was the reauthorization of the Elementary and Secondary Education Act (1965) and called for accountability of schools and school districts to states, and of states to the federal government. No Child Left Behind was formulated as a response to evidence that students were being promoted without mastering concepts and were graduating without basic literacy skills.

21ST-CENTURY KNOWLEDGE AND SKILLS

The Partnership for 21st Century Skills (P21) exerts considerable and growing influence in schools across the country. But it's not just an organization that is influencing what we teach and learn; it's the concept that our world is changing and schools need to change as well.

In Context for Change we get a sense for the complexity of life in the United States and around the world. The goal of teachers and schools should be to provide educational experiences that reflect this complexity as we equip students to live productively and positively. The present, and therefore history as well, is shaped by human responses to dilemmas. It's all about problem solving, a 21st-century skill that is more relevant than ever before.

In the 21st century, information will continue to grow at exponential rates. Teaching students how to figure out what they need to know, where and how to access it, and then how to use it effectively, should be emphasized in teaching and learning. Then wrapping this package in appreciation for, and the ability to accomplish, collaboration will help students thrive in the 21st century.

21ST-CENTURY SCHOOLS

In most schools in the United States it would be difficult to recognize change between the 1990s and the first decade of the 21st century. In some schools the classrooms may not have changed physically or in terms of learning experiences since long before 1990. Yet in others innovative technology such as SMART Boards, laptop computers, LCD projectors, and more tell the story of mushrooming technological advances.

Virtual education is becoming more widespread as educators use technology to deliver and reinforce teaching and learning. Books of all kind are available electronically, and communication with classrooms around the globe changes the way we view instruction. Although teaching is still viewed as place based in a classroom for most educators, the possibilities of using whole communities and cyberspace as learning environments are taking education into uncharted dimensions. What an exciting time to become a teacher!

How Are U.S. Schools Addressing Racial and Ethnic Diversity in the 21st Century?

The short answer to this question is "Not very well," and certainly not with consistency. For instance, research shows that 55 years after the Supreme Court declared that separate is not equal in *Brown* v. *Board of Education,* U.S. schools are more segregated now than before the Court ruling (Orfield, 2009). Of the defining issues in American education, perhaps none is so challenging as finding ways to address racial and ethnic diversity. Table 7.3 shows the percentage of students by race and ethnicity in regions of the United States.

Although American public schools have been relatively successful in educating immigrants from Europe and Asia and helping them achieve at least middle-class status in the United States, our schools have been much less successful in doing so for those students from nonwhite communities—African Americans and Hispanics (Orfield, 2009).

AFRICAN AMERICAN STUDENTS

Laws have been passed and policies have been made with the intent of fully integrating U.S. schools. In our history, African American students were not treated as benignly as Native and

TABLE 7.3 Public school student enrollment percentages by region and race/ethnicity (2006–2007)					
Region	White	Black	Latino/ Hispanic	Asian	Native American and Other
West	44.6	6.4	38.7	8.3	2
South	48.9	26.5	21.5	2.6	.5
Northeast	64	15.4	14.9	5.3	.3
National	56.5	17.1	20.5	4.7	1.2

Source: Orfield, G. (2009). *Reviving the goal of an integrated society: A 21st century challenge.* Los Angeles: The Civil Rights Project/Proyecto Derechos Civiles at UCLA.

Mexican Americans or any other racial/ethnic group. They have suffered outright and purposeful discrimination, including laws that forbade their education. Today there are no such laws, and yet in some locations and in some circumstances we still find differences in opportunities for black students, compared with white students (Banks & Banks, 2009).

One of our focus students at Cario Middle School, Patrick Sutton, is an excellent student with what appears to be an intact sense of confidence. For Patrick, as a black student, the doors of opportunity seem to be open wide. His positive experiences at Cario are what we should desire for all students, regardless of their race or ethnicity.

To watch an interview with Patrick and his mom, go to the Teaching in Focus section for Chapter 7 in MyEducationLab for this course.

HISPANIC AMERICAN STUDENTS

At the end of the first decade of the 21st century there were over 45 million Hispanic people living in the United States. Some families have been in America for centuries, and the vast majority has come here to escape some form of oppression. They have come from many countries, and thus have a variety of ethnicities, as illustrated in Figure 7.6.

Figure 7.6 Hispanic subgroups in the United States

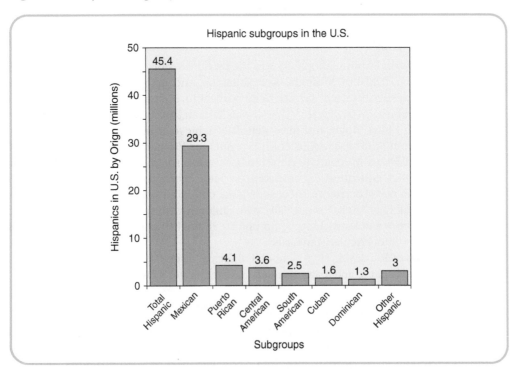

Source: U.S. Census Bureau. (2008). *American Factfinder: BO3001. Hispanic or Latino origin by specific origin.* Retrieved May 22, 2010, from http://factfinder.census.gov/servlet/DTTable?_bm=y&-geo_id=01000US&-ds_name=ACS_2008_3YR_G00_&-mt_name=ACS_2008_3YR_G2000_B03001.

History of Education in the United States

Teaching in Focus

Sara Davis Powell

Angelica Reynosa, World History, Roosevelt High School, California. *In her own words....*

I can't imagine being anywhere else professionally than in a school. My husband and I are both teachers. It is a wonderful life!

I teach in a school where minority populations are the majority. Most of my students, and indeed most of the students at Roosevelt, are Latino Americans. Some were born in America; others have been here for only a few weeks. Some have families with established careers; others have families who are undocumented workers. Regardless, they are the faces of an ever-growing Latino presence in America. Some of my students, like Hugo, have secure, loving homes headed by parents who risked their lives to come to America. Hugo will be successful. He knows it's his legacy. He attends school regularly, and he is learning English quickly.

I see my job as not only a teacher of a course for high school credit but also as an advocate for the well-being of my students, most of whom are in bilingual classes so they can learn their subjects while learning to be fluent in English. As a Spanish speaker, I am able to teach both history and coping skills in English communication. Find your special niche in education. You have unique talents and gifts that will be valuable to students. Search for those talents and develop them for the sake of the students.

The dilemmas for schools regarding the rapid increase of Hispanic students are complex. Perhaps the dilemma with the most impact on schools is that of language diversity. How do we teach the standards to children who can't understand what we say or write? Currently our schools attempt to answer this question through three basic programs: English as a Second Language (ESL), bilingual education, and Structured English Immersion (SEI). Our efforts are inadequate, particularly for any child raised in a non-English-speaking home. Read what focus teacher, Angelica Reynosa, has to say about her role as an advocate for Hispanic students in *Teaching in Focus*.

ASIAN AMERICAN STUDENTS

About half of the world's population falls into the broad category of Asian. They may live in China, Japan, India, Pakistan, Vietnam, Korea, Samoa, and many more countries. Asian Americans have vastly different experiences both before emigrating and when in the United States either legally or illegally (U.S. Census Bureau, 2009).

Students from China, Japan, and India generally achieve at high levels in U.S. schools, while students from Southeast Asian countries such as Vietnam and Cambodia tend to struggle. Many children who come to America from war-torn, trauma-filled areas find their problems within U.S. education exacerbated, or made worse, by their life experiences. Again, language is a major barrier to success. In large cities and small towns across America, teachers who speak only English work daily with children who speak a great variety of languages in their homes and struggle to communicate in English in order to learn even small bits and pieces of our curricular standards.

To review principal Romero's interview, go to Maria Romero in the Teaching in Focus section for Chapter 7 in MyEducationLab for this course.

The principal of Roosevelt High School, California, discusses her school that is populated primarily by Hispanic and Asian students in this chapter's *Diversity Dialogue*.

MIDDLE EASTERN AMERICAN STUDENTS

So often targets of prejudice in our post-9/11 world, students of Middle Eastern descent are entering our schools in increasing, yet still relatively small, numbers. They may be from countries including Egypt, Jordan, Iraq, Iran, Syria, Lebanon, and Saudi Arabia. Many are linked to Islam, the religion of people referred to as Muslim. But in reality, more Middle Eastern Americans align with Christianity than with Islam.

Maria Romero, principal of Roosevelt High School in Fresno, California, is acutely aware of the diversity in her school. She has been there in some capacity since 1986. Roosevelt students are primarily of Hispanic and Asian ancestry. But she is quick to tell us that this doesn't mean that all the Hispanics are alike; nor are all the Asians alike. Within the Hispanic population there are students whose families have lived in the United States for generations, and others who crossed the Mexican border illegally only weeks before coming to Roosevelt. Some speak fluent English, and little or no Spanish, and others who understand and speak practically no English at all. Within the Asian population, students may be Hmong, Cambodian, Laotian, and more, with very few from China, Japan, or India. They speak different languages and have a variety of dialects of each language. Most of the students at Roosevelt qualify for free or reduced-price lunch, revealing their socioeconomic status.

Sara Davis Powell

When asked by students if she is Mexican, Mrs. Romero replies that she is American, a U.S. citizen with Mexican ancestry. She tells students it is important to keep their first language, and that it is imperative for them to be fluent in English to be successful in the United States. She and her teachers have lots of lessons they want to pass on to the students at Roosevelt. Respond to the following items by writing one well-developed paragraph for each.

1. According to Mrs. Romero, why is it important for Roosevelt teachers to inspire students to believe they can be more than they thought they could be? Why is this more of a challenge at Roosevelt than in some other schools? What are two ways teachers might accomplish this given what we know about Roosevelt students?

2. Mrs. Romero tells us that unlike in many schools, Roosevelt parents put students completely in the hands of the adults in the school. They want their children to succeed, but most haven't been educated themselves. In what ways might Roosevelt teachers involve parents in the education of their children, given their parental reluctance?

Cultural norms of Middle Eastern American students are often noticeably different from the mainstream. They may talk more loudly with what sounds like an odd intonation, hold hands with same-sex friends, not consider being late a sign of disrespect, not hold females in as high regard as males, and so forth. Because these norms are counter to what we generally expect in U.S. schools, life in school may be more difficult for some. Even so, students of Middle Eastern heritage tend to do quite well in school, go to college at a higher than average rate, and live productive lives in the United States (Banks & Banks, 2009).

How Can I Be Aware of Education History in the Making?

Time gives us perspective. We can look at the history of American education and determine which of the various influences, issues, ideologies, and individuals have most affected the course of schools, teachers, and students. What is less than obvious is which of these influences, issues, ideologies, and individuals are making a difference or initiating significant change now. Fifty or 100 years from now, it will likely be evident.

Education issues come and go, often in predictable cycles. The notable individuals involved in education at any given point are numerous. Sifting through them to determine who has significant and long-term influence generally only happens with time. The danger of listing contemporary movers and shakers in any field is the inevitable omission of names. Given that risk, Table 7.4 is an attempt to provide a partial list of individuals and their contributions that are currently influencing American education. You will no doubt hear and read about these people as you pursue a degree in teaching.

Reading professional journals, continuing to take courses, attending conferences, having conversations with colleagues—all of these activities will help you stay abreast of the

Points of Reflection 7.4

Do you anticipate a diverse classroom with a sense of excitement or a nagging dread? Explain your answer. Is there anything in your background that uniquely prepares you for a diverse classroom? If so, explain.

TABLE 7.4 History in the making

Individual	Theory, Field of Research, Written Works
Mortimer Adler	Paideia Proposal; core curriculum based on Great Books
James Banks	Multicultural education
David Berliner	Educational researcher; teacher effectiveness
Marva Collins	Tireless advocate for all children; founder of Westside Preparatory School
James Comer	Comer Model; emphasis on social context of teaching and learning
Larry Cuban	Expert on change in education
Linda Darling-Hammond	*The Right to Learn*; teacher quality and preparation
Marian Wright Edelman	Children's Defense Fund; advocate for all children
Elliot Eisner	Arts education; curriculum reform
Jaime Escalante	Outstanding high school math teacher in urban Los Angeles
Paulo Freire	*Pedagogy of the Oppressed*; education gives power to the poor
Howard Gardner	Multiple intelligences theory
William Glasser	Choice theory of human behavior
John Goodlad	*A Place Called School*; democracy and education; teacher education
Maxine Greene	Existentialism; *Landscapes of Learning*
E. D. Hirsch	*Cultural Literacy: What Every American Needs to Know*
Ivan Illich	Social reconstructionism; *Deschooling America*
Herbert Kohl	*36 Children*; the value of teachers and teaching differentiated instruction
Jacob Kounin	Classroom management
Jonathan Kozol	*Savage Inequalities: Children in America's Schools*; study of urban children
Sonia Nieto	Multicultural and bilingual education
Nel Noddings	Caring in the classroom; teacher reflection
Theodore Sizer	Coalition of Essential Schools; necessity of community in school environment; *Horace's Compromise*
Robert Slavin	Success for All program; early intervention
Kay Toliver	Outstanding teacher in urban New York City
Carol Ann Tomlinson	Differentiated instruction
Grant Wiggins/Jay McTighe	*Understanding by Design*; development of curriculum, instruction, and assessment

Points of Reflection 7.5

Which educators in your school experiences have had the most positive impact on you? Explain their impact.

individuals in the forefront of our work as teachers. History is in the making all around us. In classrooms across the United States, excellent teachers are the real heroes of education. If you decide to be a teacher, then the history of American education has been changed, perhaps not in ways that will make it into history books but in ways that influence the lives of the hundreds, maybe thousands of students in your future classroom.

CONCLUDING THOUGHTS

This brief look at the history of education in the United States has been written from a majority culture viewpoint (white, middle class) primarily using sources having the same lens. Encapsulating 400 years into one brief chapter involves choices that have inherent limitations. Be aware of this when you consider any aspect of history. Understand that there's always more to the story.

American education has been more reactionary than trailblazing, more foundational than earthshaking. In an ideal world educators would be ahead of dilemmas, and the teaching and learning in U.S. schools would lead the way toward solutions to our country's problems. And indeed this is true, but in a subtle way. The adage "Teachers make all

History of Education in the United States

other professions possible" elevates teachers to indispensable heroes, although they are largely unheralded as such.

The history of education in the United States parallels the history of the country. Although once relatively simple and perceived as manageable, education in the United States is now incredibly complex and often unwieldy, with issues to match. In spite of the lessons to be learned from studying the history of American education, there remain unacceptable conditions for learning in some schools, unequal opportunities for children based on such factors as socioeconomic status and race, and international test results that show mediocre performances by U.S. students. Together we will face many challenges as we strive to effectively build on the past to do a better job of educating in, and for, the future, asking, "And how are the children? Are they all well?"

We began this chapter by considering Angelica Reynosa's classroom and teaching responsibilities at Roosevelt High School in Fresno, California. As she teaches world history, she is often reminded that the plight of many of her students resembles some in history who have suffered hardships but who also possess hope for a better life. Now as the chapter comes to an end, we join Angelica as she considers ways to make history relevant for her students. Read through *Chapter in Review* to help refresh your memory of what we have discussed, then interact with Angelica as she plans learning experiences for her students in *Developing Professional Competence*.

You watched Angelica's lesson in Chapter 3, but review it now to help you respond to these items. The lesson may be accessed in the Teaching in Focus section for Chapter 7 in the MyEducationLab for this course.

Chapter in Review

What were the major influences, issues, ideologies, and individuals in 17th-century American education?

- Many of the original colonists came to America seeking religious freedom and established schools to bolster their beliefs.
- Colonial schools primarily served white males.
- Education differed greatly among the New England, middle, and southern colonies.

What were the major influences, issues, ideologies, and individuals in 18th-century American education?

- Private academies served as secondary schools that went beyond what was taught in dame schools and town schools.
- Influential leaders, such as Benjamin Franklin, Thomas Jefferson, and Noah Webster, contributed to the expansion of educational opportunities.
- Education became a state responsibility by virtue of not being addressed in the Constitution.

What were the major influences, issues, ideologies, and individuals in 19th-century American education?

- Common schools were the first public, free American elementary schools.
- Following the Civil War, the first high schools began to flourish to meet the new economic demands of an increasingly industrialized United States.

- Kindergarten, with an activity-based curriculum, became common by the end of the 19th century.
- Teacher preparation institutions called normal schools were created to respond to the need for more teachers with increased and consistent preparation.
- Few educational opportunities existed for children with disabilities, children of color, or children of poor immigrant parents.
- Land-grant colleges were established as a result of the Morrill Acts.

What were the major influences, issues, ideologies, and individuals in 20th-century American education?

- John Dewey and the philosophy of progressive education fostered more active student participation in a school system based on democratic principles.
- Junior highs, and then middle schools, bridged the gap between elementary and high schools.
- Interest in science and math education increased following the launch of *Sputnik*.
- During the 1970s, the Education for All Handicapped Children Act and Title IX increased educational opportunities for all children.
- *A Nation at Risk* served as a wake-up call for education in the United States.
- Curriculum standards emerged in the 1990s as the defining criteria for the quality of teaching and learning.

What major influences, issues, ideologies, and individuals are we experiencing in 21st-century American education?

- The first decade of the 21st century in America was filled with turmoil.
- The No Child Left Behind Act of 2001 called for increased accountability on local and state levels and emphasized the need for all children to learn.
- The Partnership for 21st Century Skills (P21) exerts considerable and growing influence in schools across the country.
- Some schools have remained virtually unchanged for decades; others reflect the technology and strategies available for teaching and learning in the 21st century.

How are U.S. schools addressing racial and ethnic diversity in the 21st century?

- Although some strides have been made in a quest to provide equal opportunities for learning to all children in the United States, there is still much to do.
- African American students are more segregated now than they were at the time of *Brown* v. *Board of Education* when *separate but equal* was designated as unlawful.
- The Hispanic student population is rapidly growing, but our ability to improve their learning and their language skills is not keeping up with their need.
- Students from China, Japan, and India generally appear to be achieving at high levels in U.S. schools, while students from Southeast Asian countries such as Vietnam and Cambodia struggle.
- Cultural norms of Middle Eastern American students are often noticeably different from mainstream Americans, necessitating an even greater need for understanding on the part of teachers.

How can I be aware of education history in the making?

- Teachers should assume the responsibility of staying current with major shifts in educational concepts and trends. Time provides perspective. As history unfolds, those most influential will emerge in prominence.

Developing Professional Competence

Visit the Developing Professional Competence section on Chapter 7 of the MyEducationLab for this text to answer the following questions and begin your preparation for licensure exams.

Angelica Reynosa wants her students to see the big picture included in the world history curriculum and help them grasp the significance of how various forms of government enhance or inhibit people's lives. She wants them to understand how knowledge of history is meaningful for their futures and how it can give them perspective about their roots and cultural struggles.

Think about Angelica and her students as you answer the following multiple-choice questions:

1. Why is the establishment of the United States in the 17th century relevant to many of Angelica's students?
   a. The people who came to the United States from Europe did so to find refuge from a government that they found to be oppressive.
   b. It's been 400 years and we now have perspective on the early days of the United States.
   c. Many Hispanics came to America then as they do now.
   d. Mexico was experiencing a similar fight for independence in the 17th century.

2. Why is it important for Angelica's students to understand how various people throughout history have suffered oppression?
   a. They need to see that they are not alone.
   b. They will be encouraged to see how people have overcome difficulties.
   c. They need to understand it so they won't perpetuate it.
   d. It is vital to understand that history repeats itself.

3. In the lesson you observed, what purpose does the candy serve?
   a. The candy randomly given and taken shows students that they actually have very little control over their lives.

b. They are learning to cleverly hoard candy and keep it from being taken away, much as they will need to do in a capitalistic country.
c. The candy is an incentive to participate fully in the rock-paper-scissors activity.
d. The candy is randomly given and taken away, showing that in governments without freedom there is little control over one's destiny.

Now it's time for you to respond to two short essay items involving Angelica and her students. In your responses, be sure to address all the dilemmas and questions posed in each item. Your responses should each be between one half and one double-spaced page.

4. The class you observed is bilingual. How did Angelica approach the lesson to both teach the content and the English language? Why is Angelica's own ethnicity important to the teaching and learning process in her classroom?

5. As Angelica considers her students and her responsibilities, she reflects on these two NBPTS and INTASC standards. Why is each especially important to her, given that she teaches in a bilingual classroom?

NBPTS Standard 5 *Teachers are members of learning communities.*

INTASC Standard 9 Professional Commitment and Responsibilities *The teacher is a reflective practitioner who continually evaluates the effects of his/her actions on others and who actively seeks out opportunities to grow professionally.*

Where DO I Stand NOW?

In the beginning of this chapter you completed an inventory that gauged your knowledge of history of the United States and history of U.S. education. Now that you have read the chapter, completed exercises related to the content, engaged in class discussions, and so on, answer these two questions in your course notebook.

1. Explain one lesson America appears to have learned from the past and how that lesson is evident in education today.

2. Explain one lesson America appears *not* to have learned from the past. What evidence do you have that the lesson has not changed how public education functions today?

MyEducationLab

The MyEducationLab for this course can help you solidify your comprehension of Chapter 7 concepts.

- Explore the classrooms of the teachers and students you've met in this chapter in the Teaching in Focus section.
- Prepare for licensure exams as you deepen your understanding of chapter concepts in the Developing Professional Competence section.

- Gauge and further develop your understanding of chapter concepts by taking the quizzes and examining the enrichment materials on the Chapter 7 Study Plan.
- Visit Topic 7, "History and Philosophy of Education," to watch ABC videos, explore Assignments and Activities, and practice essential teaching skills with the Building Teaching Skills and Dispositions unit.

References

Adler, M. (1982). *The Paideia proposal: An educational manifesto.* New York: Simon & Schuster.

Banks, J. A., & Banks, C. A. M. (Eds.). (2009). *Multicultural education: Issues and perspectives* (7th ed.). New York: Wiley.

Bloom, B. S. (1956). *Taxonomy of educational objectives: Handbook I. Cognitive domain.* New York: Longman, Green.

Boyer, P., & Stuckey, S. (2005). *American nation in the modern era.* Austin, TX: Holt, Rinehart and Winston.

Button, W. H., & Provenzo, E. F., Jr. (1989). *History of education and culture in America.* Upper Saddle River, NJ: Prentice Hall.

Carnegie Corporation. (1989). *Turning points: Preparing American youth for the 21st century.* New York: Author.

Chartock, R. K. (2004). *Educational foundations: An anthology* (2nd ed.). Upper Saddle River, NJ: Merrill/Prentice Hall.

Cohen, S. S. (1974). *A history of colonial education, 1607-1776.* New York: Wiley.

Cubberly, E. (1934). *Public education in the United States.* Boston: Houghton Mifflin.

Dewey, J. (1956). *The child and the curriculum, and the school and society.* Chicago: University of Chicago Press.

Eisner, E. W. (2000). *Prospects: The quality review of comparative education.* Paris: UNESCO Publication, 30(3).

Franklin, B. (1931). Proposals relating to education of youth in Pennsylvania. In T. Woody (Ed.), *Educational views of Ben Franklin.* New York: McGraw-Hill.

Good, H. G. (1964). *A history of American education.* New York: Macmillan.

Gutek, G. L. (2005). *Historical and philosophical foundations of education* (4th ed.). Upper Saddle River, NJ: Merrill/Prentice Hall.

Holmes, M., & Weiss, B. J. (1995). *Lives of women public school teachers: Scenes from American educational history.* New York: Garland.

Johnson, J. A., Musial, D., Hall, G. E., Golnick, D. M., & Dupuis, V. L. (2005). *Introduction to the foundations of American education.* Boston: Allyn & Bacon.

Kaplan, L. S., & Owings, W. A. (2011). *American education: Building a common foundation.* Belmont, CA: Wadsworth, Cengage Learning.

Kneller, G. F. (1971). *Introduction to the philosophy of education.* New York: Wiley.

Loeper, J. L. (1973). *Going to school in 1776.* New York: Macmillan.

McNeil, J. D. (1995). *Curriculum: The teacher's initiative.* Upper Saddle River, NJ: Prentice Hall.

McNergney, R. F., & McNergney, J. M. (2009). *Education: The practice and profession of teaching.* Boston: Allyn & Bacon.

Montessori, M. (1967). *The discovery of the child.* Notre Dame, IN: Fides.

Ornstein, A. C., & Levine, D. U. (2006). *Foundations of education* (9th ed.). Boston: Houghton Mifflin.

Orfield, G. (2009). *Reviving the goal of an integrated society: A 21st century challenge.* Los Angeles: The Civil Rights Project/Proyecto Derechos Civiles at UCLA.

Pulliam, J., & Van Patten, J. (2007). *History of education in America* (9th ed.). Upper Saddle River, NJ: Merrill/Prentice Hall.

Rippa, S. A. (1997). *Education in a free society: An American history* (8th ed.). New York: Longman.

Stanford News Service. (1994). *Ralph Tyler, one of the century's foremost educators, dies at 91.* Retrieved March 1, 2006, from Stanford University News Service Web site: http://www.stanford.edu/dept/news/pr/94/940228Arc4425.html

Takaki, R. (1993). *A different mirror: A history of multicultural America.* New York: Little, Brown.

Tehie, J. B. (2007). *Historical foundations of education.* Upper Saddle River, NJ: Merrill/Prentice Hall.

Tyler, R. (1949). *Basic principles of curriculum and instruction.* Chicago: University of Chicago Press.

U.S. Census Bureau. (2008). *American Factfinder: BO3001. Hispanic or Latino origin by specific origin.* Retrieved May 22, 2010, from http://factfinder.census.gov/servlet/DTTable?_bm=y&-geo_id=01000US&-ds_name=ACS_2008_3YR_G00_&-mt_name=ACS_2008_3YR_G2000_B03001

U.S. Census Bureau. (2009). *Facts for features: Asian/Pacific American heritage month 2009.* Retrieved May 24, 2010, from http://www.census.gov/Press-Release/www/releases/archives/facts_for_features_special_editions/013385.html

Webb, L., Metha, A., & Jordan, K. F. (2010). *Foundations of American education* (6th ed.). Upper Saddle River, NJ: Pearson/Merrill.

Figure 8.1 Karen Heath, 2005 Vermont Teacher of the Year

Provided by the author

One of the ubiquitous rites of passage for preservice teachers is the completion of a philosophy of education. When I was a senior in college 22 years ago, having just completed my student teaching, one of the final requirements before being certified was to complete such a document. I was still a student, and much of what I thought about and wrote was largely theoretical. I wrote about the need for children's differences to be recognized, the importance of process in education, and freedom within a structured environment. "A Personal Philosophy of Education," as it was titled, went subsequently into a box in an attic while I ventured across the country and, a few years later, settled into a home in Vermont where the box was moved to a new attic, gathering dust with other college relics.

Last year when I was nominated to be Teacher of the Year, I was called upon once again to produce a philosophy of education. I sat down one weekend and wrote about what I believe to be the most important aspect of education—the heart. Years of experience have taught me that in order to be an effective teacher, my heart must be in it fully, from devotion to subject matter, to striving to keep up with best practices, and, most importantly, to having a heart connection to the children, as that is the only sure avenue to effective student learning.

It took a bit of digging, but I found the old college box, and at the very bottom of it lay my original philosophy of education. I took it like a treasure into the afternoon sun in our yard and carefully read not just a philosophy, but also the mind-set of an idealistic 21-year-old. Surprisingly, I still agreed with everything I had written, but there was a distinct lack of mention of anything having to do with relationships. I guess that is the aspect of teaching that I have truly learned over time.

Though my first written document sat untouched for 23 years and my newest one was just composed, I have always carried with me a philosophy of education. It brings stability to my work as initiatives and programs come and go. From a fairly benign population of children in a wealthy college town to an inner-city Boston high school, my philosophy is the backbone of what I do as a teacher. It directs what and how I teach and, most importantly, how I interact with my students. It is the core of who I am as a teacher.

Source: E-mail communication with Karen Heath, January 18, 2007.

Because teacher preparation puts you in a position to think about decisions relative to teaching, prospective teachers are usually asked to write a philosophy of education. This means you will look closely at established philosophical viewpoints, you will analyze what these viewpoints mean to teachers and their work, and then you will either state with which philosophy you agree or with which combination you most closely align. The philosophy of education you write before entering the classroom as a teacher will be based on limited experience and will be a work in progress. But it's a start and an important one.

An educational philosophy should not be a static document that you write because you have to and then never look at again. People change and grow, often in response to personal experiences. Your philosophy will change and grow. In Figure 8.1, read about Karen Heath's experience of writing an initial philosophy of education as a college assignment and her subsequent experiences leading her to revisit her philosophy.

What Are Four Branches of Philosophy?

There are branches of philosophy just as there are branches of medicine (e.g., cardiology, oncology, dermatology) and branches of law (e.g., civil, criminal, tax), each having its own definition. Because the study of philosophy is based on questions and the pursuit of answers, four commonly held basic branches of philosophy are best explored through the questions addressed in each. Metaphysics, epistemology, axiology, and logic each has its own unique category of questions that will aid in understanding its primary content and purposes. As you read this section, think about how the philosophical questions may apply in early childhood, elementary, middle, and high school classrooms.

METAPHYSICS

Metaphysics addresses the search for reality and purpose (Jacobsen, 2003). The word *metaphysics* means "beyond the material or the physical." Those who study metaphysics look for answers that go beyond scientific experiments. To understand more about metaphysics, first read the questions associated with this branch of philosophy, and then read about how metaphysics may be manifested in the classroom.

- What is reality?
- What is a human being in the grand scheme of things?
- Do cause-and-effect relationships exist?
- Does reality change, making the search for truth meaningless?
- What is the meaning of life?
- Are people born either good or evil?
- Does life have a purpose?

METAPHYSICS IN THE CLASSROOM. Curriculum is based on what we know about reality. Those who make decisions about what to teach are expressing a view of reality. When teachers attempt to inspire students to look to the future and find reasons for studying and learning, they are expressing metaphysics-related beliefs that life has purpose and that people can make decisions that affect the future. For instance, in a middle school career exploration class, a teacher may ask students to think about what they consider important in life. The teacher may then ask how aspects of a career in business management, for example, might help the students and others affected by a particular business to concentrate on what is considered important.

EPISTEMOLOGY

Epistemology addresses the dilemma of determining truth and ways of acquiring knowledge. The skeptic says it's impossible to know what the truth is, whereas the agnostic says there is no truth and therefore no need to look for it. Some people who are skeptics or agnostics in one area of their lives may believe that truth exists and can be determined in other areas. Consider the questions posed in the study of epistemology, and then read how epistemology may look in a classroom.

- What is truth?
- Does truth depend on circumstances or on the person seeking it?
- How do we acquire knowledge?
- What are the limits of knowledge?
- Is knowledge changing or fixed?

EPISTEMOLOGY IN THE CLASSROOM. Curriculum standards are stated as truths. When teachers consider there are absolute truths in the curriculum that students need to know, they must then deal with epistemological questions.

There are commonly held beliefs about where knowledge comes from and how it is acquired. Teachers tend to organize instruction or to use some instructional strategies more than others depending on their own views. For instance, believing that students learn best when they discover knowledge themselves will lead a teacher to practice inquiry-based strategies

Once teachers have determined what is true about their content area (or have accepted the curriculum standards as truths), they are ready to consider how they want students to know or discover these truths. Consider the following sources of knowing, based loosely on Eisner (1985):

1. We know based on *authority*. This belief puts the teacher, the textbook, and other sources of information squarely in the forefront of instruction.

Philosophical Foundations of Education in the United States

2. We know based on *experience*. This belief leads to active learning involving the students' senses and the gathering of data.
3. We know based on *reasoning and logic*. This belief says that we think through situations and problems and draw conclusions.
4. We know based on *intuition*. This belief bases truth on a feeling about the answers.
5. We know based on *divine revelation*. This belief is in the power of the supernatural to reveal knowledge or truth.

The first three ways of knowing are the ones most often employed in the classroom. Knowing based on authority leads to reading assignments, lectures, review of the appropriate literature, and many traditional ways of teaching. Knowing based on experiences would lead to the use of manipulatives in math, survey research in social studies, and experiments in science. Knowing based on reasoning is what most teachers promote in the classroom. Learning to use higher-order thinking skills and moving through Bloom's taxonomy are part of knowing based on reasoning.

AXIOLOGY

Axiology addresses values, both in ethics and aesthetics. **Ethics** is the determination of what's right and what's wrong. **Aesthetics** is the determination of what is beautiful and artistic. Both ethics and aesthetics require judgments. Consider the questions posed in the study of axiology, and then read about how axiology may look in the classroom.

- What is valuable?
- What values should a person possess?
- What is right, and what is wrong?
- What is just, and what is unjust?
- How should life be lived?
- How should we judge the quality of what we see, hear, and touch?
- What is the quality of an artistic expression?
- What is beauty?

AXIOLOGY IN THE CLASSROOM. Teachers contend daily in their classrooms with questions of axiology. Ethics deals with how students treat one another, how they respect property, and how they make decisions about right and wrong in the classroom community. When a school adopts a character education program to help students establish attitudes about respect, it is acknowledging that ethics matter.

Deciding what is aesthetically pleasing also involves axiology. Part of what teachers do is help students recognize and appreciate beauty in any form. For instance, a math teacher who encourages students to explore geometry in nature and to discover the artistry of the geometric structures is prompting them to expand their definition of what is beautiful.

School itself expresses a value. Requiring children to attend school suggests the belief that it is right to give students the opportunity to learn (Nelson, Carlson, & Palonsky, 2000). Also, teachers are expected to possess certain values and to behave in ethical ways. Focus teacher Chris Roberts tells us that teachers teach who they are, making an internalized philosophy of education even more important. Read what Chris has to say in *Teaching in Focus*.

LOGIC

Logic is reasoning that avoids vagueness and contradictions. Simply put, people use logic when they think to understand a situation, solve a problem, or draw a conclusion. Two basic kinds of reasoning, or logic, are commonly addressed in school. **Deductive reasoning** is a process that begins with a general statement, from which more specific statements are assumed to be true. **Inductive reasoning** works the other way: Given

Teaching **in** Focus

Sara Davis Powell

Chris Roberts, Grades 3-5
Multiage Classroom, Rees
Elementary School, Utah.
In his own words. . . .

I heard or read somewhere that "you teach who you are." I know, after teaching 29 years, that there is a lot of truth in those five words. I've had students return to visit me years after they've been in my class and I get invited to many of their weddings. As we catch up on the years that have passed, none of them talk about their reading or math; they tell me about me. Their memories don't focus on the great unit I taught on Native Americans, but rather on the time I told them about a trip I went on or a belief I have about life. I don't think you can be an excellent teacher if your own life is boring or "unexamined," as Henry David Thoreau would caution. Children will naturally be less interested in learning from someone they find uninteresting. Don't let the classroom, and pressures you will surely face, rule your life. Live a full life. Share with your students what you learn and experience on your amazing path.

some specific statements, a general conclusion may be assumed. Figure 8.2 illustrates these two types of logic. Consider the questions posed in the study of logic and then read how logic may look in the classroom.

- What makes sense?
- Is an idea or conclusion valid?
- How can we get from point A to point B in a way that makes sense?
- Is there a foundation for a particular argument?

LOGIC IN THE CLASSROOM. Teaching thinking skills—teaching the use of logic—is a major emphasis in many subject areas. An essay question that asks students to judge the

Figure 8.2 Deductive and inductive reasoning

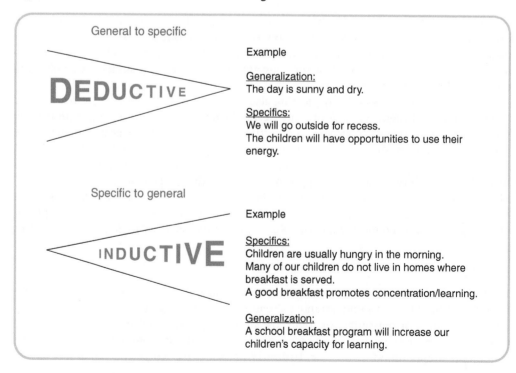

General to specific

DEDUCTIVE

Example

Generalization:
The day is sunny and dry.

Specifics:
We will go outside for recess.
The children will have opportunities to use their energy.

Specific to general

INDUCTIVE

Example

Specifics:
Children are usually hungry in the morning.
Many of our children do not live in homes where breakfast is served.
A good breakfast promotes concentration/learning.

Generalization:
A school breakfast program will increase our children's capacity for learning.

TABLE 8.1 Four branches of philosophy

Branch of Philosophy	Defining Questions
Metaphysics	What is reality? Does life have a purpose?
Epistemology	What is truth? How do we acquire knowledge?
Axiology	What is right, and what is wrong? What is beauty?
Logic	What makes sense? Is there a foundation for a particular argument?

outcome of a government program as good or bad (axiology) is asking them to use inductive reasoning as they look at individual results and draw a conclusion. A test that asks students to explain how to apply a theorem to particular variables is prompting them to use deductive reasoning. A teacher who intervenes in a student squabble and says, "Now stop and think about this" is asking students to think clearly, using logic and reasoning.

Review the four branches of philosophy and their defining questions in Table 8.1. The basic questions can be applied to the five schools of philosophical thought expressed as philosophies of education in the following section.

How Do Five Prominent Philosophies of Education Affect Teaching and Learning?

Just as knowing about individual branches helps lay the groundwork for understanding what philosophy encompasses, exploring prominent philosophies will provide a framework for understanding what they mean for teaching and learning. The five philosophies featured in this section are not the only ones that directly impact the work of teachers. A few others are discussed briefly at the end of this section.

We have explored teacher-centered and student-centered curricula and instruction. The five philosophies discussed here fall neatly into these two categories. Essentialism and perennialism are teacher-centered approaches, whereas progressivism, social reconstructionism, and existentialism are more student centered, as illustrated in Figure 8.3. Keep this

Figure 8.3 Teacher- and student-centered approaches

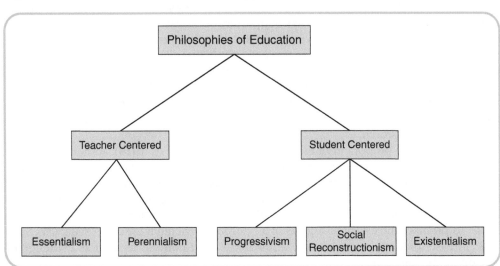

in mind as you read about the five philosophies. Also remember to think about early childhood, elementary, middle, and high school classrooms as you consider each philosophy of education.

PHILOSOPHY TREES

The discussion of each philosophy is accompanied by a diagram of a tree. The analogy of a philosophy of education to a tree is appropriate in many ways. The tree trunk represents teaching. The root system is a particular philosophy of education, or a combination of philosophies, providing the strength and foundation of the tree: The philosophy literally grounds the tree. The branches of the tree represent the work of teachers. Each trunk-attached branch supports smaller branches with plentiful leaves that represent teaching and learning.

Many aspects of a tree's growth are directly analogous to teaching and learning. Do you recall seeing a cross section of a tree trunk? Elementary students learn that you can count the rings to determine the age of a tree because each year of growth not only takes a tree skyward but also wraps another layer of life around it. So it is with teaching experience. Each year, previous experiences aren't shed but rather are wrapped in new experiences.

Trees have two kinds of roots: anchor roots, which grow deeper with time and hold the tree upright against most winds, and feeder roots, which shoot out in all directions and draw in nourishment. Have you ever noticed a makeshift fence or stakes with colored tape around the base of a tree when construction is nearby? The purpose of this barrier is to let workers know that digging closer would likely damage the tree. Although a tree can survive the loss of some feeder roots, the diameter of the feeder and anchor root system is generally the same as the diameter of the canopy of the tree's branches and leaves. Cutting away feeder roots will diminish the canopy in like proportion. The size and stability of the philosophical root system determine the effectiveness of the teaching and learning canopy. Your anchor matters; your philosophy of education affects all aspects of your success as a teacher.

ESSENTIALISM

Essentialism is a philosophy of education based on the belief that a core curriculum exists that everyone in the United States should learn. This core can shift in response to societal changes but should always be basic, organized, and rigorous. When you hear someone praise the concept of "back to basics," chances are that person is an essentialist.

Essentialism is an ancient philosophy, but in the 20th century it grew as a backlash to progressivism, the educational philosophy begun by John Dewey. Whereas progressivism puts student interests at the center of curriculum and instruction, essentialism puts little stock in what students want in terms of what and how they learn. Essentialism gained impetus from the launching of *Sputnik* by the Soviet Union in 1957 and again from the publication of *A Nation at Risk* in 1983. Supporters of the essentialist philosophy are vocal about their view that schools have dumbed down the curriculum with nonessential courses, resulting in lower test scores (Ravitch, 2000). Essentialists favor high expectations for students, along with testing to measure mastery of standards.

An essentialist philosophy of education puts the teacher front and center as an intellectual and moral role model. Direct instruction is encouraged, but other instructional methods are used if they prove effective. Students are expected to listen and learn as they follow the rules of the classroom.

One prominent proponent of essentialism is E. D. Hirsch (b. 1928), author of *Cultural Literacy: What Every American Needs to Know* (1987). Hirsch lists events, people, facts, discoveries, inventions, art, literature, and more that he believes all Americans should know about to be culturally literate. Another proponent of essentialism is Theodore Sizer (b. 1932), founder of the Coalition of Essential Schools, a group of about 200 schools that pledge to promote the essentialist goals of a rigorous curriculum based on standards. Sizer (1985) insists that students clearly exhibit mastery of content as well as evidence of developing thinking skills.

Figure 8.4 Essentialism tree

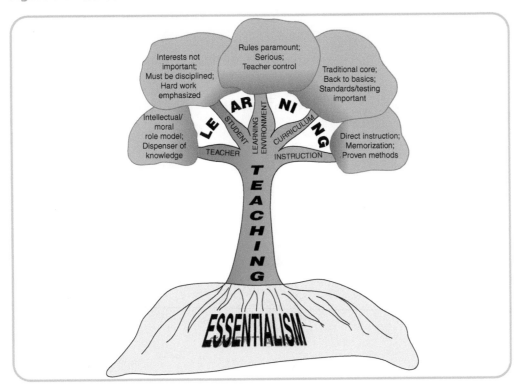

Take a few minutes to study the essentialism tree in Figure 8.4. Visualizing how teachers might translate the elements of essentialism into their classrooms will help you understand this philosophy of education.

PERENNIALISM

Perennialism is a philosophy of education based on a core curriculum, and in that regard it is similar to essentialism. The difference lies in what constitutes the core. The word *perennial* means "everlasting" and is often used when talking about plants. A perennial flower blooms in season, is dormant for a time, and then blooms again, year after year. A flower that is not a perennial is an annual that must be replanted each year. Perennialism, as a philosophy of education, says there is a curriculum with themes and questions that endure, that are everlasting. In contrast, the curriculum of essentialism is considered basic and core, but its components may change as society changes and, as such, the essentialist curriculum is more comparable to an annual.

Perennialists believe that even as life changes and times change, the real substance and truths of life remain the same. The wisdom students need may be obtained through the study of **Great Books,** the writings of those considered to be the great thinkers through the history of Western civilization, such as Homer, Shakespeare, Melville, Einstein, and many others. Perennialists do not endorse choices in the curriculum or elective courses, and they ascribe to a rigid curriculum for elementary, middle, and high schools.

Teachers who practice perennialism as a philosophy of education want to be in control of the classroom. They dispense knowledge and lead discussions of classics that require rigorous, logical thought by students. Differences in students are rarely considered, as all are expected to learn from the classics (Webb, Metha, & Jordan, 2010).

Mortimer Adler (1902–2001), author of the *Paideia Proposal* (1982), is perhaps the best known recent proponent of perennialism as a philosophy of education. The word *paideia* refers to a state of human excellence. Adler said that schools should use intense study of the classics to strive for excellence in students (Pulliam & Van Patten, 2007). Adler

Points of Reflection 8.1

Do you identify with some of the elements of essentialism? If so, which ones? Do some of the aspects of essentialism in the classroom, illustrated in Figure 8.4, appeal to you as a prospective teacher? Are there some aspects that do not appeal to you? If so, which ones?

Figure 8.5 Perennialism tree

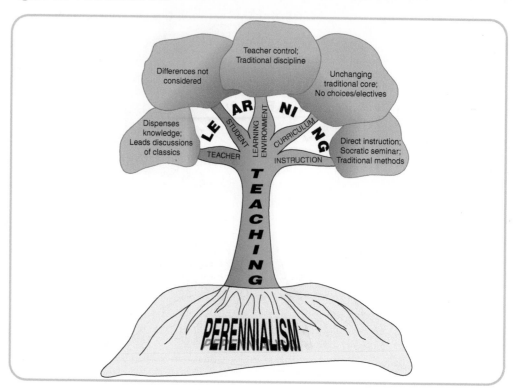

Points of Reflection 8.2

Do you identify with some of the elements of perennialism? If so, which ones? Do some of the aspects of perennialism in the classroom, illustrated in Figure 8.5, appeal to you as a prospective teacher? Are there some aspects that do not appeal to you? If so, which ones?

founded the Great Books of the Western World program at the University of Chicago in 1930 (Adler, 1982).

Take a few minutes to study the perennialism tree in Figure 8.5. Visualizing how teachers might translate the elements of perennialism into their classrooms will help you understand this philosophy of education.

PROGRESSIVISM

Progressivism is a student-centered philosophy of education that focuses on a curriculum of interest to students. To progressivists, education is more than preparation for the future: It is life itself. The progressive philosophy of education endorses experiential learning full of opportunities for student discovery and problem solving.

Constructivism and pragmatism are philosophies of education that fall within the broader philosophy of progressivism. Constructivism, an inquiry-based way of approaching instruction, builds on progressivism because students are challenged to construct, or discover, knowledge about their environments. Process is valued in progressivism, often more than product. The theory is that students who learn through the processes of construction, discovery, and problem solving will be better able to adapt to a changing world. Another philosophy, **pragmatism,** says that student-centered perspectives integrated with first-hand experiences are the most effective (Chartock, 2004).

Teachers who ascribe to progressivism act primarily as facilitators of learning, serving as resources and guides to students who explore, gather evidence, and draw conclusions. Real-world problem solving is intended to promote individual student development (Gutek, 2005).

John Dewey (1859–1952) was the most prominent of all the proponents of progressivism, beginning in the late 19th century and continuing well into the 20th century. Dewey supported a balance between valuing established content with structured learning activities and planning experiences that interest, motivate, and actively involve students. Although progressivism fell out of favor in a call for more rigor in the late 1950s, many tenets of the philosophy continue to be part of today's most widely used instructional strategies.

Philosophical Foundations of Education in the United States

Take a few minutes to study the progressivism tree in Figure 8.6. Visualizing how teachers might translate the elements of progressivism into their classrooms will help you understand this philosophy of education.

SOCIAL RECONSTRUCTIONISM

More than any other philosophy of education, **social reconstructionism** looks to education to change society, rather than just teach about it. Social reconstructionism as a philosophy of education calls on schools to educate students in ways that will help society move beyond all forms of discrimination to the benefit of everyone worldwide. This philosophy addresses such topics as racial equality, women's rights, sexism, environmental pollution, poverty, substance abuse, homophobia, and AIDS. Proponents of other educational philosophies often avoid such topics, thus relegating the topics to the null curriculum.

Encouraging students to engage in learning and express themselves is part of the philosophy of progressivism.
Rebecca Dunbar

According to some educators, Theodore Brameld (1904–1987) founded the philosophy of social reconstructionism following World War II. Brameld (1956) based the philosophy on two premises: (1) people now have the capacity to destroy civilization, and (2) people have the potential to create a civilization marked by health and humanity. The basic tenets of social reconstructionism, however, go back to the early Greeks and, more recently, to Karl Marx, who called for a social revolution that would bring about equity among all people (Jacobsen, 2003).

Teachers who ascribe to social reconstructionism promote active student involvement in societal problems. They plan experiences for students to explore issues and possible

Points of Reflection 8.3

Do you identify with some of the elements of progressivism? If so, which ones? Do some of the aspects of progressivism in the classroom, illustrated in Figure 8.6, appeal to you as a prospective teacher? Are there some aspects that do not appeal to you? If so, which ones?

Figure 8.6 Progressivism tree

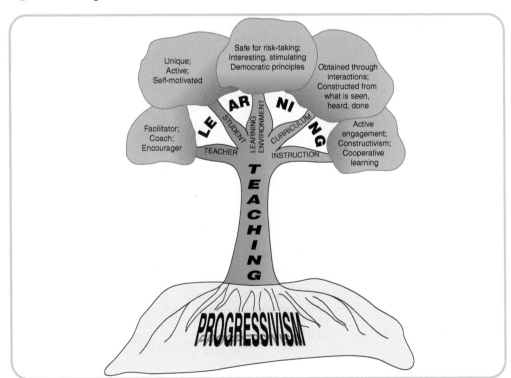

Philosophical Foundations of Education in the United States

solutions, but avoid moralizing. They promote democracy and freedom to make choices while helping students discover the consequences of particular lines of reasoning and action. All of this occurs within an educational context that focuses on reading comprehension, research techniques, analysis and evaluation skills, and writing as a form of persuasive communication.

Major proponents of social reconstructionism as a philosophy of education include George Counts (1907-1974), Paulo Friere (1922-1987), and Ivan Illich (1926-2002). In his book *Dare the School Build a New Social Order?* (1932), Counts wrote about his view that schools should equip students to deal with world problems. Friere, in *Pedagogy of the Oppressed* (1970), wrote about his personal experiences in working with poor illiterate peasants that led him to the philosophy that education is the key to empowering the poor to control and improve their lives. In his book *Deschooling Society* (1971), Illich promoted a radical view. He wrote that schools as we know them should be eliminated because they do nothing to decrease poverty. He contended that schools actually prevent what he saw as real education, a process he viewed as happening in more informal ways. While "deschooling" American society will likely not happen, the social reconstructionist views of Illich have prompted important questions about the role of public education (Chartock, 2004).

Points of Reflection 8.4

Do you identify with some of the elements of social reconstructionism? If so, which ones? Do some of the aspects of social reconstructionism in the classroom, illustrated in Figure 8.7, appeal to you as a prospective teacher? Are there some aspects that do not appeal to you? If so, which ones?

Take a few minutes to study the social reconstructionism tree in Figure 8.7. Visualizing how teachers might translate the elements of social reconstructionism into their classrooms will help you understand this philosophy of education.

EXISTENTIALISM

The primary emphasis of **existentialism** is on the individual. As a philosophy of education, existentialism contends that teachers teach the whole person, not just math, reading, science, or any other particular subject. Each student searches for personal meaning and personal understanding. If learning about a subject increases a student's sense of self, then it's worthwhile. Practices such as standardization, tracking, and testing do not fit into an existentialist viewpoint. Because meaning is personal, each student has the freedom and the subsequent responsibility to make his or her own choices. Existentialism rejects traditional

Figure 8.7 Social reconstructionism tree

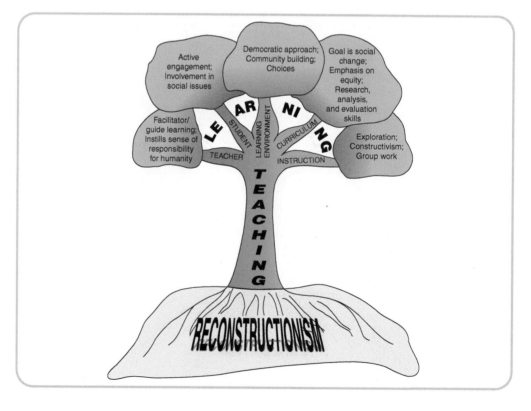

education. Few schools practice existentialism as an educational philosophy, and most that do are private. However, there are teachers in both public and private classrooms who practice some elements of existentialism.

The existentialist teacher honors individual students by arranging for learning experiences from which each student may choose. The classroom atmosphere is supposed to be stimulating and full of choices. The student's job is to make choices and then take responsibility for those choices. Teachers and students have a great deal of individual contact, participating in learning that is self-paced and self-directed (Greene, 1978). A teacher who follows existentialism as a philosophy of education teaches best by being a role model and demonstrates the importance of a discipline by pursuing academic goals related to the subject area.

A. S. Neill (1883–1973) was one of the most influential proponents of existentialism. He founded the Summerhill School in England following World War I. Learning by discovery was the primary feature of Summerhill. The student as an individual was emphasized and exploration for the sake of learning had few restrictions (Neill, 1960).

Maxine Greene (b. 1917) is the most well-known proponent of existentialism. She refers to a heightened level of personal awareness as "wide-awakeness." Greene refutes critics of existentialism who say that the philosophy in practice allows children to run free and out of control. She maintains that freedom has rules that allow others to be free as well (Greene, 1995).

Take a few minutes to study the existentialism tree in Figure 8.8. Visualizing how teachers might translate the elements of existentialism into their classrooms will help you understand this philosophy of education.

Although focus teacher Craig Cleveland does not completely fit the existentialist profile, we see that many of the ways Craig approaches his teaching responsibilities mirror an existentialist philosophy. Read more about Craig as you consider this chapter's *Diversity Dialogue*.

As we established early in this chapter, we all have philosophies. They may be consciously held, or they may just be "how we are" or "what we think." But one thing's for sure, our philosophies become evident when an issue arises. In this chapter's *Letter to the Editor*, a citizen expresses his philosophy concerning the current state of public schools.

Points of Reflection 8.5

Do you identify with some of the elements of existentialism? If so, which ones? Do some of the aspects of existentialism in the classroom, illustrated in Figure 8.8, appeal to you as a prospective teacher? Are there some aspects that do not appeal to you? If so, which ones?

Figure 8.8 Existentialism tree

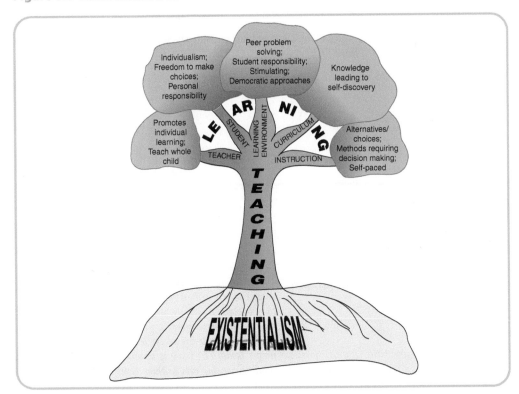

Philosophical Foundations of Education in the United States

DIVERSITY DIALOGUE

Craig Cleveland's philosophy of education is evident in everything he does at Roosevelt High School. He is intense and focused in his efforts to help students find their voice. Craig continually seeks to know his students as individuals with their own unique gifts and needs. He believes strongly in differentiating instruction.

Sara Davis Powell

For Craig to address diversity and emphasize the value of each individual, he must have competency in the subject he teaches. He abides by this INTASC standard:

INTASC Knowledge Principle 1
The teacher understands major concepts, assumptions, debates, processes of inquiry, and ways of knowing that are central to the discipline(s) s/he teaches.

"Ways of knowing" is a defining piece of epistemology. Teachers deal with this every day, whether consciously or unconsciously. Craig is very conscious of the more complex nature of history and its implications than many other teachers. He knows his subject: the major concepts, assumptions, debates, and processes of inquiry. He also believes that many of these aspects change as society changes, although the basic historical events may not.

Another standard that resonates with Craig is part of the principles of the National Board of Professional Teaching Standards (NBPTS) that says,

Accomplished teachers are models of educated persons . . . and the capacities that are prerequisites for intellectual growth: the ability to reason and take multiple perspectives, to be creative and take risks, and to adapt to an experimental and problem solving orientation.

One issue Craig is determined to help change is that in most arenas of the United States, white voices are more likely to be heard than those of minorities. As he looks around his classroom, Craig sees few white faces. To him, his mission is clear: help empower all his students to find and express their values and beliefs, to speak in their own voices and be heard.

1. What are two ways Craig encourages his students to find and express their voices in his classroom? Explain each.

2. How does Craig inform his own opinions and grow professionally? Explain.

3. With regard to how Craig views the subject he teaches, with which philosophy of education would he closely align? Why?

4. With regard to instruction, with which philosophy of education would he closely align? Why?

You watched Craig's interview, room tour, and lesson in Chapter 3. Reviewing all three brief videos will help you think more clearly about Craig and the questions concerning how his philosophy is manifested in his classroom. The videos are in the Teaching in Focus section for Chapter 8 in MyEducationLab for this course.

Letter to the Editor

This letter appeared in the Greensboro, North Carolina, newspaper, the *News & Record*. The writer is expressing a philosophy about the purposes of school.

AUGUST 1, 2010 SCHOOLS' FIRST PRIORITY SHOULD BE ON ACADEMICS

In the last 57 years, reading, writing and arithmetic have become collateral damage in a public school system increasingly devoted to solving social problems ranging from hunger to teen pregnancy.

Providing security for students and teachers on the same campus with at-risk populations warehoused until they become dropouts strains local police and school administration resources.

This is not a racial issue. This is not a socioeconomic issue. The issue is about the priority placed on reading, writing and arithmetic in a public system that

(Continued)

is broken. We can continue to bus children to achieve racial diversity. We can continue to let school boards tell parents what's best for their children. If we cannot find another venue to deal with social problems, we will be having this same harangue 57 years from now, probably in Chinese.

Joe Exum
Snow Hill

Now it's your turn. Write a letter to the editor from the perspective of a future teacher expressing your philosophy about the purposes of school. The following questions may help you frame your thinking but should not limit nor determine what you write.

1. Which of the five philosophies of education is the letter writer expressing in the first sentence? Which philosophy do you think he is definitely opposed to? How does what he's expressing fit with what you believe? Is there a happy medium you might express?

2. Mr. Exum is expressing his belief that some students are too at risk to be in regular school settings, that they require excessive effort on the part of administration and police. Does he have a valid point? As a teacher, what comment would you make to address this point?

3. Mr. Exum expresses that the public education system is broken. Do you agree? If not, what might you write to express to the public that education in America is *not* broken?

4. Mr. Exum seems to think that finding solutions to social problems outside the school system is the only way to save life as we know it in America. Is this a justified concern or an exaggeration?

Write your letter in understandable terminology, remembering that readers of newspaper Letters to the Editor are citizens who may have limited knowledge of school practices and policies.

OTHER PHILOSOPHIES

Other "isms" may impact educational philosophy. Let's look briefly at some of them.

Idealism is a philosophy based on the belief that ideas are the only reliable form of reality. Idealists believe that because the physical world changes continually, ideas are what should be taught. Taking the opposite stance, **realism** is based on the belief that some facts are absolutes whether recognized by all or not. Realists contend that the only way to know these absolutes is to study the material world.

Romanticism, or naturalism, as a philosophy of education contends that the needs of the individual are more important than the needs of society. Many early childhood and elementary educators incorporate into their classrooms the tenets of romanticism that say young children are born good, pure, and full of curiosity and that their individual interests should be validated with opportunities to explore and manipulate elements of their environment.

Postmodernism grew out of a sense that those in power control those who don't have power. Postmodernists believe this control is manifested through major institutions such as schools. The decades of the 1960s and 1970s were times of unprecedented outcry for justice and equality through the civil rights movement, the feminist movement, and a renewed concern for the poor. Postmodernist philosophy grew as a response to these cultural stirrings. The postmodern curriculum includes perspectives on history and literature by a variety of authors representing different lifestyles. Proponents of postmodernism contend they are attempting to strike a balance of power among all people and that intellectual growth from multiple perspectives is one avenue for doing so. Critics of postmodernism contend that the philosophy seeks to promote political purposes rather than intellectual purposes (Ozmon & Craver, 2008).

You will likely encounter other philosophies as you participate in future teacher preparation courses. The ones you have read about so far provide many choices for you to consider as you begin the process of writing your own philosophy of education.

How Do I Begin to Develop My Personal Philosophy of Education?

When it comes to developing a philosophy of education, balance is important. If you found yourself aligning with parts of one and parts of another as you read about the prominent philosophies of education, and thinking, "How will I weigh all this and decide?" you are

Philosophical Foundations of Education in the United States

Figure 8.9 Brenda's philosophy tree

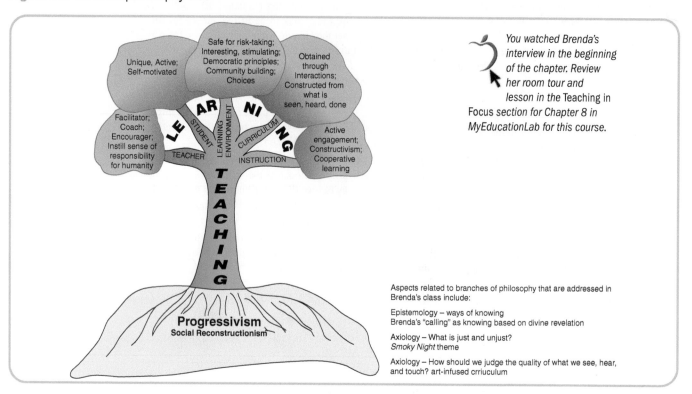

You watched Brenda's interview in the beginning of the chapter. Review her room tour and lesson in the Teaching in Focus section for Chapter 8 in MyEducationLab for this course.

Aspects related to branches of philosophy that are addressed in Brenda's class include:

Epistemology – ways of knowing
Brenda's "calling" as knowing based on divine revelation

Axiology – What is just and unjust?
Smoky Night theme

Axiology – How should we judge the quality of what we see, hear, and touch? art-infused crriuculum

Brenda, one of the focus teachers at Rees Elementary, demonstrates her skills during a field trip with her students. Provided by the author

certainly not alone. Very few educators can place themselves squarely in one camp or another. Picking and choosing from among the components of several philosophies is referred to as taking an *eclectic approach.* This entails balance. It's natural for teachers to lean toward one philosophy or approach more than another, but prescribing to only one philosophy will not serve the needs of all children. Chartock (2004) states, "For every belief there is an equal and opposite belief and data to support both. That's why the field of education is never dull" (p. 136). Never dull, indeed.

Reread the opening scenario of this chapter about Brenda Beyal. The philosophy tree in Figure 8.9 represents Brenda's philosophy. As you examine the tree, think about evidence, given what you know about Brenda, to support the elements on the tree.

YOUR TURN

Now it's your turn to grow a philosophy tree. The root system will consist of an anchor philosophy, the philosophy with which you most closely align. There's no need to ascribe to every tenet of this anchor philosophy, but it should express most of your current beliefs about teaching and learning. Other philosophies may be part of the feeder root system. The branches and leaves of the tree's canopy will be a mix of what you believe about the roles of teacher, students, the learning environment, the curriculum, and instruction. Keep in mind that the deeper and wider the philosophy root system, the stronger and more stable the trunk will grow and the richer and more extensive the canopy will be.

Figure 8.10 is a tree waiting for you to make it your own. Your philosophy tree can be a valuable component of the teaching portfolio you will no doubt develop as part of your teacher preparation.

One approach to begin examining your own philosophy is to study the content of Table 8.2 carefully. Considering the responses to the questions in the table that relate

Philosophical Foundations of Education in the United States

Figure 8.10 My philosophy tree

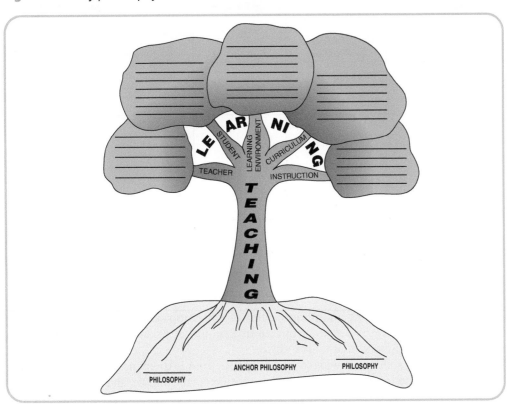

TABLE 8.2 Sample questions and philosophical responses					
Question (Branch)	Essentialism	Perennialism	Progressivism	Reconstructionism	Existentialism
What is real? (metaphysics)	Elements of core curriculum; may change	Elements of core curriculum; unchanging	What can be verified through the senses	What can be verified through research and analysis	Based entirely on the individual's perspective and experience
How do we acquire knowledge? (epistemology)	From a combination of the classics and science	From the never-changing classics	From individual experiences and discovery	From individual and group searches for meaning and justice	Through individual quests; making choices
What is valuable? (axiology)	Core of knowledge that responds to some societal shifts	Changeless core of knowledge	Determined by individual interacting with own culture	Whatever makes society more just and equitable	Whatever leads to greater self-knowledge
What makes sense? (logic)	Classics provide generalizations; specifics are deduced; observation and analysis of specifics may lead to generalization	Deductive reasoning from truths of classics	Discovered through problem solving	Weighed against potential benefit or harm to society	Whatever enhances individual freedom and increases personal responsibility

Philosophical Foundations of Education in the United States

TABLE 8.3 My favorite teachers' philosophical bents						
Teacher's Name	Teacher's Role	Interactions with Students	Learning Environment	Curriculum	Instruction	Aligned with Which Philosophy?

the branches of philosophy and philosophies of education will help you examine your philosophical views. There are many questions that may be asked, with each philosophy of education contributing unique responses.

Another approach to growing your philosophy tree is to spend some time thinking about your favorite teachers in early childhood, elementary, middle, and high school. Why did you admire them? What made them special? Your answers need to go beyond "She was so nice" or "He just stands out in my mind." To help you think through the reasons particular teachers had positive effects on you, put a special teacher's name on the chart in Table 8.3. Then think about how this person appeared to view his or her roles as a teacher, including relationships with students, the creation of the learning environment, and approaches to curriculum and instruction. Table 8.3 will help organize your recollections.

A sincere, honest start to the development of a philosophy of education will help grow you into the teaching profession. Having opportunities to talk about your philosophy and listen to your classmates, your instructor, and teachers in the field will make you more comfortable articulating your stance. The more you think, talk, and listen, the more confident you will become that you are grounded in your reasons for how you approach your role, your students, the learning environment, curriculum, and instruction.

CONCLUDING THOUGHTS

Chances are that a philosophy of education is not something you've ever seriously considered. Now you have some background about major branches of philosophy, as well as philosophies of education. You have been prompted to think about, and tentatively declare, which philosophy represents your primary beliefs about teaching and learning. You also know that an eclectic approach is not only natural but will actually benefit the diverse groups of students you will no doubt encounter.

Thoughtful teachers are not necessarily swayed by gimmicks and fads, they have basic beliefs about teaching and learning that guide their practice, and they can articulate the bases for decisions. These are teachers who will positively affect student learning throughout their careers. This applies to early childhood, elementary, middle, and high school teachers equally. A carefully considered philosophy of education provides a solid foundation for professionals in the classroom.

After reading the *Chapter in Review,* read more about Brenda and respond to items in this chapter's *Developing Professional Competence*.

Chapter in Review

What is a philosophy of education?

- We all have philosophies that guide our decisions, attitudes, and actions.
- A teacher's philosophy of education affects every decision about teaching.

What are four branches of philosophy?

- Metaphysics addresses the search for reality and purpose.
- Epistemology addresses the dilemma of determining truth and ways of acquiring knowledge.
- Axiology addresses values, in both ethics and aesthetics.
- Logic is reasoning that avoids vagueness and contradiction.

How do five prominent philosophies of education affect teaching and learning?

- Essentialism is a philosophy of education based on the belief that there is a core curriculum that is responsive to the times and that every American should know.
- Perennialism is a philosophy of education based on the belief that there is a changeless core curriculum that every American should know.
- Progressivism is a philosophy of education that focuses on a curriculum of interest to students and experiential learning.
- Social reconstructionism is a philosophy of education that endorses a curriculum that benefits society by promoting equity.
- Existentialism is a philosophy of education that focuses on the individual's search for meaning.

How do I begin to develop my personal philosophy of education?

- Incorporating components of more than one philosophy of education into your personal philosophy is an eclectic approach.
- Growing an effective philosophy tree requires a strong root system with philosophical grounding to enhance both teaching and learning.

Developing Professional Competence

Visit the Developing Professional Competence section on Chapter 8 of the MyEducationLab for this text to answer the following questions and begin your preparation for licensure exams.

Brenda ascribes to a very student-centered philosophy of education, as we have seen in her interview, room tour, lesson, philosophy tree in Figure 8.9, and what we have read in *Teaching in Focus*. She knows the content she teaches and works very hard to be the best teacher she can be. The one thing that continually bothers Brenda is the fact that we are in an era of standards, where curriculum is prescribed and teaching is on a fast-paced schedule. Add to this the week of standardized tests she must monitor every spring, and we find Brenda seeking balance for her students and innovative ways to accomplish what is expected of her while paying attention to individual student needs.

One of Brenda's favorite authors is Vito Perrone (1991). Here is an excerpt that is particularly poignant for her.

To engage students constructively, the school day needs more continuities, not more fragmentation. Work that can truly be valued takes time, sometimes hours and days. It is hardly reasonable to expect a child to complete a fine piece of artwork in ten- or twenty-minute intervals, twice a week, or produce a well-organized, thoughtful description, a poetic or narrative story within ten minutes. Teachers know this but claim that in this current basic skills, testing, "academic" environment, they don't have the time any more for work of that quality. (p. 33)

Given what we know about Brenda, answer these multiple-choice questions.

1. What do you think Brenda considers a source of fragmentation of her teaching day?
   a. District administrative guidelines that outline the time to be spent each day on language arts, reading, math, science, and social studies.
   b. Her students go to dance/movement class with Chris Roberts in the morning and to music/theater class with Tim Mendenhall in the afternoon.
   c. She has an early lunch time with her class.
   d. Rees incorporates two recess times a day.

2. Brenda attributes her agreement with Perrone's point about what's valuable to her Native American heritage. What might be the best of these four options for Brenda to let students know about her opinion?
   a. She could teach the students some of the soothing chants and tunes Native American mothers sing to their children.
   b. She could share artifacts and talk with students about how they are preserved.
   c. She could tell them stories about patience and perseverance from Native American folklore.
   d. She could explain to students the meaningfulness of the sundial and how Native Americans have historically honored the sun.

Now it's time for you to respond to three short essay items involving Brenda. In your responses, be sure to address all the dilemmas and questions posed in each item. Your responses should each be between one half and one double-spaced page.

3. Which do Brenda and Vito Perrone appear to value more: progress of a group or progress of the individual? Explain your response.

4. Perrone writes about "continuities." What kinds of activities do you think Brenda would put in this category? Explain two continuities you would expect to see in her classroom.

5. How might Brenda incorporate balance into the day as she teaches the standards while valuing quality and creativity?

Where DO I Stand NOW?

In the beginning of this chapter you completed an inventory that helped you discover your own philosophy of education. Now that you have read the chapter, completed exercises related to the content, engaged in class discussions, and so on, answer the following questions in your course notebook.

1. If you fell into the teacher-centered philosophy in *Where Do I Stand?* do you still think that essentialism and perennialism are the philosophies that most closely align with you and your beliefs? Why or why not? What has strengthened or weakened your alignment with a teacher-centered philosophy?

2. If you fell into the student-centered philosophy in *Where Do I Stand?* do you still think that progressivism, social reconstructionism, and existentialism are the philosophies that most closely align with you and your beliefs? Why or why not? What has strengthened or weakened your alignment with a student-centered philosophy?

3. What is one aspect of education philosophy that has surprised you or had an impact on you in large measure, and why?

MyEducationLab

The MyEducationLab for this course can help you solidify your comprehension of Chapter 8 concepts.

- Explore the classrooms of the teachers and students you've met in this chapter in the Teaching in Focus section.
- Prepare for licensure exams as you deepen your understanding of chapter concepts in the Developing Professional Competence section.

- Gauge and further develop your understanding of chapter concepts by taking the quizzes and examining the enrichment materials on the Chapter 8 Study Plan.
- Visit Topic 7, "History and Philosophy of Education," to watch ABC videos, explore Assignments and Activities, and practice essential teaching skills with the Building Teaching Skills and Dispositions unit.

References

Adler, M. (1982). *The Paideia proposal: An educational manifesto*. New York: Simon & Schuster.

Brameld, T. (1956). *Toward a reconstructed philosophy of education*. New York: Holt, Rinehart and Winston.

Chartock, R. K. (2004). *Educational foundations: An anthology* (2nd ed.). Upper Saddle River, NJ: Merrill/Prentice Hall.

Counts, G. (1932). *Dare the school build a new social order?* New York: John Dey.

Eisner, E. (Ed.). (1985). *Learning and teaching the ways of knowing: The eighty-fourth yearbook of the National Society for the Study of Education*. Chicago: University of Chicago Press.

Friere, P. (1970). *Pedagogy of the oppressed*. New York: Herder and Herder.

Greene, M. (1978). *Landscape of learning*. New York: Teachers College Press.

Greene, M. (1995). What counts as philosophy of education? In W. Kohli (Ed.), *Critical conversations in philosophy of education*. New York: Routledge.

Gutek, G. L. (2005). *Historical and philosophical foundations of education* (4th ed.). Upper Saddle River, NJ: Merrill/Prentice Hall.

Hirsch, E. D. (1987). *Cultural literacy: What every American needs to know*. Boston: Houghton Mifflin.

Illich, I. (1971). *Deschooling society*. New York: Harper & Row.

Jacobsen, D. A. (2003). *Philosophy in classroom teaching: Bridging the gap* (2nd ed.). Upper Saddle River, NJ: Merrill/Prentice Hall.

Neill, A. S. (1960). *Summerhill: A radical approach to child rearing*. New York: Hart.

Nelson, J. L., Carlson, K., & Palonsky, S. B. (2000). *Critical issues in education: A dialectic approach* (4th ed.). New York: McGraw-Hill.

Ornstein, A. C. (2003). *Pushing the envelope: Critical issues in education*. Upper Saddle River, NJ: Merrill/Prentice Hall.

Ozmon, H., & Craver, S. (2008). *Philosophical foundations of education* (8th ed.). Upper Saddle River, NJ: Merrill/Prentice Hall.

Perrone, V. (1991). *A letter to teachers: Reflections on schooling and the art of teaching*. San Francisco: Jossey-Bass.

Pulliam, J., & Van Patten, J. (2007). *History of education in America* (9th ed.). Upper Saddle River, NJ: Merrill/Prentice Hall.

Ravitch, D. (2000). *Left back: A century of failed school reforms*. New York: Simon & Schuster.

Sizer, T. R. (1985). *Horace's compromise*. Boston: Houghton Mifflin.

Webb, L., Metha, A., & Jordan, K. F. (2010). *Foundations of American education* (6th ed.). Upper Saddle River, NJ: Merrill/Prentice Hall.

Figure 10.1 National Education Association Code of Ethics

Preamble

The educator, believing in the worth and dignity of each human being, recognizes the supreme importance of the pursuit of truth, devotion to excellence, and the nurture of the democratic principles. Essential to these goals is the protection of freedom to learn and to teach and the guarantee of equal educational opportunity for all. The educator accepts the responsibility to adhere to the highest ethical standards.

The educator recognizes the magnitude of the responsibility inherent in the teaching process. The desire for the respect and confidence of one's colleagues, of students, of parents, and of the members of the community provides the incentive to attain and maintain the highest possible degree of ethical conduct. The Code of Ethics of the Education Profession indicates the aspiration of all educators and provides standards by which to judge conduct.

The remedies specified by the NEA and/or its affiliates for the violation of any provision of this Code shall be exclusive and no such provision shall be enforceable in any form other than the one specifically designated by the NEA or its affiliates.

PRINCIPLE I

Commitment to the Student

The educator strives to help each student realize his or her potential as a worthy and effective member of society. The educator therefore works to stimulate the spirit of inquiry, the acquisition of knowledge and understanding, and the thoughtful formulation of worthy goals.

In fulfillment of the obligation to the student, the educator—

1. Shall not unreasonably restrain the student from independent action in the pursuit of learning.
2. Shall not unreasonably deny the student's access to varying points of view.
3. Shall not deliberately suppress or distort subject matter relevant to the student's progress.
4. Shall make reasonable effort to protect the student from conditions harmful to learning or to health and safety.
5. Shall not intentionally expose the student to embarrassment or disparagement.
6. Shall not on the basis of race, color, creed, sex, national origin, marital status, political or religious beliefs, family, social or cultural background, or sexual orientation, unfairly—
   a. Exclude any student from participation in any program
   b. Deny benefits to any student
   c. Grant any advantage to any student
7. Shall not use professional relationships with students for private advantage.
8. Shall not disclose information about students obtained in the course of professional service unless disclosure serves a compelling professional purpose or is required by law.

PRINCIPLE II

Commitment to the Profession

The education profession is vested by the public with a trust and responsibility requiring the highest ideals of professional service. In the belief that the quality of the services of the education profession directly influences the nation and its citizens, the educator shall exert every effort to raise professional standards, to promote a climate that encourages the exercise of professional judgment, to achieve conditions that attract persons worthy of the trust to careers in education, and to assist in preventing the practice of the profession by unqualified persons.

In fulfillment of the obligation to the profession, the educator—

1. Shall not in an application for a professional position deliberately make a false statement or fail to disclose a material fact related to competency and qualifications.
2. Shall not misrepresent his/her professional qualifications.
3. Shall not assist any entry into the profession of a person known to be unqualified in respect to character, education, or other relevant attribute.
4. Shall not knowingly make a false statement concerning the qualifications of a candidate for a professional position.
5. Shall not assist a noneducator in the unauthorized practice of teaching.
6. Shall not disclose information about colleagues obtained in the course of professional service unless disclosure serves a compelling professional purpose or is required by law.
7. Shall not knowingly make false or malicious statements about a colleague.
8. Shall not accept any gratuity, gift, or favor that might impair or appear to influence professional decisions or action.

Source: National Education Association. Retrieved May 27, 2005, from http://www.nea.org/aboutnea/code.html?mode=print.

Ethical and Legal Issues in U.S. Schools

Laws do not dictate these actions; ethical attitudes and beliefs call for them. Similarly, Derek Boucher's attitudes and actions—both in and outside the classroom—with regard to the teaching profession stem from his ethics.

Let's bring these concepts into the reality of the classroom by examining what it means to be an ethical teacher. Regardless of what our students learn, they learn *us*. We either represent, or *mis*represent, ethical behavior in the classroom.

ETHICS FOR TEACHERS

An ethical teacher is guided by a set of beliefs that leads to attitudes and actions focused on what's best for students. Being ethical means taking the high road and behaving professionally in the midst of big issues as well as in everyday decision making in the classroom.

Howe (1996) tells us that six characteristics form a conceptual basis for making ethical decisions. The first characteristic, appreciation for moral deliberation, means understanding that situations are complex and part of our obligation is to ensure that the rights of all involved are protected. The second characteristic, empathy, refers to the ability to put oneself mentally in the place of others to appreciate a variety of perspectives. Knowledge, the third characteristic, is necessary to have a clear view of the dilemma at hand. Dealing with knowledge requires reasoning, the fourth characteristic, and courage, the fifth characteristic, is needed to act on that reasoning. Finally, the sixth characteristic, interpersonal skills, allows teachers to communicate effectively with others about their ethical deliberations. These six characteristics are described in Figure 10.2. Characteristics 2 through 6 are self-explanatory. This doesn't diminish their value, but we more often know what they look like in practice than characteristic number 1.

Cultivating an "appreciation for moral deliberation," as Howe puts it, is a career-long area of growth for teachers. When we have big decisions to make, we generally see the right and wrong sides pretty clearly. We know there are consequences for our choices and we usually recognize many of them. This is a good thing. But what about the seemingly little decisions and actions, the things we do, or don't do, on a regular basis? Is it possible that these less-than-life-changing situations have "complex moral dimensions" and require that we have a "realization that care is needed to protect the rights of all parties"? Bringing higher-order thinking and problem-solving skills to bear on dilemmas, big and small, is what teachers must do.

In Table 10.1 you'll find some sample attitudes and decisions leading to actions, along with questions a teacher might consider. Could a teacher be dismissed because of these? Maybe, but probably not. Would a teacher's reputation suffer in the eyes of some? Maybe, and probably so. Every teacher could name similar, as well as very different, scenarios from personal experience if prompted to think about it. Perhaps there's the dilemma: *if prompted to think about it*. When our actions go unexamined, we are less likely to consider moral deliberation and therefore not be the ethical teachers we might otherwise become.

When we habitually apply ethical thinking and actions (the "shalls" referred to earlier) to situations, we are contributing to the development of students who ideally will do the same. As we model morally sound decision making, it is helpful to have a vision of desirable

Figure 10.2 Six desirable characteristics for teachers as they make ethical judgments

1. Appreciation for Moral Deliberation—ability to see complex moral dimensions of a problem and realization that care is needed to protect the rights of all parties
2. Empathy—ability to "get inside the skin of another"
3. Knowledge—facts to enable us to put issues in context
4. Reasoning—reflecting systematically on an issue and moving step by step to a conclusion
5. Courage—the willpower to act in what we perceive to be the right way, rather than just the comfortable way
6. Interpersonal Skills—communicating about issues sensitively and tactfully

Source: Howe, K. R. (1996, May/June). A conceptual basis for ethics in teacher education. *Journal of Teacher Education, 37*, 6.

TABLE 10.1 Recognizing ethical dilemmas

Attitudes/Decisions/Actions	Thinking It Through
With a wink, I say to a few students that I think I'm coming down with something. I return 48 hours later with an obvious skier's sunburn.	Is it OK to indicate to students that I am going to call in sick when I'm really planning to go on a ski trip? What lesson are they learning from me about responsibility and honesty?
A spelling bee competition is planned for tomorrow in which all the students in each class must participate. I have three students who are English language learners. I really want to win this bee since I am a candidate for my school's Teacher of the Year award. I casually mention to the three students that tomorrow would be a great day to stay home and enjoy the new fallen snow since it's Friday and they won't miss much.	Have I let my desire to look good get in the way of doing what's right for my students? Without these three students, my fifth grade class has the best chance of winning our grade-level bee. Winning will be a big boost for my students. So am I justified in encouraging these three students to stay home? After all, it's Friday before winter vacation and not much will go on that's academic in nature besides the spelling bee. They won't miss much . . . or will they?
On a field trip to a local museum I decide to buy each student a cold drink from a vending machine. I drop in two quarters and out pops not just one soda, but three. I laugh and say this must be my lucky day.	It's only a dollar loss for the vending company, but am I setting a good example for students? If I think that cheating the system makes me lucky, what message am I giving my students?
I just started a landscaping business that hopefully will occupy my weekends and give me extra income. I have developed an advertising flyer that I will distribute in the community. Because I haven't made much money yet, I decide to use the school copier one late afternoon to make a thousand flyers.	The students will likely never know I did this. But if another teacher walks into the workroom and sees what I'm doing, will my reputation be somewhat affected?
A parent generously donated $200 for me to buy a classroom set of a novel to use in spring semester. She determined the donation amount by going to a local bookstore. Knowing that I would get a 10% teacher discount, she gave me a check rather than buying the books herself. I go online and find the books for $150 and order them. I decide that it was my ingenuity that resulted in the discount and decide to keep the extra $50 for my trouble.	It's unlikely that anyone will ever know about this, so why should I care? After all, I work very hard as a teacher and this is just a small perk. Is $50 worth living with a small voice inside that says I should have spent the money on something for my classroom?
It's time for the first-quarter grades to be submitted just as football season has become very exciting. Our team is looking promising as a contender for the district championship. Mike has a 68% in my class, making him ineligible to play in a big rivalry game Friday night. He's had a lot to do with practice every afternoon and he's a really good guy. I decide to make his grade a C− instead of a D.	I didn't make this adjustment for several other students who struggled, or maybe didn't struggle enough, to make a C−. Because I insist that all my students keep up with their grade averages, Mike will know that I changed his grade. What message am I sending him about doing just enough to get by and then receiving "gifts"? If he brags about this, what about the other students, both those who didn't get the extra boost and others who do fine in my class but will know that I fudged on Mike's grade? Will some parent discover what I have done and complain to my principal?
It's time once again to promote the sale of wrapping paper to earn money for school projects. I send a letter home encouraging parents to join in. I e-mail parents each day reminding them to help their students sell the paper. I promise the students a party, but only for those who bring in orders for $100 of paper. The students feel the pressure, as do the parents.	Because my class is composed of kids from a wide range of socioeconomic-level homes, am I unduly putting pressure on some families who don't know many people with discretionary money to spend on fancy wrapping paper? If I still like the party idea, how might I design the party incentive so that particular students would not be ostracized?
Because fund-raising efforts have been disappointing in recent years, and our school improvement team wants to landscape the courtyard, our principal decides to give each student who brings a $20 donation 10 points to be used on any test in any class during the quarter.	At first I buy into this plan, not considering the fairness or morality of it. Then a student comes to me and complains that being able to give $20 will be difficult. Suddenly I see this initiative as very unfair and fundamentally misguided. Should I express this to my principal? Should I tell my students that I won't honor the 10-point bonus?

Ethical and Legal Issues in U.S. Schools

traits we want to promote in those we profoundly influence through ethical teaching. In writing about her vision of young adolescents, Donna Marie San Antonio (2006, p. 7) simply and eloquently describes some desirable traits. We want students to be

- smart but not arrogant
- flexible but not easily deterred from their hopes and dreams
- compassionate toward others but not overly accommodating
- self-confident but not too preoccupied with themselves
- proud but not exclusive

Points of Reflection 10.1

What are your memories of teachers who promoted ethical behavior? Describe a scenario from your PreK–12 school experiences.

What are your memories of teachers who displayed unethical attitudes and actions? Describe a scenario from your PreK–12 school experiences.

Helping students build these traits is a tall order and one we must fulfill with ethical attitudes, decisions, and actions. The results will be positive and cumulative.

Now that you have considered what it means to be an ethical teacher and some of the ways ethics guide classroom practice, it's time to look at more concrete guidelines that determine actions.

How Do Laws Affect Schools, Teachers, and Students?

The U.S. government, its legal system, and the laws that affect schools, teachers, and students are based on a balance of rights and responsibilities. The government and legal system achieve a viable balance of power through the interaction of the three branches of government: executive, legislative, and judicial. Since the founding of the United States of America, four basic sources of law have directly impacted the everyday work of all teachers: the U.S. Constitution, federal laws, state and local laws and policies, and case law.

U.S. CONSTITUTION

The Constitution does not specifically mention education. However, certain amendments directly impact teachers and schools.

FIRST AMENDMENT. The First Amendment to the Constitution, shown in Figure 10.3, guarantees, among other things, freedom of speech and religion and prohibits government (i.e., public school) advancement of religion. The relationship between law and religion is discussed later in this chapter.

Freedom of speech, as guaranteed in the First Amendment, applies to schools. As you read this chapter you'll recognize how often the First Amendment is cited as a guide in decision making on educational issues. The Association for Supervision and Curriculum Development (ASCD) established The First Amendment center to help educators better understand how to apply the tenets of this amendment in schools. The Web site www.firstamendmentschools.org is designed to provide resources to assist schools in implementing the guiding principles of the First Amendment.

FOURTH AMENDMENT. The Fourth Amendment protects citizens from unreasonable search and seizure and, in doing so, protects the basic privacy and security of all people, including students' rights to privacy. For instance, do students have the right to keep whatever they want in a locker assigned to them? Under what circumstances can adults examine the locker contents? This topic is discussed later in the chapter.

Figure 10.3 First Amendment

Congress shall make no law respecting an establishment of religion, or prohibiting the free exercise thereof; or abridging the freedom of speech, or the press; or the right of the people peaceably to assemble, and to petition the government for a redress of grievances.

FOURTEENTH AMENDMENT. The Fourteenth Amendment protects the rights of due process and guarantees equal protection to all citizens. For teachers, this amendment pertains to job security and the right to be heard if charges are made against them. Later in the chapter we examine how this amendment affects both teachers and students.

The general guidelines of the U.S. Constitution, specifically the First, Fourth, and Fourteenth Amendments, provide the framework for the federal laws that affect schools, teachers, and students.

FEDERAL LAWS

The federal statutes written and passed by Congress (the legislative branch of the U.S. government) have a major impact on the daily work of teachers and the operation of schools.

Here are examples of federal laws impacting education:

- The National Defense Education Act (1958) established curricular priorities, placing math, science, and foreign language at the top.
- The Civil Rights Act (1964) officially ended more than 50 years of overt racial segregation in public schools by declaring, "No person in the United States shall on the grounds of race, color, or national origin, be excluded from participation in or be denied the benefits of, or be subjected to discrimination under any program or activity receiving federal financial assistance." Unfortunately, however, segregation still exists in public schools in many areas.
- The Elementary and Secondary Education Act (1965) was originated to benefit children in low socioeconomic settings. This act created Title I funding and has been reauthorized several times.
- The Bilingual Education Act (1968) proposed that students be taught in their native languages while they learned English.
- Federal Title IX legislation (1972) opened many doors, specifically to girls, by prohibiting discrimination based on gender.
- The Individuals with Disabilities Education Act (1975, 1990, 2004) guarantees the rights of students with disabilities to a free education in the least restrictive environment.

Another federal law you've read about many times throughout this text is the 2001 reauthorization of the Elementary and Secondary Education Act, known from 2001 through 2010 as No Child Left Behind. The federal law has significantly impacted schools so far in the 21st century.

STATE AND LOCAL LAWS AND POLICIES

The U.S. Constitution stipulates that anything not specifically addressed by it becomes a state issue. Consequently, laws and policies affecting education vary from state to state, and from district to district within each state. Some of the issues addressed by state and local laws and policies include curriculum standards and assessment mandates, as well as funding and governance. The guidelines for teacher certification are left up to states, with some federal stipulations.

CASE LAW

Many legal decisions concerning education are based on precedence—what has been done in the past and what the judicial system has decided with regard to specific rights and responsibilities. The cases brought before the courts are deliberated and settled based on what the U.S. Constitution says, what federal law dictates, and what state and local governing bodies have established. All of these aspects are considered, ideally with heaping doses of common sense, as decisions are made by the courts.

Case law is based on the doctrine of *stare decisis*, a Latin phrase meaning "let the decision stand." This means that once a decision is made in a court of law, that decision sets a

Figure 10.4 Relationship of law and ethics

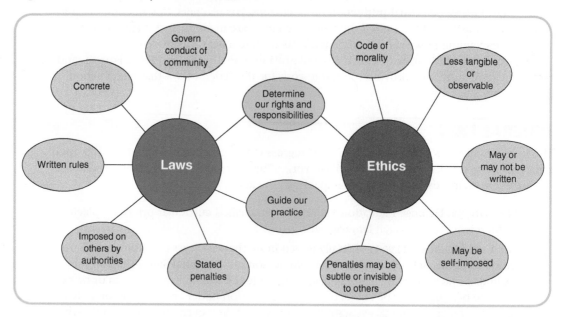

precedent for future cases of a similar nature until challenged or overturned. There is a large body of federal case law on which state and local cases rely for precedence. A decision made by the U.S. Supreme Court establishes case law until either the Supreme Court changes the ruling or an amendment to the Constitution alters the decision. Unfortunately, many school and local government officials have not abided by this principle. Because the Supreme Court doesn't have an enforcement arm, continued court action is sometimes necessary to bring school districts into compliance. For instance, the famous *Brown* v. *Board of Education* (1954) court decision ruled that separate schools are not equal and opened many schoolhouse doors for African Americans. Occasionally during the last 50 years, however, decisions have been made that do not comply with the *Brown* results, and more court action has been needed (LaMorte, 2008).

Throughout this chapter, discussions of the legal rights and responsibilities of teachers, the rights of students, and the relationship between schools and religion will cite sample case law. Read these highlighted cases carefully.

Before addressing the rights and responsibilities of teachers and students, consider the relationship between laws and ethics. Take a few minutes to examine Figure 10.4 that shows how laws and ethics differ in a number of ways, yet still share some qualities.

What Are the Legal Rights of Teachers?

Teachers in the United States are entitled to the same rights as other Americans. However, some rights are occasionally tempered by the opinions of either the community or the court when there is concern that teachers' individual rights may impact classroom effectiveness. In addition, certain legal rights apply specifically to the teaching profession. Most teachers will never find themselves in positions where their legal rights are threatened in any way. The day-to-day realities of teaching rarely involve legal challenges.

EMPLOYMENT LEGALITIES

Being employed by a school district entails understanding your rights and responsibilities. You will sign a contract, possibly have tenure in your future, and have procedures for filing grievances if things go wrong or if dismissal is threatened.

TEACHING CONTRACTS. A **contract** is an agreement between parties that states the rights and responsibilities of each. A teacher signs an initial contract and then signs again

Ethical and Legal Issues in U.S. Schools

each year to continue in the same position. Teaching contracts typically include a formal offer of employment, the salary, and a description of the position. When you sign a teaching contract, you state that you will abide by district policies. It is very important to carefully read and understand the policies and the contract. Both are extensive and may be written in complex language. Don't hesitate to ask for an explanation.

Contracts are binding on both parties. If you sign a contract and then back out or take a different job, or if the district backs out, you or the district can be sued for damages involving **breach of contract.**

TENURE. Continuing contract status is known as **tenure.** A teacher with tenure is entitled to a contract each year unless the district has reason not to renew it or the teacher decides to go elsewhere. In most states tenure doesn't guarantee a particular position in a particular school, but it does guarantee employment in the district.

Some object to the concept of tenure because it requires more steps to dismiss an ineffective teacher who has it. However, even teachers with tenure cannot keep their jobs if they are shown to be incompetent, display immoral behaviors, are insubordinate, or are involved in any of a wide array of behaviors considered unprofessional conduct.

DISMISSAL. Teachers have been dismissed for many reasons, some of which sound outrageous to us today. Historically, teachers have been dismissed for not attending a particular church, for wearing pants in public (a female teacher), for marrying or becoming pregnant during the school year, and even for moving to a neighboring town. More recently the courts have ruled for dismissal due to, among others, the following reasons:

- insubordination
- neglect of duty
- conduct unbecoming a teacher
- incompetence
- physical or mental health problems
- engaging in illegal activities
- causing or encouraging disruptions

The general direction of court cases that consider dismissal tends today more toward a teacher's personal liberty than in the past. Here are two overriding questions asked when considering dismissal:

- Is the educational process significantly disrupted by the action?
- Is the teacher's credibility significantly harmed among students, colleagues, families, and the community?

Some teacher offenses are considered by the courts to be remediable, meaning that given assistance and time, a teacher may be able to correct the problem and be effective in the classroom. For instance, if a district begins dismissal procedures because a tenured teacher's classroom management skills are considered very poor, the court will likely say the teacher has a right to try to remediate those skills. On the other hand, some actions are considered irremediable in that they are so unprofessional that a district is not obligated to provide assistance. Conviction in a criminal case and having a sexual relationship with a student are two examples of actions for which districts may begin immediate procedures toward dismissal.

Most districts require teachers to serve successfully for about 3 years before offering them a continuing contract, or tenure. During these first 3 years or so, teachers can be dismissed for suspected incompetence or because of a general **reduction in force** of the district teacher population. Such a reduction may result from lower student numbers, budget cuts, or program cancellation. Reduction in force (rif) may also apply to tenured teachers. However, the general rule of "riffing" is that the last hired are the first to go.

Ethical and Legal Issues in U.S. Schools

DUE PROCESS. When a tenured teacher is threatened with dismissal, the steps the district must take to pursue the charges against the teacher are called **due process.** Due process is an important principle that requires guidelines to be followed to ensure that individuals are protected from arbitrary or capricious treatment by those in authority. The procedures of due process vary by state, but generally a teacher must be

1. notified of the proposed charges
2. given reasonable time to examine evidence
3. told who will be called as witnesses and given the right to legal representation
4. provided with a hearing before an impartial jury, panel, and/or judge
5. given the opportunity to call witnesses and cross-examine the district's witnesses
6. afforded a decision based on evidence
7. provided a transcript of the proceedings
8. given the right to appeal

Even though due process has been in force for many years and will likely continue to be part of the profession, outcomes of hearings based on due process may vary by location and according to the times (LaMorte, 2008). For instance, until the 1970s, if an unmarried teacher lived with someone of the opposite sex, the teacher could go through due process procedures and be dismissed. Today, it would be very rare for a teacher's living arrangements to serve as grounds for dismissal.

Points of Reflection 10.2

How do you feel about teachers going on strike and removing themselves from the classroom for a period of time during which collective bargaining takes place? Should teachers be allowed to strike because of grievances about their work environment (salary, hours, class size, etc.) if it means closing schools during the process? Why or why not?

UNIONS AND COLLECTIVE BARGAINING. Although not exclusively related to getting and keeping a job, collective bargaining is a right practiced in most states by teacher unions. States often allow unions to negotiate with school boards concerning elements of teacher contracts and working conditions. The two major teacher organizations that act as unions are the National Education Association (NEA) and the American Federation of Teachers (AFT). States have their own affiliates of NEA or AFT to represent teachers in more local ways. Individual teachers and groups of teachers can file **grievances,** or formal complaints against a district. NEA and AFT, or their state affiliates, often represent teachers who file grievances. NEA and AFT, as unions, can also call for teacher strikes when collective bargaining does not result in changes that satisfy the large groups of teachers who affiliate with the unions.

Teachers affiliated with unions may go on strike when collective bargaining does not result in satisfactory changes.
Philip James Corwin/CORBIS-NY

FREEDOM OF EXPRESSION

There are many ways to express opinions and beliefs, including symbolic, written, and verbal expression. Symbolic expression generally involves making a statement by what is worn—a style of clothing, a political button, particular colors, an armband, a ribbon. Some symbolic statements are socially acceptable, even desirable. For instance, ribbons showing support for breast cancer research or bracelets commemorating important days in history are considered appropriate. However, wearing an armband to protest an ongoing war or a shirt with inflammatory or offensive words or pictures may be legal outside school but ruled unacceptable in school and can serve as possible grounds for dismissal. For teachers, freedom of symbolic expression has limits, especially if it disrupts the school or classroom.

As with symbolic expression, written and spoken expression must not interrupt the education process. Teachers have the right to express themselves through letters to the editor, written articles, conversations, speeches, and debates. Since the often-quoted case of

Ethical and Legal Issues in U.S. Schools

Pickering v. *Board of Education,* 1968, the courts have generally ruled on the side of teachers' rights to freedom of spoken and written expression, even when that expression involves harsh criticism of a school, district, or personnel connected to education. In *Pickering,* an Illinois teacher wrote a sarcastic letter to the editor criticizing the school superintendent and school board for funding practices. The board fired Pickering, and the state supreme court upheld the dismissal. Pickering appealed to the U.S. Supreme Court. Justice Thurgood Marshall stated that the problem was one of balance between personal rights of the teacher and the district's right to promote efficient public service through its employees. The court ruled in favor of Pickering and his right to openly debate questions without fear of retaliatory dismissal.

If a teacher's expression is intended to incite unprofessional behavior, the courts may rule against the teacher. John Stroman was fired for encouraging teachers to call in sick as a form of protest against some administrative decisions. In *Stroman* v. *Colleton County School District,* 1992, the Supreme Court ruled in favor of the school district on grounds that encouraging others to lie is unprofessional.

ACADEMIC FREEDOM

Academic freedom is a form of expression that allows teachers to use their judgment in making decisions such as what to discuss, what to assign as readings, and what teaching strategies to employ. Like the other freedoms, academic freedom has limits that courts have upheld in many cases.

One recurring issue involves the courts' attempts to balance the right of academic freedom with a district's desire for students to learn a specific curriculum. Districts and states set the curriculum teachers must teach. When teachers exercise academic freedom and go beyond or eliminate parts of this curriculum, problems occur because either (1) including the additional topics does not leave time for the prescribed curriculum, or (2) the nonprescribed topics are controversial and may be deemed inappropriate.

In this era of standards and high-stakes testing, failing to teach the prescribed curriculum is likely to become evident, but it may take time. The line between what is appropriate in the classroom, and what is not, is the most common cause of disagreements between districts and teachers with regard to academic freedom. Some of the topics deemed inappropriate in the public school classroom when they are not part of the curriculum include sexuality-related issues, gun control, abortion, some political issues, and any topic involving offensive language. For instance, in *Keefe* v. *Geanakos,* 1969, a Massachusetts high school English teacher assigned an article from the *Atlantic Monthly* that contained offensive language. He was fired because he would not agree never to give the assignment again. A court decision gave Keefe his job back and stated that because some of the school's library books contained the same words and students would likely not be shocked by them, parental complaints about the words did not dictate what was proper in the classroom.

Some teaching methods may be deemed inappropriate if a teacher cannot substantiate the approach using professional opinions and research. In *Murray* v. *Pittsburgh Board of Education,* 1996, a teacher used a motivational technique called "Learnball" with at-risk high school students involving dividing the class into teams. Competition between teams involved rewards, such as listening to the radio and shooting baskets with foam balls. The school board ordered the teacher not to use the method. Murray sued the board but lost. The courts determined that the school board had the right to set policy against particular teaching methodologies.

Summaries of the four cases in this section concerning freedom of expression, plus two others of interest, are in Figure 10.5.

TEACHERS' PERSONAL LIVES

A teacher has a right to a personal life. However, the notion that teachers are role models entails some limits that have been upheld in courts. As late as the 1960s, teachers were quickly and without challenge fired for adultery, drunkenness, homosexual conduct, illegal drug use, cohabitation with the opposite sex, or becoming pregnant while single. To lend

Points of Reflection 10.3

Are there issues about which teachers should not talk or write about if it means the community will be aware of his or her views? If not, justify your answer. If so, what is one issue and why?

If you felt strongly about teaching a particular topic in an advanced high school class, but the district said that you should not spend time on the topic even though it was not offensive, how would you respond?

Figure 10.5 Case law: Freedom of expression

Pickering **v.** *Board of Education* (1968)
Teacher kept job after publicly criticizing school board.

Keefe **v.** *Geanakos* (1969)
Teacher keeps job after assigning controversial readings.

Kingsville Independent School District **v.** *Cooper* (1980)
Teacher uses role play to teach about racial relations
A teacher was dismissed when she refused to stop using role-play simulations to teach about post–Civil War American history. Parents complained that the activity caused racially charged sentiments in their children. The Court of Appeals reinstated the teacher, with back pay. The court determined that the district violated the teacher's First Amendment rights.

Krizek **v.** *Cicero-Stickney Township High School* (1989)
Teacher showing R-rated movie
A teacher was dismissed for showing an R-rated movie to her class as a modern-day parallel to *Our Town* by Thornton Wilder. She apparently told her students they would be excused if their parents objected, but she did not communicate directly with parents. The court upheld Ms. Krizek's dismissal saying the movie was a planned event, and not an inadvertent mistake, and that her methodology was problematic.

Stroman **v.** *Colleton County School District* (1992)
Teacher fired for encouraging others to lie.

Murray **v.** *Pittsburgh Board of Education* (1996)
Teacher may not use instructional strategy considered unorthodox by school board.

Sources: Dunklee, D. R., & Shoop, R. J. (2002). *The principal's quick-reference guide to school law: Reducing liability, litigation, and other potential legal tangles.* Thousand Oaks, CA: Corwin Press. LaMorte, M. W. (2008). *School law: cases and concepts* (9th ed.). Fischer, L., Schimmel, D., & Stellman, L. R. (2007). *Teachers and the law* (7th ed.). Boston: Allyn & Bacon.

some perspective to this discussion, take a look at an excerpt from an actual teacher contract from the 1920s, shown in Figure 10.6.

PERSONAL CONDUCT AND JOB PERFORMANCE. The notion that teachers can be automatically fired for what is considered by the community as immoral behavior was rejected by the California Supreme Court in *Morrison* v. *State Board of Education,* 1969. The court found that grounds for dismissal must include evidence that the personal conduct of a teacher adversely affects job performance. The Morrison case involved a teacher who had a brief homosexual relationship with another teacher. When the superintendent found out, Morrison's teaching license was revoked on the grounds that his immoral conduct was contrary to the moral standards of the people of California. However, the court ruled in favor of Morrison and said the term *immoral* was interpreted too broadly. No evidence was found to connect Morrison's personal life and his professional work.

In *Morrison,* the California Supreme Court said it was dangerous to allow the terms *immoral* and *unprofessional* to be interpreted too broadly. The court established that immoral conduct means vastly different things to different people. To some immoral behavior includes laziness, gluttony, selfishness, and cowardice, and unprofessional conduct for teachers may include signing controversial petitions, opposing majority opinions, and drinking alcoholic

Figure 10.6 Excerpt from 1920s teacher contract

I promise to abstain from all dancing, immodest dressing, and any other conduct unbecoming a teacher and a lady. I promise not to go out with any young men except in so far as it may be necessary to stimulate Sunday School work.

I promise not to fall in love, to become engaged, or secretly marry.

I promise to sleep at least eight hours at night [and] to eat carefully . . . in order that I may be better able to render efficient service to my pupils.

Source: Fischer, L., Schimmel, D., & Stellman, L. R. (2007). *Teachers and the law* (7th ed.). Boston: Allyn & Bacon.

Ethical and Legal Issues in U.S. Schools

beverages. The court ruled that a teacher should not be fired because someone disapproves of the teacher's personal life unless it directly relates to his or her professional work and that today's morals may well be considered absurd in the future (Fischer, Schimmel, & Stellman, 2007). Generally the courts have ruled that teachers have the right to privacy in regard to procreation, marriage, child rearing, and other activities in the home (Underwood & Webb, 2006).

Since 1969 other cases have been brought to courts by teachers who felt they were wrongly dismissed. The courts continue to look for evidence that particular conduct adversely affects job performance. In *Eckmann* v. *Board of Education,* 1986, an Illinois teacher was fired when she became pregnant while unmarried and decided to raise the child as a single parent. The judge found in favor of the teacher and said that she had a due process right to conceive and raise her child, even out of wedlock, and without school board intrusion (Fischer et al., 2007). In contrast, and in what may seem like a frivolous situation, a high school teacher was not rehired because she refused to stop wearing short skirts. In *Tardif* v. *Quinn,* 1976, the court recognized the teacher's constitutional right to choose her grooming but ruled that the right did not extend to wearing whatever she pleased during the school workday.

As with personal conduct, if a district wants to fire a teacher for health reasons (e.g., obesity, disabilities, AIDS), it must show a direct link between the health problem and impaired classroom function. And there is a considerable gray area when it comes to the following situations:

- conviction of a misdemeanor or felony
- possession or use of illegal drugs
- overuse of alcohol

Figure 10.7 summarizes the cases in this section along with several others that concern teachers' personal lives.

Points of Reflection 10.4

Do you think the role of teacher carries with it personal restraints? Would you be willing to alter your lifestyle somewhat to conform with what a particular community considers moral and professional behavior?

Figure 10.7 Case law: Teachers' personal lives

Morrison v. *State Board of Education* (1969)
Teacher keeps position because behavior does not directly affect job performance.

Tardif v. *Quinn* (1976)
Teacher challenges dress code but does not keep job.

Thompson v. *Southwest District* (1980)
Teacher unmarried cohabitation
A female teacher was fired because she lived with her boyfriend. Although she didn't particularly keep the arrangement a secret, when the school board suspended her for immorality, they publicized it. The court ruled that it was unfair to make the issue public in an attempt to gain support. In addition, the court found that living with her boyfriend did not diminish the teacher's classroom effectiveness. The board lost and the teacher kept her job.

Eckmann v. *Board of Education* (1986)
Single teacher raising child keeps job.

Ware v. *Morgan County School District* (1988)
Teacher using obscene language toward students
A Colorado high school music teacher took a misbehaving student outside and used obscene language to tell him he was a disgrace to the band. The teacher was fired and the court sided with the school district.

Elvin v. *City of Waterville* (1990)
A divorced female fourth grade teacher was fired for having sexual relations with her 15-year-old neighbor boy. Although he had never been her student, the court agreed with the school district's decision to fire her saying she had proven herself unfit to teach. The judge added that public awareness of her conduct undermined her ability to deal with students and parents.

Sources: Dunklee, D. R., & Shoop, R. J. (2002). *The principal's quick-reference guide to school law: Reducing liability, litigation, and other potential legal tangles* by D. R. Dunklee and R. J. Shoop, 2002. Thousand Oaks, CA: Corwin Press. LaMorte, J. W. (2008). *School law: Cases and concepts* (9th ed.). Boston: Allyn & Bacon. Fischer, L., Schimmel, D., & Stellman, L. R. (2007). *Teachers and the law* (7th ed.). Boston: Allyn & Bacon.

Ethical and Legal Issues in U.S. Schools

MISCONDUCT WITH STUDENTS. The most clear-cut decisions involving the firing of teachers on moral grounds involve misconduct with students. When a teacher's personal life or habits intersect a student's in illegal or morally questionable ways, it is relatively easy for a school district to dismiss a teacher for

- sexual relations with students
- profane, abusive language directed at students
- allowing students to drink alcohol
- encouraging students to be dishonest

What Are the Legal Responsibilities of Teachers?

Teachers have many responsibilities, some dictated by laws and others by state, district, or school policies. Some responsibilities are governed by ethical and professional guidelines.

LIABILITY

To be **liable** means to be responsible for. We generally hear the term in a negative sense, for instance, "He was found liable for the accident" or "That will raise my liability insurance premium." In a positive sense, though, liability is what teaching is all about—accepting responsibility for students while they are under our supervision. This is why we study such aspects as child development, subject matter, instructional and assessment strategies, guidelines for health and safety, and school law. However, being held liable when something goes wrong is far from positive. Depending on the severity of the issue, liability for a situation can end a career.

Teachers serve *in loco parentis*, "in place of parents." They are bound by law to care for and protect children in the school setting as a parent would and are held to a standard of reasonableness. Teachers, schools, and districts are frequently sued over issues related to liability. For a school employee to be considered liable for something, the following four components must be proven to be present:

1. The person has a legal duty to protect students.
2. The person fails to act within reason and provide the appropriate standard of care.
3. There is a causal connection between the person's conduct and the result of the injury.
4. Actual damage occurs to the injured person. (LaMorte, 2008)

In the case of *Mancha* v. *Field Museum of Natural History,* 1971, students ages 12 to 15 went on a field trip with teachers to the Chicago Natural History Museum. The students were allowed to tour the exhibits on their own. One student was beaten up by teenagers from another school. In this case, the teachers had a legal duty to protect students (1), and there was actual damage (4). The court had to decide if the teachers failed to act within reason and provide an appropriate standard of care (2) and if there was a causal connection between the teachers' conduct and the injury (3). The teachers were not held liable for the student's injuries because the court determined there was minimal risk at the museum, and the teachers could not reasonably have been expected to directly supervise them.

In a similar case the same year, an eighth grader sustained a severe eye injury when a student threw rocks during a baseball game. The teacher involved in *Sheehan* v. *St. Peter's*

Focus teacher Chris Roberts believes in teaching through a variety of experiences. He is responsible for student safety when he takes his class on field trips. Provided by the author

Ethical and Legal Issues in U.S. Schools

Catholic School, 1971, had accompanied the students outside but then returned to the building. The courts determined that the teacher left the area and therefore was not properly supervising the students. She was found liable for leaving students alone in a potentially dangerous setting.

Teachers can take some precautions that will lessen the causal connection between their actions and any harm that may come to students. Here are a few to consider:

- Be 100% present when with students. Limit personal distractions and remain focused.
- Think through situations and, if possible, avoid those that have unusual potential for danger.
- Establish routines and rules that make safety a habit among students.
- Remind students of appropriate behavior to help them remain safe.

Accidents happen—in the classroom, the hallway, the cafeteria, the science lab, the gym, on school grounds, and on field trips. Additional cases involving teacher liability are summarized in Figure 10.8. Using good judgment in the *in loco parentis* role will be enough for most teachers. But occasionally students are injured and teacher liability may be questioned. Liability insurance is a good idea. Teacher organizations offer reasonably priced policies that are recommended even for student teachers. These organizations often also provide legal assistance to members who find themselves involved in a school-related lawsuit.

Points of Reflection 10.5

Have you considered the many ways things may go wrong for teachers and students? Were you ever involved in a situation where a teacher's liability was questioned? If so, what were the circumstances?

COPYRIGHT LAWS

Copyright laws provide guidelines for authorized use of someone else's intellectual property and are intended to protect the rights of creators of intellectual property by preventing others from copying or distributing it without permission. Intellectual property includes written material, original audio and visual work, and computer programs.

Copyrighted materials may be used under three conditions: the user has permission from the copyright owner, the work is in the public domain, or the use is considered "fair

Figure 10.8 Case law: Teacher liability

Kaufman v. City of New York **(1961)**
Teacher supervising basketball
A boy was seriously injured when he bumped heads with another boy during a basketball game. The court ruled that any amount of supervision could not have prevented the accident and that the school and teacher were not liable.

Morris v. Douglas County School District **(1965)**
Teacher's lack of caution on field trip
A first grade teacher took her students on a field trip to the Oregon coast. While students waded in the water, a large wave washed a log onto a student causing serious injury. The court found that the teacher was liable because this kind of injury was not uncommon and the teacher was responsible for the safety of the young children in her care.

Mancha v. Field Museum of Natural History **(1971)**
Teacher allowing students to "self-guide" during field trip is not held liable for injury.

Sheehan v. St. Peter's Catholic School **(1971)**
Teacher leaving students on field
The teacher had accompanied the students outside but then returned to the building. The courts determined that the teacher left the area and therefore was not properly supervising the students.

Station v. Travelers Insurance Co. **(1974)**
Teacher leaving students during class is held liable for student injury.

Sources: LaMorte, J. W. (2008). *School law: Cases and concepts* (9th ed.). Boston: Allyn & Bacon. Fischer, L., Schimmel, D., & Stellman, L. R. (2007). *Teachers and the law* (7th ed.). Boston: Allyn & Bacon.

Figure 10.9 Guidelines for classroom copying

1. A single copy may be made of any of the following for your own scholarly research or use in teaching:
   - a chapter from a book
   - an article from a periodical or newspaper
   - a short story, short essay, or short poem
   - a chart, graph, diagram, drawing, cartoon or picture from a book, periodical, or newspaper.

2. Multiple copies (no more than one per student) may be made for classroom use if each copy gives credit to the copyright holder and passes three tests.
   - The brevity test includes guidelines such as poems of fewer than 200 words and prose of fewer than 2,500 words.
   - The spontaneity test generally says that you are inspired to copy and use material for the sake of teaching effectiveness and there was not time to ask and receive permission.
   - The cumulative effect test generally restricts the length of time copied material is used and how many instances of copying take place in a period of time.

3. Teachers cannot copy individual works and put them together to serve as an anthology.

4. Students cannot be charged for the photocopying of copyrighted works.

Source: Underwood, J., & Webb, L. D. (2006). *School law for teachers: Concepts and applications.* Upper Saddle River, NJ: Merrill/Prentice Hall.

use." A work is in the **public domain** if it is more than 75 years old or is published by a government agency. **Fair use** allows the nonprofit reproduction of certain materials in the classroom without permission of the copyright owner (Underwood & Webb, 2006, p. 87). Generally, fair use stipulates that the material copied must be for educational purposes and that the amount copied must fall within certain guidelines, some of which are listed in Figure 10.9. Teachers may not, however, make copies of consumable products such as textbooks, workbooks, and standardized test materials. If copies could be freely made of these kinds of materials, then their creators and publishers would lose money because the need for them would diminish.

Because teachers often want students to create work using certain computer software, it is important to know that computer software is copyrighted and that fair use guidelines do not apply. Some software publishers allow one backup copy to be made, but more than this is illegal. Additionally, commercially produced videos may not be copied. Copies made of television programs can be kept for 45 days and then must be erased or destroyed.

With the Internet serving as a major research tool in classrooms today, teachers must be aware that what is on the Internet is not in the public domain. Because the Internet is international, laws governing its use are somewhat unclear. Following fair use guidelines is a safe way to use Web resources.

Whether using written works, audiovisual materials, computer software, or information from the Internet, teachers must take copyright laws seriously. School districts have policies based on fair use guidelines. A school's media specialist is often a helpful, knowledgeable source of information about what is lawful and what is not. Teachers should ask if there is any question about how they plan to use any form of intellectual property.

REPORTING SUSPECTED CHILD ABUSE

A teacher who has a reasonable suspicion of child abuse or neglect has a legal obligation to report it to a school counselor or administrator, who in turn will report it to a social services agency or the police. Teachers don't have to be certain that they are correct. They are granted immunity and may not be sued for reporting their suspicions (Fischer et al., 2007).

It is a good idea for teachers to keep lists of signs of abuse and neglect handy for easy reference. Teachers should never become too busy to be observant. Physical abuse may be visually evident and difficult to miss. However, sexual abuse may be more subtle in terms of symptoms, and emotional or mental abuse may be even more difficult to detect. Reviewing the signs periodically, watching for behavioral or emotional changes, and reporting suspicions of abuse or neglect to administrators or school counselors will help protect students. This is a teacher's legal and ethical responsibility—and simply the right thing to do.

Teacher responsibilities obviously include protecting their students however and whenever they can. Teacher responsibilities also include safeguarding students' rights.

How Does the Law Impact the Relationship Between School and Religion?

The First Amendment makes it clear that the founders of the United States did not want government to have any say in how or whether citizens worship. Because public schools are government entities, they may neither establish religion nor interfere with the free exercise of it. As clearly stated as it is in the Constitution, the issue is anything but clear cut in practice. Few topics are as charged with emotion and passion, and hence with such potential to polarize people, as religion.

Let's establish some basic dos and don'ts for teachers and students with regard to religion and education. In 1998 President Clinton asked Secretary of Education Richard Riley to prepare guidelines based on law and court decisions to help educators determine the rights of students and staff regarding religion and public schools. For easy reference, these guidelines are adapted to question format in Figure 10.10.

Figure 10.10 Guidelines for religious expression in public schools from the U.S. Department of Education

Can students pray in school?
Yes. Students may pray individually or in a group as long as they are nondisruptive. For instance, students may pray before meals or tests to the same extent they may engage in comparable nondisruptive activities.

Can students read religious materials and discuss religion among themselves?
Yes. Students may read and talk about religion to the same extent as they may read and talk about anything else in school.

Can students meet to express their religious beliefs during the school day and on school grounds?
Yes. Students may meet for nondisruptive purposes during their lunch periods or other noninstructional time during the school day, as well as before and after the school day. This includes religion-related meetings.

Is it legal to have organized prayer at sporting events or other school functions?
No. Under current Supreme Court decisions, school officials may not mandate or organize prayer at any school-sponsored event or graduation.

Can teachers participate in religious meetings while at school?
No. Teachers and school administrators, when acting in those capacities, are representatives of the state and are prohibited from soliciting or encouraging religious activity, and from participating in such activity with students.

Can teachers teach about religions in school?
Yes. Teachers may teach *about* religion, including the Bible or other scripture: the history of religion, comparative religion, the Bible (or other scripture)-as-literature, and the role of religion in the history of the United States and other countries. They may also prompt students to consider religious influences on art, music, literature, and social studies.

Can teachers display religious-related holiday items or encourage the celebration of religious holidays in school?
No. Although public schools may teach *about* religious holidays, including their religious aspects, and may celebrate the secular aspects of holidays, schools may not observe holidays as religious events or encourage students to do so.

(continued)

Figure 10.10 Continued

Is it acceptable for students to express religious beliefs in school assignments?
Yes. Students may express their beliefs about religion in the form of homework, artwork, and other written and oral assignments free of discrimination based on the religious content of their work. The assignments should be graded according to the standards the lesson is intended to address.

If a lesson may be considered offensive by a student and/or the student's family, can the student opt not to participate?
Yes. Schools can excuse individual students from lessons that are objectionable to the student or the students' parents on religious or other conscientious grounds.

Can students opt out of a particular dress code or uniform for religious reasons?
Legally, the answer is no. However, schools have discretion to interpret this in ways that make sense in their communities.

Can students wear religious messages or symbols on their clothes?
Yes. The restrictions are the same as for any other comparable messages. Schools can not single out religion-related messages and symbols to prohibit.

Source: Adapted from Riley, R. W. (1998). *Secretary's statement on religious expression.* Retrieved November 12, 2006, from www.ed.gov/inits/religionandschools.

RELIGION AND COMPULSORY EDUCATION

Compulsory education laws require students to attend school through a certain age. *Pierce* v. *Society of Sisters,* 1925, established that compulsory education laws could be met through attendance at private or parochial schools. In the 1970s, Amish families asked to be exempt from compulsory education beyond eighth grade on the grounds that attendance in upper grades would have a negative effect on their traditions and way of life. The Supreme Court ruled in their favor in *Wisconsin* v. *Yoder,* 1972. This ruling is known as the "Amish exception." If non-Amish parents wish to isolate their children from public or private school beyond a particular grade (under age 16), they must show that school will somehow destroy their religion. Homeschooling is a legal option with very few requirements or constraints. Because families aren't required to supply a reason for homeschooling, it is unknown how many families use their right to homeschool their children as a way to avoid compulsory education laws.

Students may pray together on school grounds, as long as it is not disruptive to the education process.
Valerie Berta/Journal-Courier/The Image Works

PRAYER IN SCHOOL

Students may pray silently or quietly in small groups in school. But that's it. Legally there may be no school-sponsored public prayer, even nondenominational prayer (Underwood & Webb, 2006). This prohibition includes prayer at gatherings such as graduation ceremonies, football games, and assemblies. In *Santa Fe Independent School District* v. *Doe,* 2000, a Texas school district allowed students to vote on whether to have prayer and who would deliver it before football games. Groups of Mormon and Catholic students, alumni, and parents filed a suit claiming the district was violating the First Amendment. The U.S. Supreme Court ruled against the district, contending that the school would be endorsing a specific religion depending on who delivered the prayer.

Some communities choose to violate the First Amendment principle of separation of church and state by endorsing prayer in school-related settings. If challenged, they would likely lose in court. Some school boards even begin their meetings with prayer, often careful not to use language that would offend Christians or Jews. However, these prayers may offend Muslims,

Buddhists, and other religious groups, as well as atheists. Regardless of who is present, prayer is not legal in public education meetings.

RELIGIOUS ORGANIZATIONS MEETING ON SCHOOL GROUNDS

If a school building is used before or after hours for organizations of any kind, it may also be used for organizations that are religious in nature. In *Good News Club* v. *Milford Central School,* 2001, the Supreme Court ruled that a private Christian organization for children ages 6 to 12 in New York could use a public school for weekly after-school meetings. Although some lower courts have ruled that teachers may be involved in student religious organizations on their own time, generally school employees may not sponsor the groups (Fischer et al., 2007).

RELIGIOUS HOLIDAYS. Observing specific religious holidays in class is not allowed. This is a visible and controversial aspect of mixing school and religion. The longest traditional school breaks or vacations (other than summer) occur during Christian celebrations—December break at Christmas and spring break at Easter. What was once called Christmas break is now generally referred to as the winter holiday. The traditional holiday student presentation once called the Christmas Program is now the choral/band event that may be referred to as the Holiday or Winter Program. Students may sing Christmas songs with religious messages, such as "Silent Night," but these songs may not dominate the program.

Holiday displays that depict Christian or Christmas symbols may be used if they are balanced with other cultural symbols such as a Jewish menorah. The displays must be temporary and help show diversity (Underwood & Webb, 2006). Parents and students may request to be exempt from activities focused on holidays.

RELIGION AND CURRICULUM. Must schools do away with all reference to religion to separate church and state? The answer is no. It is permissible to teach about religion but not with the purpose of convincing students that a particular belief should be followed. Use of the Bible, Talmud, Koran, and other religious books for teaching literature and history is permissible as long as one is not endorsed over another.

Perhaps the greatest point of tension concerning religion and curriculum is the theory of evolution. In the so-called Scopes Monkey Trial, 1925, a high school teacher was convicted of violating a Tennessee regulation against teaching anything that contradicted the biblical Genesis account of the creation of humans. Although the conviction was overturned on a technicality, controversy over the teaching of evolution in schools has continued. In 1982 Louisiana passed the Balanced Treatment Act, which required the teaching of both creationism and evolution. The U.S. Supreme Court ruled the act illegal because it endorsed creationism, a Christian view, to the exclusion of other views. Some school districts, and even whole states, have attempted to give equal time to what some Christians believe about creation as embodied in the literal translation of the Bible and to evolution. Some districts have attempted to outlaw the teaching of evolution or to require a disclaimer stating that it is only a theory, one of many that tries to explain the origin of humans.

Figure 10.11 summarizes the cases in this section plus two others that affect how religion and schools coexist.

As you can see, the rights and responsibilities of teachers and students often intersect at the delicate point of separation of church and state. In some communities, and at some times of the year, preserving this separation is challenging.

What Are the Legal Rights of Students?

Students do not leave their constitutional rights at the schoolhouse door. You may notice that there isn't a section of this chapter devoted to students' legal responsibilities. If there were, the section would be short. Students have the responsibility to go to school as long as it is compulsory (usually to age 16, but to age 18 in some locations). That's about it in terms of legal responsibilities. Although we hope students take responsibility for their learning

Points of Reflection 10.6

Did you or your family ever have religion-based views that conflicted with events at your school? Were your views conservative (opposition to dancing, nonacceptance of evolution theory, nonparticipation when certain movies were shown, etc.)? Were there restrictions imposed that you believed unnecessary?

Figure 10.11 Case law: Religion in schools

Wisconsin **v.** *Yoder* **(1972)**
Amish allowed to end formal education at eighth grade.

Stone **v.** *Graham* **(1980)**
Parents protest posting of Ten Commandments
A Kentucky statute required the posting of the Ten Commandments on the wall of every public school classroom. The plaques were purchased with private funds and had a notation describing them as secular. The posting was declared unconstitutional on the grounds that merely stating that the Ten Commandments (rooted in Judeo-Christian beliefs) were secular did not make it so.

Herdahl **v.** *Pontotoc County School District* **(1996)**
Parent protested prayer in public school
A Mississippi mother sued a K–12 school for having prayers following morning announcements on the intercom. The court ruled that the practice violated separation of church and state because the students are a captive audience. This case was an example of violations of already established law that continue to go through our judicial system.

Santa Fe Independent School District **v.** *Doe* **(2000)**
Public prayer at school events violates the First Amendment because the school would be endorsing a specific religion, depending on who delivered the invocation.

Good News Club **v.** *Milford Central School* **(2001)**
Student Christian group allowed to use school facilities.

Sources: Fischer, L., Schimmel, D., & Stellman, L. R. (2007). *Teachers and the law.* Boston: Allyn & Bacon. McNergney, R. F., & McNergney, J. M. (2009). *Education: The practice and profession of teaching.* Boston: Allyn & Bacon.

and behavior, unless their behavior is deemed illegal or extremely disruptive, there are no other laws binding them.

FREEDOM OF EXPRESSION

Before 1969 students were not recognized as having First Amendment rights to freedom of expression. The U.S. Supreme Court's decision in *Tinker* v. *Des Moines Independent Community School District,* 1969, provided a clear message that a student is entitled to freedom of expression (LaMorte, 2008). The case involved three students who wore armbands to protest the war in Vietnam. They were suspended and subsequently sued the district. In this monumentally important case the U.S. Supreme Court ruled that teachers and students do not "shed their rights to freedom of speech or expression at the schoolhouse gate." The *Tinker* case has been cited repeatedly since 1969.

However, court challenges since *Tinker* have served to balance the rights of students to express themselves and the necessity of limiting personal freedom to ensure the safety and well-being of others. For students, understanding the need for this balance is a lesson in the principles of democracy.

FREEDOM OF SYMBOLIC EXPRESSION. The *Tinker* decision so influenced how students are viewed in relation to freedom of expression that it is known as the *Tinker doctrine.* This doctrine extends to symbolic freedom. As with other rights, students are allowed to express their views symbolically through what they wear as long as it doesn't disrupt the educational process.

Dress Codes. Since the 1960s, numerous lawsuits have been initiated over the restrictions imposed by dress codes, but the U.S. Supreme Court has not ruled on the issue. In 1972 Justice Black wrote that the U.S. Constitution doesn't require the courts to bear the burden of supervising clothing or hairstyles.

However, schools are concerned about immodest dress and unusual hairstyles because they could disrupt the educational atmosphere of the classroom as well as lead to more serious issues. For instance, violence generated by gangs and groups such as the "trench coat mafia" (the students associated with the 1999 Columbine school shootings) has prompted

Ethical and Legal Issues in U.S. Schools

educators to identify and attempt to ban insignia clothing and hats associated with specific groups. LaMorte (2008) lists the following as school concerns:

- T-shirts depicting violence, drugs (e.g., marijuana leaves), racial epithets
- ripped, baggy, or saggy pants or jeans
- colored bandanas
- baseball or other hats
- words shaved into scalps
- brightly colored hair
- exposed underwear
- tattoos, . . . pierced noses
- decorative dental caps (p. 172)

These forms of symbolic expression are not protected by the First Amendment because they may contribute to school unrest. Most dress codes outlaw some or all of the items in LaMorte's list. However, because some of the items are associated with particular cultures, it is difficult for schools to designate them without appearing to be biased. Rules designating shirt length, requiring belts, and prohibiting exposed midriffs are more generic but still hard to enforce.

Students often enjoy expressing personal taste in their choices of clothing and shoes. Sara Davis Powell

Uniforms. Dress codes are often ambiguous, leaving much room for interpretation. They can infringe on learning time if teachers are expected to watch for and report violations. Thus some schools and entire districts choose to impose a uniform policy, giving students several modest, relatively plain choices of clothing. Currently, more than half the states have schools with uniform policies. Some large cities, such as Long Beach, Chicago, and San Antonio, require at least elementary students to wear uniforms. In 2002 Memphis, Tennessee, became the nation's first large public school district to adopt a uniform policy in all of its 175 schools.

Public schools that impose uniform policies must provide an opt-out clause for parents who don't want their children to participate. For instance, some parents may not want their children to wear a uniform because it conflicts with the clothing traditions of their religion. Other parents may request to be exempt simply because their children don't want to wear the uniform and are persistently making that clear. Private schools do not receive government support and, unlike public schools, may impose a uniform policy on all students without allowing them to opt out.

Before we discuss student freedom of speech, consider this chapter's **Diversity Dialogue** (p. 288) involving focus teacher Brenda Beyal and a dilemma she faced that began with symbolic freedom. Reflect on the opportunities for Brenda and her students to learn about aspects of culture and a belief system with which they are not familiar.

FREEDOM OF SPEECH. The freedom of speech implied in *Tinker* was challenged in 1986 when a student made a speech containing sexual innuendo in a high school assembly. He was reprimanded and subsequently sued the school, claiming that his freedom of speech was denied. The case, *Bethel School District No. 403* v. *Fraser,* 1986, went to the U.S. Supreme Court, where the adolescent lost. The court ruled that a school does not have to accept indecent or offensive speech.

Although students enjoy free speech, it does have limits. An individual student's freedom of speech, as well as freedom of the press, must be balanced against the school's ability to maintain a safe and civil atmosphere, where all students are shown respect.

FREEDOM OF THE PRESS. School publications have long been fertile ground for disputes about students' rights to express themselves. In attempts to make school newspapers relevant and truly student owned, students tend to write about what's on the minds of classmates, no matter how controversial. However, it is clear from court decisions such as

Points of Reflection 10.7

Did your schools have dress codes or uniforms? What do you remember about them? Did you feel that your freedom of expression was restricted by what the schools said you could and couldn't wear?

As a future teacher, do you like the idea of dress codes or uniforms? Why or why not? Are they more important at particular levels of school?

Ethical and Legal Issues in U.S. Schools

Sara Davis Powell

DIVERSITY DIALOGUE

Brenda Beyal, as a teacher in a multiage classroom, enjoys the fact that her school, colleagues, and students are open minded and accepting of differences. She also enjoys the status of her school as an arts-focused elementary. The arrival of fifth grade twin girls in Benda's classroom 2 weeks after school began proved to be both a challenge and an opportunity.

Amira and Farah were the first children of traditional Muslim parents to attend Brenda's school. These 11-year-old twins walked into Brenda's classroom one Friday morning in September. They wore loose-fitting pants and long tunic tops, along with scarves on their heads that completely covered their hair. Amira and Farah smiled sweetly and took their seats at a table with three other children. Brenda welcomed them and invited the girls to introduce themselves to the class. Amira went first and explained that her name means *princess* in Islam. Then Farah followed suit by saying that her name means *happiness*.

Brenda had been told she would have two new students, but she had not been told that the girls were part of a very traditional Muslim family and that there would be some challenges because of their presence as the first students of Islamic faith. Here are some of the challenges Brenda faced:

- A school rule states that headgear may not be worn in the school building. The girls wore *hijab*, traditional Muslim headwear.

- Amira and Farah arrived in the middle of Ramadan, a Muslim month in which believers fast during daylight hours.

- Amira and Farah are required to pray five times a day, and two of the times fall within the school day.

- The parents of Amira and Farah talked with Principal Larsen and told him they are aware that his school is known for the arts. They have concerns because (in their tradition) dance serves no purpose and needlessly causes girls and boys to come in contact, they find some music offensive, and Muslim children are not allowed to draw human figures.

- Sentiment in the United States is generally unfavorable toward people of the Muslim faith, especially following the events of 9/11. The uncle of one of Brenda's students was killed in the New York City bombing of the World Trade Center.

Think about Brenda's challenges and opportunities to help all her students learn from, and about, each other's similarities and differences. Respond to these items by writing one well-developed paragraph each.

1. Is it legal for Amira and Farah to pause twice each day for prayer and refuse to eat lunch during Ramadan? If not, why? If so, how might Brenda explain this to her students?

2. Should the school rules be relaxed to allow Amira and Farah to wear *hijab*? If not, how should Brenda handle the situation? If so, how might Brenda explain this rule variation to her students?

3. On September 11 of each school year, a tradition at Rees consists of students reading stories written by children about the heroes of 9/11. Laura, the niece of a firefighter who lost his life in the World Trade Center bombing, brings a picture of her uncle each year as part of a memorial. When Amira and Farah arrive at Rees, the commemoration is only a few days away. Brenda anticipates there will be questions from students, perhaps expressed privately to her, about whether the new girls are part of the group responsible for the tragedy. What are three points Brenda should make to her students?

Hazelwood School District v. *Kuhlmeier,* 1988, that teachers and administrators may exercise editorial control over school publications. In this case, two articles written by students for a Missouri high school newspaper were deleted by the principal. The main topics of the articles were teen pregnancy and divorce, and they contained references to sexuality the principal thought inappropriate for younger students. In addition, even though their names

Ethical and Legal Issues in U.S. Schools

were changed, the principal was concerned that students written about in the articles were identifiable. The Supreme Court ruled in favor of the district, stating that educators may exercise substantial control over school-sponsored publications and events.

For all three forms of expression—symbolic, speech, and written—students' rights must be balanced with what is in the best interest of the school population. The adults in charge—school board members, district personnel, administrators, and teachers—must be vigilant and protect student rights while also protecting those who may be adversely affected by the exercise of those rights.

THE RIGHT TO BE PROTECTED

Freedom of expression refers to what students may do. The right to be protected is freedom from actions that may be imposed on students.

SEARCH AND SEIZURE. The Fourth Amendment provides for citizens to be secure from unreasonable search and seizure. This right applies to students in schools—to a point. The courts have attempted to balance the student's right to privacy and the school's need to know. The key term is *reasonableness*. In *New Jersey* v. *T.L.O.,* 1985, two high school girls were accused of smoking in the bathroom. One admitted it, and one (T.L.O.) denied it. In the principal's office T.L.O. was asked to empty her purse. In it were cigarettes, cigarette-rolling paper, marijuana, a pipe, a roll of money, and a list titled "People who owe me money." The student was turned over to juvenile court. She sued the school for invasion of privacy. The U.S. Supreme Court ruled against her and maintained that the search and seizure were reasonable.

In most cases the courts have ruled against schools that arbitrarily and routinely search lockers, use drug-sniffing dogs, and search through students' clothes. Privacy is upheld as a right unless a search is deemed reasonable. But school lockers are part of school property. If there are reasonable suspicions of contraband in lockers, they may be searched.

Drug testing as a form of search of students remains controversial among the general public. However, since about 2000 most court decisions have ruled that drug testing is permissible for all students who participate in extracurricular activities, making no distinction between basketball and debate teams.

If there is reasonable suspicion for a search, the search itself must be reasonably conducted. Age and gender need to be considered. Walking through a metal detector or putting a book bag through a detector is noninvasive and considered reasonable if there have been problems with weapons at the school. Searching lockers, either by hand or using dogs, is more invasive but reasonable if there is suspicion. Asking students to empty their pockets and take off coats may be called for and is reasonable. However, strip searches are very invasive and should only be done if there is probable cause (more stringent than reasonable suspicion) and by proper authorities, not by teachers. The courts have been split on the legality of strip searches. In elementary school strip searches are typically supported by the courts, whereas in middle and high school they are sometimes not supported by court decisions. This kind of intrusive search should not be done by teachers alone under any circumstances.

SEXUAL HARASSMENT. According to the American Association of University Women (AAUW) (2001), **sexual harassment** is behavior with sexual implications that is neither wanted nor welcome. It interferes with a person's life. Sexual harassment may include obvious looks with lewd intent, taunts with sexual innuendo, touching, kissing, groping, and any actions or behaviors that have sexual connotations. The AAUW conducted a survey in 1993, and again in 2001, of eighth and eleventh grade students to gauge the extent of sexual harassment in schools. The survey revealed that 80% in both grade levels experienced sexual harassment. The results served as a wake-up call for schools as sexual harassment came into the public eye. However, a positive change is that in 2001, 69% of respondents, as opposed to only a small percentage in 1990, reported knowing about school policies against sexual harassment and the consequences for harassing. Awareness has increased, but the problem persists.

This chapter's Letter to the Editor highlights an incident of sexual harassment that occurred in 2006 in Mt. Lebanon, Pennsylvania. Excerpts from two articles published in the *Pittsburgh Post-Gazette,* shown in Figure 10.12, set the stage for the letter. Although one or

Did you ever sense that your freedom of speech or press was restricted in some way in high school? Were you on a newspaper staff? Did anyone censor or limit in any way how students could express themselves in the paper? If so, how? What was your reaction?

Points of Reflection 10.9

Did you ever experience any form of search as a student in K–12 schools? What experiences do you recall of teachers or administrators acting on their suspicions of contraband? Have you or has anyone you know been subjected to a locker or clothing search? If so, what were the circumstances and how did you or the other person respond?

Do you think teachers and administrators should be able to conduct random searches?

Figure 10.12 Articles dealing with sexual harassment

Explicit ranking of high school girls sparks outrage in Mt. Lebanon

'Top 25' list details students' looks, bodies

Wednesday, April 26, 2006

By Mary Niederberger and Nikki Schwab, *Pittsburgh Post-Gazette*

The Mt. Lebanon School District and Mt. Lebanon police are investigating the distribution of an anonymous document that features sexually explicit descriptions of 25 girls at the high school.

The document, titled "Top 25 in 2006," ranks the girls in order from one to 25. It includes their names, grade levels and photos.

Each girl is assigned a letter grade for her breasts, buttocks and face, followed by a brief description of each girl in crude and vulgar terms.

There are references to girls performing oral sex and comments about their height and weight. . . . "I think that it's outrageous, the equivalent of a written rape on our daughter," said the father of one girl, who didn't want his name published to protect his daughter's identity.

He and another parent said they are frustrated that the district hasn't disciplined the students who created the publication. . . .

The second father said he has done some investigating and talked to students, including his children, who told him that ballots to choose the "Top 25" were circulated at high school basketball games and that students had been seen reading the list in the school cafeteria.

He said he embarked on his investigation after [the] Mt. Lebanon High School principal . . . told him that the list was not a district matter because none of the activities involved with it took place on school grounds. . . .

Mt. Lebanon Police Chief Thomas A. Ogden Jr. said the "Top 25" list is "in very poor taste," but that his department could not substantiate that any crime had been committed. . . .

[School officials] said the district is examining to see whether the publication violates the district's sexual harassment policy. . . .

Mt. Lebanon suspends student for role in list

'Too little, too late,' one girl's father says

Friday, May 05, 2006

A Mt. Lebanon High School student has been suspended for his involvement with a vulgar "Top 25" list of female students.

School officials wouldn't comment on any action taken, beyond a letter issued yesterday by Superintendent George D. Wilson, which states:

"Those proven to be responsible will receive consequences that include disciplinary action, a requirement for atonement and character education. However, since this is a student disciplinary matter, I am prohibited from releasing any confidential information."

The letter was mailed to high school parents and posted on the district's Web site. . . . Although the disciplinary action wasn't announced, the district must follow procedures set in state law when a student is removed from school.

If a suspension is longer than three school days, the student and parents must be offered an informal hearing within five days of the suspension. Formal hearings are required for expulsions, which by definition are longer than 10 school days.

The fathers of two of the girls whose names were on the list were angry when they read Dr. Wilson's letter.

"Way too little, way too late," said one of the fathers, who repeatedly has criticized the superintendent for not taking immediate action on the list when it was presented to him in early April. . . .

In his letter, Dr. Wilson said he was "appalled" by the actions of any student who participated "in any way." . . .

The superintendent's letter said the district will reinforce with all students "the importance of treating each other with respect and dignity. . . . Schools cannot control popular culture, but, together with the home, we exert a strong influence on how our students conduct themselves." The district has a policy prohibiting sexual harassment.

Ethical and Legal Issues in U.S. Schools

Letter to the Editor

This *Letter to the Editor* appeared in the Pittsburgh, Pennsylvania, newspaper, the *Post-Gazette*. It was written in response to the situation at Mt. Lebanon High School described in Figure 10.12.

MAY 6, 2006 WOMEN OBJECTIFIED

It is a sad comment on the state of our society that young men from a highly rated school district find nothing wrong in objectifying young women, humiliating them and possibly betraying their trust.

Does it really matter whether the list was compiled on school property? Obviously the school district and the parents of these young men fell down on the job when it came to instilling respect and good values in these young men.

And one has to wonder if the list had been a ranking of male students, teachers, administrators and/or police officers based on parts of their anatomies, whether the uproar and response would have been swifter, with more concern for the victims.

Celia Shapiro

Now it's your turn. These questions will help you write your own Letter to the Editor.

1. Would it be possible to determine if the list was made on school grounds? Even if the list was not written on campus, is it the school's responsibility to investigate and discipline students?
2. Whose responsibility is it, as the writer puts it, to instill respect and values? Who should be held responsible for the actions of the perpetrators? Why?
3. Do you agree that a similar incident with male victims might have received swifter action? Why or why not?
4. The articles refer to due process rights in disciplinary actions. Do you have a sense that these rights will be granted? Why or why not?
5. Are the parents overreacting? Explain your reasoning.
6. The superintendent says there will be a "requirement for atonement." What do you envision this might be?

Your letter should be in response to the *Pittsburgh Post-Gazette* letter: supporting it, adding information, or refuting it. Be prepared to share your letter. Write your letter in understandable terminology, remembering that readers of newspaper Letters to the Editor are citizens who may have limited knowledge of school practices and policies.

---

more high school students described in the articles may have been dismissed by some with the attitude of "Oh, well, boys will be boys," the young women, their families, and the community were clearly outraged by the sexual harassment perpetrated by these students.

When students report incidents that appear to be sexual harassment, teachers must take their complaints seriously. The ruling in *Davis* v. *Monroe County Board of Education*, 1999, determined that educators can be held liable if they do not respond to complaints of sexual harassment. A fifth grade girl in Georgia was groped and verbally harassed by a classmate. She and her parents repeatedly reported it to the school, but it continued. The family filed a lawsuit, and 6 years later the U.S. Supreme Court ruled in a 5-to-4 decision that the school failed to act appropriately to protect the girl.

Teachers must also be conscious of their own behavior with students to prevent it from being misconstrued as harassment. In the 2001 AAUW survey, 7% of the respondents said that teachers sexually harassed them. Teachers must be constantly aware of how students may perceive their actions.

When sexual harassment is detected, the school is likely to take disciplinary action. The range of possibilities, governed by both common sense and lawful procedures, is broad.

DISCIPLINARY ACTION. The U.S. court system has been clear that schools have the right to administer a variety of punishments based on policy. Relatively minor rule infractions call for relatively minor consequences or punishment that may be administered at the classroom or school level. Rule infractions that are more serious require more serious consequences.

CORPORAL PUNISHMENT. Fewer than half of states allow corporal punishment. Individual districts may choose not to allow corporal punishment even if allowed by the

Points of Reflection 10.10

Have you ever experienced sexual harassment? What were the circumstances? Was it addressed by anyone, or did it go unnoticed by everyone but you? How did it make you feel? Have you ever been guilty of sexually harassing someone else?

state. People who are in favor of corporal punishment say it's necessary and educationally sound, while those who oppose it call it archaic, cruel, inhumane, and unjustifiable (LaMorte, 2008).

In *Ingraham* v. *Wright,* 1977, the Supreme Court found that corporal punishment does not violate the tenets of the Constitution. In this case two boys were paddled, causing bruises that kept them out of school for a few days. The court commented that schools can be held liable for injuries, but that students are not entitled to due process before district- or state-sanctioned corporal punishment is administered. The most common restrictions in states that permit corporal punishment are that only an administrator can spank or paddle a student, and there must be an adult witness. Teachers can lose their jobs if they violate state laws or local policies related to corporal punishment (Fischer et al., 2007).

EXCLUSIONARY PUNISHMENT. Exclusionary discipline, or discipline that takes students out of school, such as suspension and expulsion, carries with it the need for student due process, or steps that protect student rights (Pauken, 2006). Excluding students from school through suspension or expulsion has been ruled a denial of property rights to an education. Suspension is time out of school that may range from 1 day to less than a semester but is usually 10 days or less. Expulsion is more permanent and is generally for a semester or for an indefinite period.

Exclusionary punishment carries possible long-term consequences that may exceed the seriousness of the original offense. Any time away from school can be harmful to students in many ways. For instance, if a brief suspension causes a student to miss an exam, grades will suffer. Being out of school more than 10 days makes it almost impossible for a student to catch up. An expulsion almost always means a grade must be repeated. For some students a lengthy suspension or expulsion may make admission to college difficult or impossible.

Students are entitled to due process when exclusionary punishment is imposed or when the rule infraction and resulting punishment will become part of a student's permanent record. In the case of *Goss* v. *Lopez,* 1975, several Ohio high school students were suspended for up to 10 days without receiving a hearing. The students maintained complete innocence and were never informed of what they were accused of doing. When a federal district court agreed with the boys in their suit against the school, administrators appealed to the U.S. Supreme Court, where the decision went in favor of the students again. The justices wrote that students have a property right in school and that they may not be withdrawn without due process that includes

- written notification of time and place of hearing, along with a description of the procedures to be followed
- list of evidence to be presented and names of witnesses
- description of the substance of witnesses' testimonies
- taped or written record of the proceedings and findings
- notification of the right to appeal (Fischer et al., 2007)

STUDENT RIGHT OF NONPARTICIPATION. Students have a right to refuse to participate in some activities, including these that have been upheld in the courts.

- Students may refuse to recite the Pledge of Allegiance.
- Students may refuse to dance, even when it is part of the physical education curriculum.
- Students may have other literature substituted for the planned curriculum if they object for religious or other reasons.
- Students may opt out of certain courses (usually dealing with sex education) if they and their parents object to content.
- Parents may refuse to follow guidelines that require students to be immunized.

Have you ever received corporal punishment in a school setting? If so, how did it make you feel? Have you ever been suspended or expelled? If so, did the exclusionary punishment take care of whatever behavior it was intended to curb?

Are corporal punishment, suspension, and expulsion ever justified? If not, why not? If so, under what circumstances?

Ethical and Legal Issues in U.S. Schools

This list will no doubt grow as parents and students have their voices heard in the courts. Administrators and teachers need to be aware of students' rights to nonparticipation, or at least question the legitimacy of insisting on compliance with school policies and traditions.

STUDENT RECORDS: ACCESS AND PRIVACY. The **Family Educational Rights and Privacy Act (FERPA) of 1974,** commonly called the **Buckley Amendment,** allows parents and guardians access to their students' academic records and requires written parental permission for the records to be shared with anyone else. When students turn 18, they have control over who sees their records.

The Buckley Amendment establishes the minimum standards of privacy of records, with some states and districts going beyond to allow students access to their own records. Some items, however, are not subject to student or parent viewing. For instance, teachers' grade books, notes kept by teachers for their own use, and the private notes kept by school law enforcement teams typically remain inaccessible to others.

The extent to which student records must be kept private was tested when an Oklahoma parent challenged the long-standing practice of students grading each others' work in *Owasso Independent School District* v. *Falso,* 2002. The parent sued an Owasso school saying peer grading was embarrassing and often inaccurate. Because of conflicting court actions the case ended up in the U.S. Supreme Court, which ruled unanimously that day-to-day grading is not covered by FERPA.

RIGHT TO NONDISCRIMINATION. Students may not legally be discriminated against by public schools. Discrimination cases that have been tested in U.S. courts have resulted in the following principles:

- Students of any race, religion, or disability may attend U.S. public schools.
- Students who are married, are parents, or are divorced may attend the same public schools as those who are not.
- Students with HIV/AIDS pose no significant risk to others and may attend public schools.

Not only are all students guaranteed the right to attend public schools, but the right has also been extended to extracurricular activities.

Figure 10.13 summarizes the cases in this section plus others that deal with students' rights.

Figure 10.13 Case law: Student rights

***Tinker* v. *Des Moines Independent Community School District* (1969)**
The rights of students to wear arm bands to protest the war in Vietnam was upheld.

***Goss* v. *Lopez* (1975)**
Students suspended without due process. Court ruled that school attendance is a property right.

***Ingraham* v. *Wright* (1977)**
Corporal punishment may be administered without due process in states that allow it.

***New Jersey* v. *T.L.O.* (1985)**
Student's purse searched after she was caught smoking. Court ruled search was reasonable.

***Bethel School District No. 403* v. *Fraser* (1986)**
Student reprimanded for lewd language. Court said school has the right to censor to avoid school disruption.

***Hazelwood School District* v. *Kuhlmeier* (1988)**
Schools have the right to censure controversial articles in school publications.

(continued)

Ethical and Legal Issues in U.S. Schools

Isaacs v. *Board of Education of Howard County* (1999)
Student protesting "no hats" rule
A high school girl in Maryland was not allowed in school because she wore a head wrap to celebrate her cultural heritage in violation of the "no hats" rule. A judge ruled in favor of the school and for the following reasons:

1. hats increase horseplay and conflicts
2. hats block teachers' and students' views in classrooms
3. hats allow students to hide drugs and other contraband
4. hats foster a less respectful learning climate

The judge concluded that it was unrealistic to expect schools to make hat-by-hat decisions.

Davis v. *Monroe County Board of Education* (1999)
Student was sexually harassed. Court ruled the school failed to act to protect her.

Sources: Dunklee, D. R. & Shoop, R. J. (2002). *The principal's quick-reference guide to school law: Reducing liability, litigation, and other potential legal tangles.* Thousand Oaks, CA: Corwin Press. LaMorte, M. W. (2008). *School law: Cases and concepts* (9th ed.). Boston: Allyn and Bacon. Fischer, L., Schimmel, D., & Stellman, L. R. (2007). *Teachers and the law* (7th ed.). Boston: Allyn & Bacon.

CONCLUDING THOUGHTS

Controversial issues, such as sex and AIDS education, Internet usage, school choice, high-stakes testing, school uniforms, protection for homosexual students, and funding for public education, continue to emerge and will no doubt prompt legal questions. The courts will interpret the Constitution or rely on case law to settle disputes. Teachers need to stay current on how laws affect what takes place in classrooms and schools.

When you choose to teach you make a commitment to a service profession. You take on the serious responsibility not only to abide by laws but to continually promote what is ethical for students and for yourself in the big issues as well as in the seemingly minor issues that test you every day. You commit to thoughtful and deliberate decision making, the courage to do what's right for students, and the good sense to ask for advice and guidance when needed.

We began this chapter by considering Derek Boucher and his classroom at Roosevelt High School in California. Now as the chapter comes to an end we join Derek as he addresses issues that have come about as he sponsors a newsletter written by students in his reading remediation class. Read through *Chapter in Review* to help refresh your memory of what we have discussed, and then interact with Derek as he confronts challenges in *Developing Professional Competence.*

Chapter in Review

What does it mean to be an ethical teacher?

- Laws tell us what we can and can't do. Ethics tell us what we should and shouldn't do.
- The National Education Association provides a professional code of ethics for educators.
- To be an ethical teacher means to be guided by a set of beliefs that lead to attitudes and actions focused on what's best for students.
- Six characteristics that help teachers make ethical decisions include appreciation for moral deliberation, empathy, knowledge, reasoning, courage, and interpersonal skills.
- Ethical attitudes, decisions, and actions involve both major and seemingly minor issues.

- It is important to have a vision of the characteristics we want to help cultivate in our students.

How do laws affect schools, teachers, and students?

- The laws that affect schools, teachers, and students are based on a balance of rights and responsibilities.
- Four basic sources of law directly impact the work of teachers: the U.S. Constitution, federal laws, state and local laws and policies, and case law.

What are the legal rights of teachers?

- The legalities of employment include contracts, tenure, and dismissal.

- Due process involves a set of guidelines that must be followed to ensure that individuals are protected from arbitrary or capricious treatment by those in authority.
- Teachers enjoy the same rights as other citizens, including freedom of expression, whether symbolic, written, or spoken, but with restraints based on the responsibilities of teaching.
- Academic freedom is a form of expression that allows teachers to use their judgment concerning what and how to teach.
- Teachers have some restrictions on their personal lives that other people do not have because of the nature of the profession.

What are the legal responsibilities of teachers?

- Teachers serve *in loco parentis* and are responsible to care for and protect the students they supervise.
- Among other things, teachers have the legal responsibility to avoid liability, abide by copyright laws, and report suspected child abuse.

How does the law impact the relationship between school and religion?

- The First Amendment says that government (public schools) can neither establish religion nor interfere with the free exercise of it.

- Public prayer is illegal in public school. Religious organizations may meet and pray in school facilities outside regular school hours.
- It is permissible to teach about religion but not with the purpose of persuading students to believe in a particular religion.

What are the legal rights of students?

- Court decisions attempt to balance the rights of students to express themselves and the necessity of limiting personal freedom to ensure the safety and well-being of others.
- Students have freedom of symbolic expression, speech, and the press.
- Student privacy is protected from unreasonable search and seizure.
- Students have the right not to be sexually harassed.
- Students have due process rights when facing serious disciplinary action.
- Students and parents have rights concerning privacy and access to records.
- Students may not legally be discriminated against by public schools.

Developing Professional Competence

Visit the Developing Professional Competence section on Chapter 10 of the MyEducationLab for this text to answer the following questions and begin your preparation for licensure exams.

Derek Boucher's mission to ensure literacy for all his students at Roosevelt High School often leads him to be quite innovative. Because most of the students in his sophomore reading remediation class speak Spanish as their primary language, one of his ideas led to the development of a newsletter written for, and by, Latino students. The purpose of the newsletter is to encourage English-language learners to write articles that the students who are also learning to speak English would enjoy reading.

Derek followed the proper channels to get permission to initiate the newsletter and to use school supplies to publish it twice a month. Things went fine for 3 months, and Derek was quite pleased with how much his students were learning about writing and editing and, as an added bonus,

about expressing themselves in English. Articles ranged from reporting of some school and local issues to movie reviews to opinion pieces. After school every other Thursday when the pieces were due, Derek would read them for content and mechanics, make notes, return them Friday at the beginning of class, and then spend all of the Friday class period helping with rewrites and putting the pieces together in the four-page format in which it would be published.

Although most of the content of the student-written articles proved to be noninflammatory, one Thursday Derek found in the stack of articles two pieces that implicated several students in marijuana possession and sales. No names were given as the authors of the two pieces spoke out against the illicit drug activity, but from what Derek knew about the kids at Roosevelt and what the authors implied, he was fairly certain he could identify the culprits. Although students knew Mr. Boucher had the ultimate responsibility to edit what they wrote, censorship had not yet been a

Ethical and Legal Issues in U.S. Schools

115

topic of discussion. Now Derek faced a number of serious questions about how he would proceed.

Think through this scenario and answer the following multiple-choice questions:

1. The student newsletter is a good idea for all of these reasons except which one of the following?
   a. Students saw a purpose for writing.
   b. Students learned to communicate better in their native language.
   c. The newsletter helped give Latino students an identity on campus.
   d. Derek was able to build literacy skills in a way that engaged his students.

2. Derek had a right as a teacher to censor the content of the student-generated newsletter because of which of the following case law precedents?
   a. *Pickering v. Board of Education*
   b. *Brown v. Board of Education*
   c. *Tinker v. Des Moines Independent Community School District*
   d. *Hazelwood School District v. Kuhlmeier*

3. Derek knows that if he tells Ms. Romero or Mr. Lael, the principal and assistant principal at Roosevelt, they will have the right to search the lockers of students who are implicated in drug possession and sale. The case that grants school officials the right to search lockers of students if they have reasonable suspicion is
   a. *New Jersey v. T.L.O.*
   b. *Hazelwood School District v. Kuhlmeier*
   c. *Tinker v. Des Moines Independent Community School District*
   d. *Pickering v. Board of Education*

4. The most meaningful reason Derek demonstrates one of the six characteristics of teachers who make ethical judgments, *appreciation for moral dilemma*, is
   a. Derek believes strongly that marijuana use is wrong.
   b. Derek believes that any lengths he may go to in order to encourage reading and writing are justified.
   c. Derek recognizes that this situation is complex and that the rights of everyone involved should be protected.
   d. Derek is concerned that the way he communicates his concerns to the administrators does not imply his students are involved.

Now it's time for you to respond to two short essay items involving the scenario. In your responses, be sure to address all the dilemmas and questions posed in each item. Your responses should each be between one half and one double-spaced page.

5. Is Derek obligated to reveal what he knows to the administration? How is Derek's decision related to his personal code of ethics? If, from an administrator's viewpoint, the newspaper is somehow fueling problems at Roosevelt and Derek is asked to stop publishing it, how might Derek defend the newsletter as a valuable teaching tool?

6. Derek knows that he has to talk with the students in his reading remediation class. When should he approach the subject? What should he say about his right and responsibility to act as a censor of newsletter content? How could he encourage his students to continue to write about relevant issues now that they know he can block items if he sees the need?

Where DO I Stand NOW?

In the beginning of this chapter you completed an inventory that gauged how closely your opinions matched laws regarding education. Now that you have read the chapter, completed exercises related to the content, engaged in class discussions, and so on, complete the following items in your course notebook.

1. List the items in *Where Do I Stand?* on which you indicated 3 rather than 4. Then choose one of the items and explain if your stance has changed from "I agree" to "I strongly agree" or if you still have slight reservations about the statement.

2. List the items in *Where Do I Stand?* on which you indicated 2 rather than 4. Then choose one of the items and explain if your stance has changed from "I don't have an opinion" to "I agree" or "I strongly agree" or if you still don't agree or disagree with the statement.

3. List the items in **Where Do I Stand?** on which you indicated 0 or 1 rather than 4. Then choose one of the items and explain if your stance has changed from "I disagree" or "I strongly disagree" to "I agree" or "I strongly agree" or if you still do not agree with the law.

4. Were you surprised to read about any of the issues and/or laws in this chapter? If so, which ones and why?

MyEducationLab

The MyEducationLab for this course can help you solidify your comprehension of Chapter 10 concepts.

- Explore the classrooms of the teachers and students you've met in this chapter in the Teaching in Focus section.

- Prepare for licensure exams as you deepen your understanding of chapter concepts in the Developing Professional Competence section.

- Gauge and further develop your understanding of chapter concepts by taking the quizzes and examining the enrichment materials on the Chapter 10 Study Plan.

- Visit Topic 4, "Ethical and Legal Issues," to watch ABC videos, explore Assignments and Activities, and practice essential teaching skills with the Building Teaching Skills and Dispositions unit.

References

American Association of University Women. (2001). *Hostile hallways: Bullying, teasing, and sexual harassment in school.* New York: Harris Interactive.

Dunklee, D. R., & Shoop, R. J. (2002). *The principal's quick reference guide to school law: Reducing liability, litigation, and other potential legal tangles.* Thousand Oaks, CA: Corwin.

Fischer, L., Schimmel, D., & Stellman, L. (2007). *Teachers and the law* (7th ed.). Boston: Allyn & Bacon.

Howe, K. R. (1996). A conceptual basis for ethics in teacher education. *Journal of Teacher Education, 37,* 6.

LaMorte, M. W. (2008). *School law: Cases and concepts* (8th ed.). Boston: Allyn & Bacon.

McNergney, R. F., & McNergney, J. M. (2009). *Education: The practice and profession of teaching.* Boston: Allyn & Bacon.

National Education Association. (2005). *About NEA.* Retrieved May 27, 2005, from http://www.nea.org/aboutnea

Pauken, P. D. (2006). Student rights. In C. Russo (Ed.), *Key legal issues for schools: The ultimate resource for school business officials.* Lanham, MD: Rowman & Littlefield Education.

Riley, R. W. (1998). *Secretary's statement on religious expression.* Retrieved November 12, 2006, from www.ed.gov/inits/religionandschools

San Antonio, D. M. (2006). Broadening the world of early adolescents. *Educational Leadership, 63*(7), 8–13.

Underwood, J., & Webb, L. D. (2006). *School law for teachers: Concepts and applications.* Upper Saddle River, NJ: Merrill/Prentice Hall.

Governing and Financing Public Schools in the United States

Provided by the author

Most teachers get to know the system of public school governance and funding only when a particular issue demands their attention. Developing an overview now will help you put in context what you read in the newspaper or see on TV about issues such as school board proceedings, hiring of administrators, legislative decisions, and test score reports. As we explore the complex array of individuals and groups that have governing and financial authority over public schools in the United States, we consider the following questions:

✦ How does the federal government influence public education in the United States?

✦ What is the state's role in public education?

✦ How do school districts function?

✦ What is the management structure of individual schools?

✦ What other entities impact the governance of public schools in the United States?

✦ How are public schools financed?

✦ How are funds for education spent?

Before we discuss the governance and financing of public schools, explore your own views in this chapter's *Where Do I Stand?*

Shutterstock

From Chapter 11 of *Your Introduction to Education: Explorations in Teaching*, 2/e. Sara Davis Powell.

Where DO I Stand?

This inventory involves your general perceptions about which level of authority would best address a variety of responsibilities. The complexity of governing and financing schools makes both topics controversial. After reading an item, indicate your level of agreement by choosing a number 0 to 4 and placing it in the blank before the statement. Following the inventory are directions for how to organize your responses and what they may mean in terms of where you stand. You'll notice that this inventory frequently uses the word should. Some of what you read in the items actually happens, while other statements don't depict what is typically practiced. But remember that just because something occurs doesn't mean that it should, and, conversely, just because something doesn't occur, it doesn't mean it shouldn't.

4   I strongly agree
3   I agree
2   I don't have an opinion
1   I disagree
0   I strongly disagree

_____ **1.** The federal government should play an increasingly significant role in the functioning of schools.

_____ **2.** The state legislature is the place where most budgetary decisions should be made for schools.

_____ **3.** Decisions about curricula should be made at the district level.

_____ **4.** Principals and teachers are the appropriate people to be in charge of how schools operate and are assessed for effectiveness.

_____ **5.** A governor, as the leader of a state, should have extensive influence on the schools of the state.

_____ **6.** A school district, as an organizational structure of local schools, should be in charge of how schools operate and are assessed for effectiveness.

_____ **7.** School budgets should be handled at the federal level.

_____ **8.** An important leadership role of the president is to guide education in the United States.

_____ **9.** A state department of education is the organization to determine what it takes to qualify for a teaching position.

_____ **10.** School budgets should be handled by principals and teachers.

_____ **11.** District personnel should have extensive influence on local schools.

_____ **12.** A principal is the right person to oversee every aspect of school life.

_____ **13.** School budgets should be handled at the district level.

_____ **14.** A state department of education should make curricular decisions for schools.

_____ **15.** The federal government should have the right to take over the operation of a school, or even an entire school district, that is deemed unsatisfactory.

_____ **16.** Principals should function in the role of instructional leader of schools.

_____ **17.** School district personnel know what's best for local schools.

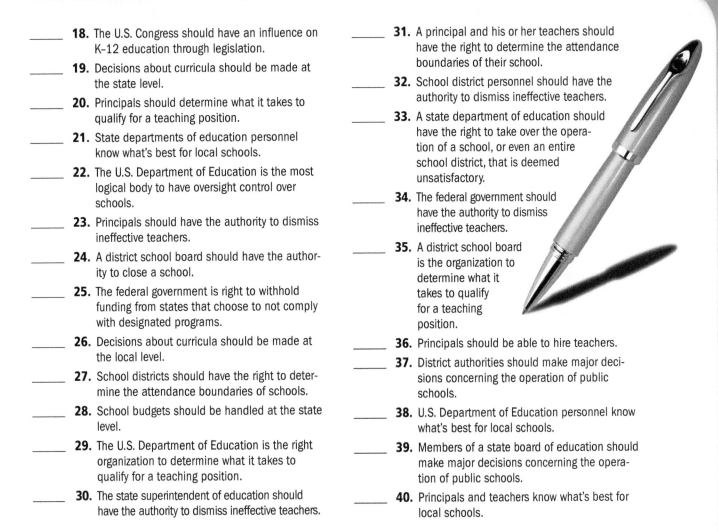

_____ **18.** The U.S. Congress should have an influence on K-12 education through legislation.

_____ **19.** Decisions about curricula should be made at the state level.

_____ **20.** Principals should determine what it takes to qualify for a teaching position.

_____ **21.** State departments of education personnel know what's best for local schools.

_____ **22.** The U.S. Department of Education is the most logical body to have oversight control over schools.

_____ **23.** Principals should have the authority to dismiss ineffective teachers.

_____ **24.** A district school board should have the authority to close a school.

_____ **25.** The federal government is right to withhold funding from states that choose to not comply with designated programs.

_____ **26.** Decisions about curricula should be made at the local level.

_____ **27.** School districts should have the right to determine the attendance boundaries of schools.

_____ **28.** School budgets should be handled at the state level.

_____ **29.** The U.S. Department of Education is the right organization to determine what it takes to qualify for a teaching position.

_____ **30.** The state superintendent of education should have the authority to dismiss ineffective teachers.

_____ **31.** A principal and his or her teachers should have the right to determine the attendance boundaries of their school.

_____ **32.** School district personnel should have the authority to dismiss ineffective teachers.

_____ **33.** A state department of education should have the right to take over the operation of a school, or even an entire school district, that is deemed unsatisfactory.

_____ **34.** The federal government should have the authority to dismiss ineffective teachers.

_____ **35.** A district school board is the organization to determine what it takes to qualify for a teaching position.

_____ **36.** Principals should be able to hire teachers.

_____ **37.** District authorities should make major decisions concerning the operation of public schools.

_____ **38.** U.S. Department of Education personnel know what's best for local schools.

_____ **39.** Members of a state board of education should make major decisions concerning the operation of public schools.

_____ **40.** Principals and teachers know what's best for local schools.

ITEM	MY #	ITEM	MY #	ITEM	MY #	ITEM	MY #
1		2		3		4	
7		5		6		10	
8		9		11		12	
15		14		13		16	
18		19		17		20	
22		21		24		23	
25		28		27		26	
29		30		32		31	
34		33		35		36	
38		39		37		40	
Sum		Sum		Sum		Sum	
÷ 10	F =	÷ 10	S =	÷ 10	D =	÷ 10	L =

Now plot F for Federal, S for State, D for District, and L for Local on this number line.

A complex system of people and policies make it possible for teachers to teach and students to learn. This number line indicates your opinion concerning which level of governance should have the greatest authority over public schools. The closer each sum is to 4, the more authority you would give the federal, state, district, and local levels.

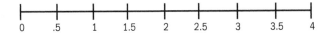

0   .5   1   1.5   2   2.5   3   3.5   4

Teaching in Focus

Chris Roberts, Brenda Beyal, and Tim Mendenhall teach in multi-age classrooms of third, fourth, and fifth graders at Rees Elementary, Utah. They function beautifully as a team and enjoy working together as they shape their multiage program. Because multiage education is not the norm, teachers and administrators must have an interest in initiating the concept. Chris, as a former special education teacher, is very aware that students of different ages can actually learn at the same level and rate. Brenda and Tim, teachers who routinely find ways to individualize instruction, know that the learning capabilities of students the same age can vary widely. Experience has taught all three that 8- to 12-year-olds may be able to grasp some concepts at the same time from basically the same experiences, whereas other concepts may come easily or prove more difficult for individual students regardless of age. This knowledge prompted them to establish multiage classrooms.

As accomplished and respected teachers, Chris, Brenda, and Tim had workable plans to go with their idea. They learned a lot about district governance policies as they worked through the approval process, beginning with their principal, then the district director of elementary education, and, finally, the school board and superintendent. After hours of talking and preparing, district authorities approved the idea of multiage education. Although school board approval was almost certain once the district director of elementary education endorsed the plan, Chris, Brenda, and Tim still needed to present their ideas in a formal meeting of the board and superintendent.

To learn more about Chris, Brenda, and Tim's philosophies of teaching, go to the Teaching in Focus section for Chapter 11 in MyEducationLab for this course and watch their interviews.

How are the geographic boundaries that determine who attends your school drawn? If the principal is your boss, who is the principal's boss, and what's the chain of command? Who decides whether your school building gets a new wing and how it is financed? Who decides what standardized tests your students take? Why do you have so many forms to fill out? Who pays for special programs for kids in low socioeconomic settings? These questions, and a myriad more, are all related to the governing and financing of public schools in the United States. Figure 11.1 shows the four basic governing levels of public schools, and this chapter explains at what levels particular decisions are made.

How Does the Federal Government Influence Public Education in the United States?

Because education is not addressed in the Constitution, it has historically been basically a state's responsibility. However, the federal government's involvement in the functioning of schools through the institutions and agencies shown in Figure 11.2 has increased in recent decades.

Figure 11.1 Overview of American public school governance

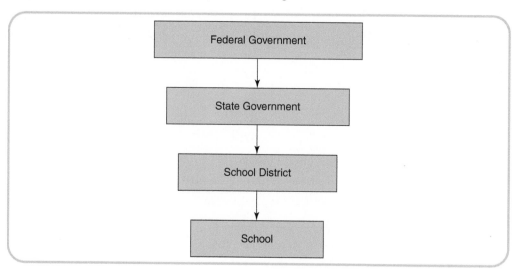

Governing and Financing Public Schools in the United States

Figure 11.2 Federal government role in American public school governance

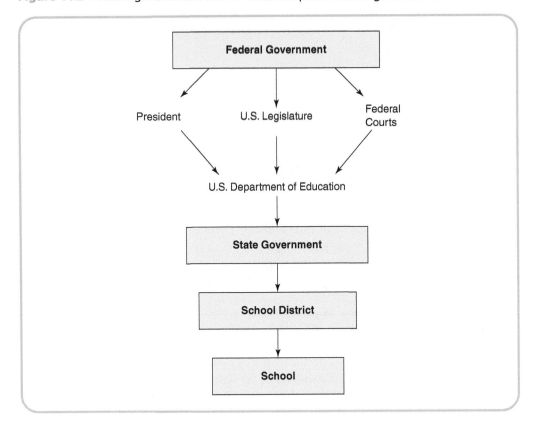

PRESIDENTIAL INFLUENCE

Almost every presidential candidate in the 20th century included education in his or her campaign platform; most had boldly articulated plans and promises. From its establishment in 1857 until 1980, the U.S. Department of Education served in an advisory capacity with little impact on public schools. President Ronald Reagan (1980–1988) was the first president to experience the department as a cabinet-level agency, an impact resulting from President Jimmy Carter's administration in 1979. Since 1980 the influence of the U.S. Department of Education has steadily increased. President Bill Clinton (1992–2000) worked vigorously toward achieving the objectives of *Goals 2000,* an ambitious list of goals for students in U.S. public schools. President George W. Bush's legacy (2000–2008) regarding education is the No Child Left Behind Act of 2001, discussed throughout this text.

President Barack Obama declared his commitment to public education on Inauguration Day 2009. On the official White House (2010) Web site we read,

> Providing a high-quality education for all children is critical to America's economic future. Our nation's economic competitiveness and the path to the American Dream depend on providing every child with an education that will enable them to succeed in a global economy that is predicated on knowledge and innovation. President Obama is committed to providing every child access to a complete and competitive education, from cradle through career.

> The American Recovery and Reinvestment Act of 2009 invests heavily in education, both as a way to provide jobs now and to prepare for the future, with almost $100 billion pledged as additional support for public education, including emphasis on teacher effectiveness, early learning programs, programs for children with special needs, and greater achievement in low-performing schools. The Obama administration is working to ensure that teachers are supported as professionals and that they are held accountable for student learning. One means of accomplishing both aims is to provide

competitive funding to states with innovative plans to deliver a 21st-century education that prepares all children for success in a global workplace, with teachers both qualified and responsible. This funding is delivered in the form of *Race to the Top* grants (White House, 2010).

CONGRESS AND THE COURTS

The U.S. Congress has passed many influential laws regarding education, and the federal court system has made numerous rulings impacting education. For example, the Bilingual Education Act of 1968 made provisions for English-language instruction. The Education for All Handicapped Children Act of 1975 was the first to guarantee a free public education for students with disabilities. The No Child Left Behind Act of 2001 has impacted K–12 schools, teachers, and students, with mixed and impassioned reviews.

U.S. DEPARTMENT OF EDUCATION

The U.S. Department of Education has had some influential secretaries over the years. The term *secretary* as used here indicates the head of a presidential cabinet-level department. The secretary of education is chosen and appointed by the president, making the position political. The incumbents' favor with citizens and educators rises and falls with the popularity of the president and the party in power. The secretary of education influences policies established by the U.S. Department of Education, which has a sizable budget and exercises its power through these policies and programs. The federal government sponsors programs that impact schools and students. For instance, Head Start and the National School Lunch Program benefit children in low socioeconomic settings.

Funding provided to schools by the federal government is distributed in the form of assistance to implement approved programs and to conduct educational research. The funds are also used as leverage to help ensure that state departments of education comply with specific mandates, such as guidelines and policies related to attempts to equalize educational opportunities for all children, and the use of widespread testing programs. In some cases states may choose whether to comply with U.S. Department of Education policies. However, the federal government withholds funds from states and their schools when they choose not to comply.

What Is the State's Role in Public Education?

Governors, legislators and judges, as well as state boards of education, state departments of education, and state superintendents, have much influence on public schools. Figure 11.3 is an overview of the basic state structure that impacts schools in the United States.

BALANCE OF POWER AT THE STATE LEVEL

States use a balance of power with three major branches of government, similar to what exists at the federal level. Governors have executive authority, legislatures have lawmaking authority, and state courts uphold and interpret laws, as well as establish constitutional guidelines.

GOVERNORS. Governors, as leaders of state governments, potentially have tremendous impact on public schools. A governor's attitude toward education has far-reaching influence on policies and laws. In many states the governor appoints the state's superintendent of education, as well as members of the state board of education. In addition, governors make budgetary recommendations that impact schools.

The National Governors Association (NGA) was founded in 1908 and serves as the collective voice of the nation's governors. The NGA Center for Best Practices is an online clearinghouse that provides governors and the public with information about public education, including such topics as disparities in academic achievement, turning around low-performing schools, and quality of teaching. The organization describes policy options for states, identifies how states cope with dilemmas pertaining to education, helps governors

Figure 11.3 State government role in American public school governance

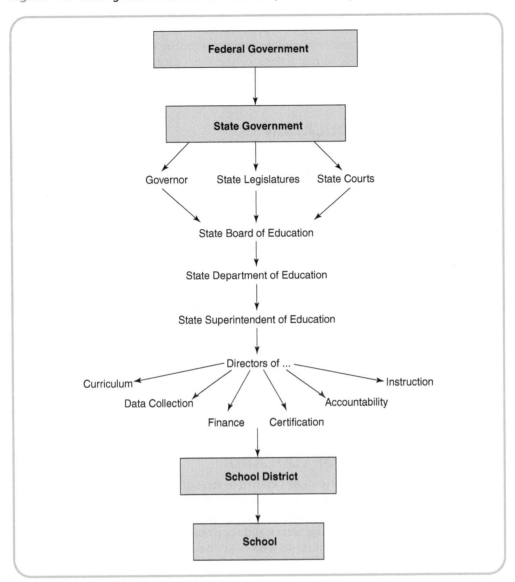

establish and maintain quality education in their states, and counsels them on how to work effectively with state legislatures (National Governors Association [NGA], 2010).

STATE LEGISLATURES. Members of state legislatures have significant influence on public education. State legislators impact schools as they determine

- state laws that affect every aspect of public education
- how state chief officers of education and state school board members are selected
- responsibilities of state-level school officials
- how taxes are used to support schools
- the general direction of the curriculum
- the length of the school day and year
- aspects of teacher employment, including issues involving tenure, retirement, and collective bargaining

There are no requirements in terms of educational background or experience for state legislators. Teachers and school administrators frequently question the wisdom of decisions made in the legislature. Having conversations, inviting legislators to visit schools, and writing letters are vehicles for influencing legislative viewpoints.

STATE COURTS. When state laws require interpretation, or when there is a question of conflict with state laws, federal regulations, or the U.S. Constitution, state courts impact public education. State courts hear arguments and make decisions about school compliance with state laws that are often written in broad terms.

STATE BOARD OF EDUCATION

Almost every state has a **state board of education,** generally composed of seven to nine volunteers who are either elected or appointed by the governor. State legislatures give state boards oversight authority; in other words, state boards act in regulatory and advisory capacities. State boards of education make major decisions concerning the operation of public schools as they

- set goals and approve standards and assessments for schools
- establish the standards by which schools are accredited (allowed to function)
- advise the governor and the legislature on educational issues
- make many of the decisions about how state funds are used
- represent and report to the public on education issues
- serve as the governing body of the state department of education (National Association of State Boards of Education, 2005)

The state board of education is primarily a policy-making body with broad responsibilities. The many detailed responsibilities that deal with education on a statewide basis are overseen by the state's department of education.

STATE DEPARTMENT OF EDUCATION

A **state department of education** (also known as state office of education or department of public instruction) operates under the guidance of the governor, legislature, and state board of education. These state agencies are large, with a complex array of responsibilities and employees. Governors, state legislators, and state board members may not have expertise in education. However, most of those who hold nonclerical positions within a state department of education are professional educators. There is one notable exception. The chief state officer, or state superintendent of education, is likely to be either publicly elected or a political appointee and may not be a professional educator.

STATE SUPERINTENDENT OF EDUCATION. The one person with responsibility for managing the state department of education may be called **state superintendent,** chief state education officer, or commissioner of education. This person may either be elected by the voters or appointed by the governor or state school board, depending on the state's policy (Council of Chief State School Officers, 2006). The state superintendent position is both public and political. The superintendent is in charge of the bureaucracy that is usually centralized in the state's capital city and travels throughout the state as the acknowledged authority on how schools operate and are assessed for effectiveness.

STATE DEPARTMENT OF EDUCATION RESPONSIBILITIES. The state superintendent of education generally has a large staff of individuals with varied expertise. The people who work as department directors are in charge of divisions within the state department that address, among other issues,

- teacher certification (or licensure)
- curriculum standards and accountability
- instruction (usually a director for each content area)

- special education
- school levels (high, middle, elementary, early childhood)
- technology
- charter schools
- teacher professional development
- state budget funds
- communication and public relations
- collection and reporting of school data

Although not commonly done, a state department of education may take over the operation of a school, or even an entire school district, that is deemed unsatisfactory.

How Do School Districts Function?

A **school district** is an organizational structure of local schools defined by geographic boundaries. Figure 11.4 provides an overview of the basic structure that exists in most school districts.

School districts have at least one **feeder system** of schools, early childhood/elementary schools that feed into middle schools that feed into a particular high school. There are

Figure 11.4 School district role in American public school governance

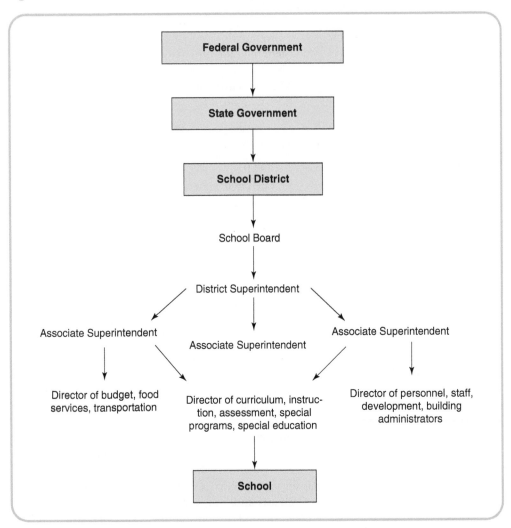

over 15,000 school districts in the United States. In the early to mid-20th century, there were almost 10 times as many. The decrease occurred as officials realized it was more efficient to combine small districts and share services and administration. Interestingly, the entire state of Hawaii is one school district, whereas the state of Texas has more than a thousand separate districts (National Education Association [NEA], 2009).

School districts vary greatly in size, from one building that houses all grade levels, as in Gilpin County School District in Colorado with about 300 students, to New York City public schools, with over 1 million students. Small and large districts each have distinct advantages as well as limitations. Small and medium districts have the advantage of accessibility. Teachers feel as though they can be heard in policy matters, and parents often sense a distinct connection to the schools and faculty. In very large districts teachers may sense that they are far removed from where policy decisions are made. Large districts generally have the advantage of availability of numerous services and specialists to oversee the many aspects of life in schools and classrooms. In small and medium districts, individuals tend to have an array of duties, and fewer curricular and service options are offered. Regardless of size or complexity, each district has a school board and a superintendent who function as leaders of central administration.

Points of Reflection 11.1

Were your K–12 experiences in a small, medium, or large district? What advantages or limitations because of the size of your district were you aware of? Did you attend school from kindergarten through 12th grade in one feeder system, or did you move frequently?

DISTRICT SCHOOL BOARDS

District school boards are unique American institutions composed of elected citizens who volunteer their time. This form of governance originated in the locally controlled schools of the colonies and in the common schools movement. Through one reform effort after another, the basic structure of school boards has not changed. They represent democratization by linking the public to public schools. Many educators find school boards to be flawed in terms of how they govern, but most agree that they serve a worthwhile purpose (Hess, 2010). Because local schools are profoundly affected by district school board decisions, we spend more time discussing them than the other levels of governance.

Most members of public district school boards are noneducators and receive little or no compensation. A 2007 study (Nylander, 2007) involving board members from about two thousand districts yielded the information in Figure 11.5, as well as the following information about district school board members:

- Over 90% have or had children who live in the district in which they serve.
- About 25% have been teachers at some point.
- 96% say that their districts provide safe environments for teachers and students.
- 92% say that parents in their districts are not willing to serve on the school board.
- 88% have lived in their communities more than 5 years.
- 90% say they will continue to live in their districts indefinitely.

BOARD ELECTIONS. It can be costly to campaign for a school board seat, especially in medium to large districts (at least 20,000 students). The two basic kinds of school board elections are at-large and single-member elections. In **at-large elections,** voters may vote for any candidate regardless of the area in the district the candidate represents. If there are five distinct areas in a school district, each will have specific candidates who live in the areas, but *every* voter in the *entire* district may vote for their choices regardless of where they live.

In **single-member elections,** only those who live in a specific area can vote for the representatives in their area. The single-member process has the potential to elect more representative school board members because neighborhoods are more likely to have candidates and voters who share ethnicity and socioeconomic status. As you can see in Figure 11.5, often district school board members, and especially those elected in an at-large system, are not representative of the families of many students in the United States.

BOARD RESPONSIBILITIES. District school board members are responsible for setting policies that affect the operation of schools. In a poll sponsored by the National School Boards Association, the five biggest concerns and responsibilities of school board members

Figure 11.5 Profile of school board members

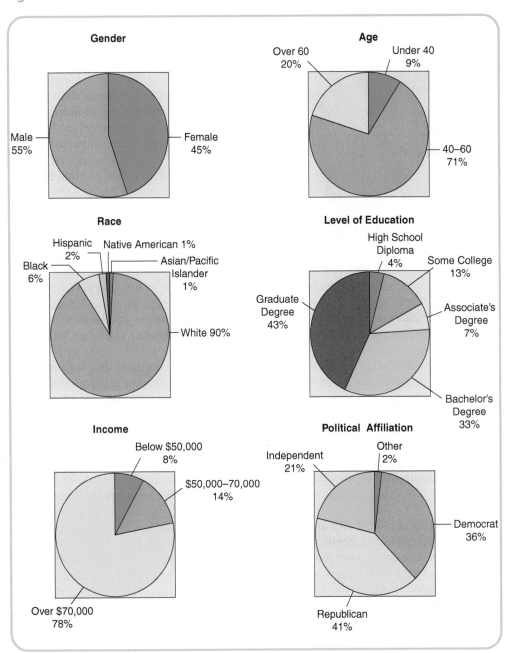

Gender

Male 55%
Female 45%

Age

Over 60 20%
Under 40 9%
40–60 71%

Race

Hispanic 2%
Native American 1%
Black 6%
Asian/Pacific Islander 1%
White 90%

Level of Education

High School Diploma 4%
Some College 13%
Graduate Degree 43%
Associate's Degree 7%
Bachelor's Degree 33%

Income

Below $50,000 8%
$50,000–70,000 14%
Over $70,000 78%

Political Affiliation

Independent 21%
Other 2%
Democrat 36%
Republican 41%

Source: Nylander, A. (2007). National School Board Survey. Accessed at: http://www.oldham.kyschools. us/files/reports/National_Surveys/National%20School%20Board%20Survey%202007%20Final%20Results_ pdf.pdf

from small, medium, and large districts were funding, student achievement, teacher quality, improving technology, and special education (Hess, 2002). Dealing with these concerns and fulfilling other duties require numerous meetings and research. Among other responsibilities, school board members

- decide how much money will be spent on teacher salaries, facilities improvement, and instructional materials
- hire and fire personnel, both professional and classified (clerical, custodial, etc.)
- approve and evaluate programs that may affect some or all schools, teachers, and students within the district

Governing and Financing Public Schools in the United States

Teachers, families, and community members voice their questions and opinions at public school board meetings. Mark Richards/ PhotoEdit

- make curricular decisions within state guidelines
- determine organizational policy

SCHOOL BOARDS AND THE PUBLIC. Controversy is never far from school boards. Members are easy targets for both oral and written chastisement by the community. It's a rare moment indeed when school board members are not perceived by some segment of the population as incompetent, downright stupid, or even evil. As trustees of public schools, their often unappreciated position requires them to make hard decisions. When one group feels slighted or excluded, the board hears its complaints, but must still make decisions that may not be satisfactory to those affected. When it makes fiscal (monetary) sense to close a school, parts of the community storm the board with emotionally charged, often valid, objections. The board listens and makes decisions. When community groups work diligently to help improve education for all students and present research and suggestions, the board listens and makes decisions. When teachers take positions on issues such as board choices to transfer administrators, or program alterations, they make their case to the school board. The board listens and makes decisions.

An ongoing challenge for school boards is to be both accountable and **transparent,** meaning that decisions are made with full disclosure of information and reasoning. With technology today, there is little justification for data not to be available to the public. Methods for making information gathered by school boards easily searchable are also possible. But this organizational structure, almost as old as the United States itself, will likely be slow in following any new guidelines calling for complete transparency. Snider (2010) tells us that organizations composed of elected citizens sometime have a sense of "we know best." This attitude may appear to permeate local school boards and, even in the second decade of the 21st century, it may take some digging to find the logic behind school board decisions.

With all this responsibility, and frequent community wrath, why would any citizen want to be a school board member? Many do it as a service to the community. They have a genuine interest in doing what they can to benefit local schools and students. Others seek the position to gain power and visibility, to further political ambition, or to advocate for a particular cause (Mizell, 2010). Regardless of their motivations, school board members dedicate long hours to the governance of public schools, including the hiring of a district superintendent.

Points of Reflection 11.2

Have you observed the functioning of a district school board, either firsthand or through television news or newspapers? What impressions did you have?

DISTRICT SUPERINTENDENT AND STAFF

A **district superintendent** functions as the school district's chief executive officer. The superintendent is hired by the board and serves at its pleasure, which means the board can also dismiss the superintendent. The superintendent is expected to both advise the board and carry out board policies. As largely noneducators, board members often choose an educator as superintendent to keep schools running smoothly on a day-to-day basis. The superintendent serves at the pleasure of the board meaning that the school board has authority over the superintendent and evaluates his or her performance. The relationship between the board and the superintendent can become awkward when school board members go beyond policy making into what is considered the authority of the superintendent. When board members get involved in day-to-day operations, it is often referred to as **micromanagement**. If tensions develop over policies or decisions, a school board may dismiss a superintendent. Generally, before things escalate to this point, the public is involved and meetings are held to discuss the situation. These can be trying times for communities.

Governing and Financing Public Schools in the United States

In small districts, superintendents may handle all the responsibilities listed in Figure 11.4. The larger the district, the more necessary it is for the superintendent to delegate. Medium to large districts have associate or assistant superintendents who handle specific duties such as supervision of the different levels—early childhood, elementary, middle, and high. They work with district curriculum and instruction directors to coordinate efforts. Larger districts also have associate superintendents in charge of areas such as personnel, facilities, and finance.

People in the community sometimes complain there are too many administrators and non-classroom teachers doing supervisory work rather than directly teaching children. Before making this judgment, citizens should recognize the complexity of operating school districts and individual schools in ways that free teachers to teach and students to learn.

What Is the Management Structure of Individual Schools?

Now we consider individual schools, the places where teachers and students interact. Within the school building, the management structure often depends on both the size and the level of the school. Figure 11.6 lists some of the people who may contribute to the management of local schools, including the one constant person in almost all building-level management structures, the principal.

PRINCIPALS

The **principal** oversees every aspect of school life and is responsible to the district for all that occurs at the school. The principal's role involves oversight of administrative tasks such as facility maintenance, attendance, discipline, parent and community relationships and communication, transportation, and all manner of paperwork. Principals also have the role of instructional leader, with knowledge of, and experience with, the teaching and learning process. Instructional leaders have the ability to make positive suggestions and model practices that enhance student learning (Sergiovani, 2001).

Figure 11.6 Local American public school governance

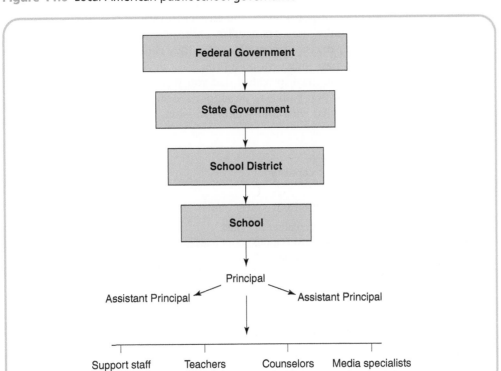

Rees Elementary principal Mike Larsen takes a personal interest in students and their success.
Sara Davis Powell

A principal who is an instructional leader focuses teachers on improved learning for all students. Many principals who are confident in their administrative and instructional leadership skills believe in the benefits of sharing leadership with teachers and members of the community.

SITE-BASED MANAGEMENT. In *Leadership Capacity for Lasting School Improvement* by Linda Lambert (2003), we are told that the most effective principals build leadership capacity in teachers and others who are sincerely interested in student learning. Site-based management is a form of local school governance that puts much of the decision-making power regarding curriculum, textbooks, student behavior, staff development, budget, and hiring in the hands of teachers, family members, and the community. Principals who want to share leadership and management of schools employ some or all of the actions listed in Figure 11.7. Serving on a site-based management team gives teachers deeper insight into the role of the principal.

From the list in Figure 11.7, perhaps the most fundamental thing principals do to empower teachers to take responsibility for student learning is the third statement: *insist that student learning is at the center of the conversation*. In other words, students take precedence and empowered teachers do what's best for them. In **Teaching in Focus,** Tim Mendenhall advises teachers to experiment to find what works for their students in their own circumstances.

UNDERSTANDING THE ROLE OF PRINCIPAL. As you beginning your teaching career, your principal will have a major impact on you. Your memories of the principals you have experienced may factor into how you view your first principal when you become a teacher. He or she will select you and ask the school board to hire you, will determine the grade level or subject you teach, will likely assign a teacher mentor for you, will evaluate your teaching performance, and will make the decision of whether to offer you a contract for the following year.

Principals have multiple responsibilities and answer to various constituencies, including superintendents, community members, families, and teachers. They are often privy to information that impacts their decisions, some of which they cannot share with their staffs. Too many teachers tend to pass judgment on a principal's decisions and sometimes hold grudges. As a new teacher you need to realize that you won't always understand why or how decisions are made. Your best path is to be supportive of your principal and helpful to the programs and people aligned with your school's mission.

Figure 11.7 Building leadership capacity

Principals who build leadership capacity in teachers and others . . .

- develop a shared vision based on community values
- organize, focus, and sustain the conversations about teaching and learning
- insist that student learning is at the center of the conversation
- protect and interpret community values, assuring a focus on, and congruence with, teaching and learning approaches
- work through the evaluation and district personnel systems to dismiss ineffective teachers
- work with all participants to implement community decisions
- develop reciprocal relationships with the larger system, such as by securing support and resources

Source: Adapted from Lambert, L. (2003). *Leadership capacity for lasting school improvement.* Alexandria, VA: Association for Supervision and Curriculum Development.

Governing and Financing Public Schools in the United States

Teaching in Focus

Sara Davis Powell

Tim Mendenhall, Grades 3–5 Multiage Classroom, Rees Elementary School, Utah. *In his own words. . . .*

I would first encourage you to follow your heart. Trust yourself and do what you feel needs to be done for your students. Don't follow a program just because it's been adopted. If there is something better for your students, use it, adjust it. Education is messy. You will try things and fail. That's how we learn.

Second, more than reading and math, teaching your students to be lifelong learners is your ultimate goal. Make your classroom fun. If you don't like a book or an activity, why do you think they will? Love what you are doing, and they will learn to love learning.

Finally, stay at teaching long enough to get the REAL pay. This could be a child bringing you a Cherry Coke (instead of an apple) every Friday. Or a former student running off the football field to talk with you when he is quarterback and supposed to be leading a play. Or a parent coming back and telling you that you are still their child's favorite teacher (even after all the years and they are now graduating from high school). The pay is great; you just have to wait for it sometimes.

Figure 11.8 illustrates gender, age, and racial characteristics of school principals at the elementary and secondary (high school/middle school) levels. You will notice that the overwhelming majority of these school leaders are white, and, overall, male and over the age of 45. Just as there is a need for a more diverse teaching force, there is also a need for principals who more closely mirror student gender, racial, and ethnic characteristics. Regardless of their gender or race, most principals in all but small schools (fewer than 400 or so students) generally receive help in fulfilling their administrative and instructional leadership roles from assistant principals.

ASSISTANT PRINCIPALS

The position of assistant principal entails a variety of duties. If there is only one in a school, then the responsibilities may be general and similar to the principal's, or as specific as the principal chooses to make them. When there are multiple assistants, they generally have designated areas of responsibility. For instance, a medium-size elementary school (400 to 700 students) may have a principal and one assistant who may do various aspects of the principal's job, depending on day-to-day needs. A large middle school (more than 1,000 students) may have a principal and three assistants, each responsible for a grade level. A principal of a large high school (more than 1,500 students) may have more than three assistants who specialize in areas such as student discipline, athletics and extracurricular activities, transportation, and materials. Teachers often work with

Points of Reflection 11.3

What do you remember about your schools' principals? Were they accessible or did they seem aloof? Did you view them as disciplinarians to be feared or as friendly adults who were helpful to teachers, parents, and students?

Assistant principals may be perceived as stern in their roles of student disciplinarian and yet be approachable as supporters of teachers. Sara Davis Powell

Governing and Financing Public Schools in the United States

Figure 11.8 Characteristics of elementary and secondary principals

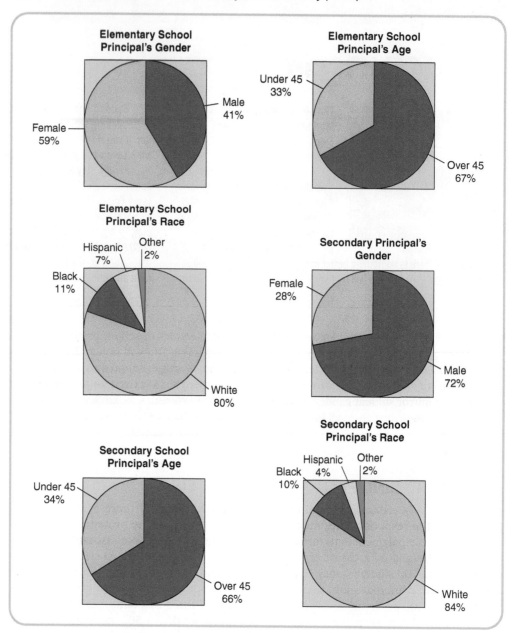

Source: U.S. Department of Education. (2009). *Characteristics of public, private, and Bureau of Indian Education elementary and secondary school principals in the United States.* Washington, DC: Author.

assistant principals. A teacher in a large school may be more connected with the assistant principal(s) than with the principal.

TEACHER LEADERS

The phrase *teacher leader* has come to mean in many circles that a teacher has taken on additional responsibilities such as chairperson of a grade level of teachers or perhaps a subject area specialist who works with other teachers to help them improve their knowledge and/or skills. But individuals can be leaders in their schools, as well as in their districts and states, simply by being dynamic, well-informed classroom teachers. They don't need official titles to impact other educators around them, their own students and others in their buildings, and their communities. An example of teacher leadership is in this chapter's *Diversity Dialogue,* featuring focus teacher Brandi Wade.

Sara Davis Powell

Brandi Wade, our kindergarten focus teacher at Summit Primary School in Ohio, believes in experiential learning. Her years in the classroom have shown her that children become more excited when they are actually involved in their own learning and engaged in activities that capture their imagination. In her classroom she tries to provide experiences that get kids moving and doing, rather than passively listening and watching.

To watch Brandi's lesson, go to the Teaching in Focus section for Chapter 11 in MyEducationLab for this course.

Brandi is researching the Columbus area for possible field trips for her students. She wants her students to experience the Heritage Gardens at the governor's residence in Columbus, the farmers market in both fall and spring, and the Franklin Park Conservatory and Botanical Garden. They'll learn so much on these adventures. But there's a problem. Field trips cost money. Some of the students in Brandi's class come from homes where paying for these trips will not pose a problem; she also knows that for at least 10 of her 24 students, it will be out of the question to ask the families to pay their part of the transportation costs and admission fees. When the children are with Brandi at Summit Primary they sense that they are all valued the same and insulated from the problems of poverty. She knows that economic dilemmas are not just affecting families who have been in low-income circumstances for a long time. With high unemployment, parents of Brandi's students are struggling financially.

Respond to these items by writing one well-developed paragraph for each.

1. A free public education is a wonderful aspect of life in America, even with the occasional fee and the tax burden. Is what Brandi wants to do with her students out of line, considering that schools and school districts may be in tough economic times? If you think her plans are justifiable, explain why. If you think Brandi is using less than optimal judgment, explain why.

2. Do you think it would be a good idea for Brandi, with the principal's approval, of course, to send a letter home to families asking for their help? They might volunteer time, materials, or money. The money could be used for transportation and admission fees for the whole class, rather than asking for specific amounts per child. What might be the benefits of this plan? What might be drawbacks?

A growing number of teachers with specialized training are relieved of some or all of their classroom teaching duties to lead a grade level or be an in-school subject area expert. For instance, a school may have an instructional coach, a teacher who works with individual teachers as they improve or add to their toolboxes of instructional strategies. Another school may have a math specialist who teaches math to all fourth and fifth graders, regardless of their homeroom. These specially designated teacher leaders may become part of the school management team along with the principal and assistant principal(s).

What Other Entities Impact the Governance of Public Schools in the United States?

The decisions about policies and laws by the individuals and groups discussed so far in this chapter are influenced by many constituencies. Among them are parents, businesses, universities, and special interest groups.

PARENTS

Parents, including stepparents, foster parents, and guardians, have the potential to be among the most influential players in the education of children. Parents, by virtue of their position, are influential in the lives of their own children and, if they are informed and involved in

Watch an interview with focus student Amanda Wiley that includes her mom, the president of the Rees Elementary PTA, in the Teaching in Focus section for Chapter 11 in MyEducationLab for this course.

schools, can make a positive difference in the lives of many children in their local schools. One question is "How can they do this?" But perhaps even more important to ask is "Why don't they do it more often?"

One way for parents to be involved in the life of the school is through the Parent Teacher Association (PTA), a national organization with millions of members at thousands of schools across the country. School PTAs have varying degrees of impact. Some groups boast large numbers of members whose only involvement is the payment of small annual dues ($2 to $10). Other groups have very active members who volunteer to help out at school in a variety of ways. Although individual PTAs contribute to school life, rarely do they impact decision-making bodies.

Parents can volunteer to help in schools and classrooms and impact the quality of students' school-related experiences. They also have opportunities to serve on committees that address school issues. In some school districts, parents are encouraged to be part of site-based management groups sometimes called School Improvement Councils (SIC) or Local School Councils (LSC). Being part of an SIC or LSC is a serious responsibility that far too few family members are willing to accept. Parents are usually busy providing for their families and often feel that their time is too limited to commit to membership in a site-based management group. Some parents may be intimidated by the process or may feel they are not qualified to represent families.

Points of Reflection 11.4

In what school activities do you recall parent volunteers participating? Were your parents members of a PTA or other organized school groups? What do you remember about their involvement?

BUSINESSES

Businesses have a vested interest in education. Having competent employees is a major key to business success, and these employees are likely to be products of public education. Large businesses and their chief executive officers are increasingly becoming involved in **education summits,** or organized meetings to advocate for school improvement. This is a positive step because business leaders can potentially support schools and students in meaningful ways.

Business leaders can be influential in supporting educational initiatives. Some businesses offer scholarships to promising students. Other businesses, whether locally owned or national franchises, form partnerships with schools to sponsor events, such as science fairs, and contribute resources to enhance school activities. Additionally, some large businesses give employees paid time off to volunteer in schools and may match funds their employees donate to school organizations.

UNIVERSITIES

Schools of education and teacher educators have important influence on schools because most classroom teachers are prepared on university campuses. Future teachers learn about the concepts in this text and more as they go through teacher preparation programs. The more teachers know, the better prepared they are to take active roles in influencing policies and working toward school improvement.

Teacher educators have the knowledge, and ideally the will, to exert influence by expressing their views to school administrators, school board members, and legislators. They can serve on School Improvement Councils, curriculum revision and textbook adoption committees, and, in general, be active in local, state, and national education associations. University faculty also have an impact on schools through research focused on classroom programs and practices and by facilitating staff development. These activities can form the foundation for recommending policy changes and promoting effective practices.

SPECIAL INTEREST GROUPS

When a group of people join together with a common mission and work to have an impact they are often called a **special interest group.** An example would be a group composed of parents of children who have special needs. Informal groups of parents of children with autism or Down syndrome, for example, may band together to help ensure more effective services for their children.

Sometimes community members join forces to form local **watchdog groups,** meaning they keep an eye on school district accountability by examining policies and practices. One such group is the Charleston Education Network (CEN). This group of citizens meets regularly to review happenings in, and policies of, the Charleston County School District in South Carolina, where one of this text's four focus schools, Cario Middle, is located. Members of CEN often fund or conduct research on issues, articulate findings and viewpoints, and lobby school board members and state legislators to bring about change. Groups like CEN offer effective services by asking hard questions and being persistent in their search for answers.

On the national level, groups like the Public Education Network (PEN) tirelessly advocate for children. In addition to activities similar to those of CEN, PEN gathers articles and research results on education issues and distributes them through its Web site to help individuals and organizations stay informed. You can subscribe for free to *PEN Weekly NewsBlast* at http://news.publiceducation.org and receive valuable updates on many education issues.

Now that we have examined governance structures of public schools and those who influence these structures, let's explore how schools are financed and how the money is spent.

How Are Public Schools Financed?

Free public education—think about it. What a remarkable and noble concept. But is it really free? Hardly. It's true that students don't pay tuition. However, their parents often pay fees for specific items, such as science equipment, gym clothes, band instruments, and workbooks, as well as vague charges for grade-level fees. Parents are also asked to supply certain materials each school year. But these expenses barely make a dent in what it costs to provide K–12 education. So where does all the money come from?

SOURCES OF EDUCATION FUNDING

Most of the funding for public education comes from federal, state, and local governments in the proportions shown in Figure 11.9. It's interesting to note how these three major sources of funding have shifted over the years from local funding as the primary source in the early part of the 20th century, to local and state sources currently sharing funding responsibilities at approximately the same levels. Figure 11.10 illustrates these historical shifts in the proportion of funding from each major source. As the number of K–12 students and the cost of educating them have grown, most states have increased both the amount and the percentage of their contributions. Although Figure 11.10 appears to indicate a decrease in local funding, that is not the case; rather, the states' average proportion of total funding has simply increased. The call for equitable funding, regardless of race, socioeconomic status, or geographic location, has led states to increase their portion of funding responsibility (Biddle & Berliner, 2002). States have also come to recognize that the quality of public education has lifestyle and economic implications. As indicated in Figure 11.10, the federal government's contribution to public schools is relatively small, with an increase occurring about the time of the release of the 1983 report *A Nation at Risk* and remaining fairly stable since then.

FEDERAL FUNDING. The federal government budget is supported through income taxes, investments, and various charges for services and goods. Federal government contributions to public education account for only about 2% of the U.S. government budget (U.S. Department of Education, 2006).

The federal government supplies a little less than 10% of the total education budget. Although this doesn't sound like a lot, federal contributions have a major impact on public schools because the money is allocated as **categorical grants,** or funds earmarked for specific purposes. Programs previously discussed like Head Start, Title I, the Bilingual Education Act, and the Education for All Handicapped Children Act are examples of categorical grants. As a group, these and other grants are referred to as **entitlements,** meaning that certain

Figure 11.9 Percentage of revenues received from federal, state, and local sources for public elementary and secondary schools

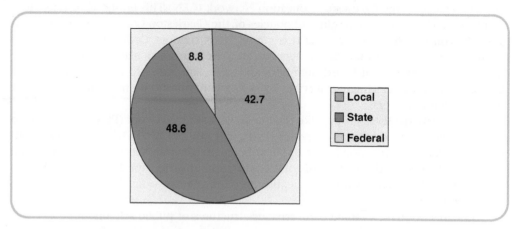

Source: National Education Association. (2009). *Rankings of states 2008 and estimates of school statistics* 2009. Washington, DC: Author. Retrieved June 18, 2010, from http://www.nea.org/assets/docs/09rankings.pdf

segments of the population have specific needs and the federal government deems these individuals as entitled to extra assistance.

The Reagan administration attempted to diminish the influence of the federal government on schools while still funding their efforts. In the 1980s, some federal funding changed from categorical grants to **block grants,** which provide funding with few restrictions for its use. This type of funding allows states and school districts the freedom to use the money in ways that meet their specific needs.

Figure 11.10 Revenues for public schools, by source of funds, 1920–2008

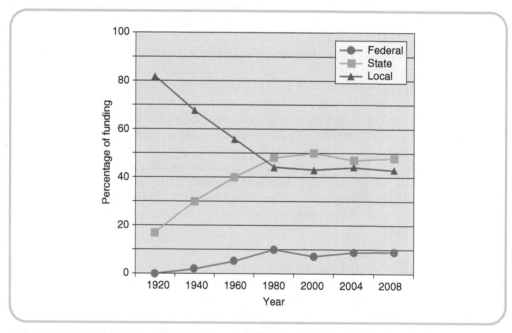

Sources: U.S. Department of Education (2001b). *Statistics of state school systems: Revenues and expenditures for public elementary and secondary education.* Washington, DC: U.S. Department of Education, National Center for Education Statistics. Retrieved August 2, 2006, from http://www.nces.ed.gov. National Education Association. (2009). *Rankings of the states 2008 and estimates of school statistics 2009.* Retrieved June 18, 2010, from http://www.nea.org/assets/docs/09rankings.pdf

Governing and Financing Public Schools in the United States

The No Child Left Behind Act of 2001, as a reauthorization of the 1965 Elementary and Secondary Education Act, involved federal funds tied to school improvement as prescribed by the act's specific guidelines. Schools were required to meet the mandates of NCLB to receive the funds. In most cases, states attempted to protect federal funding by complying with the mandates.

STATE FUNDING. About half of the funding for public education comes from state sources. State money for schools is basically raised through taxes, such as:

- state income tax based on personal earnings
- state corporate tax based on company earnings
- state sales tax added as a percentage of the cost of goods and services
- **excise tax,** or tax on luxury items such as boats and travel trailers
- **"sin" tax** on items some consider vices, such as alcohol and cigarettes

As of 2010, 44 states had lottery games with portions of the funds specifically earmarked for education (North American Association of State and Provincial Lotteries, 2010). Although lottery-based funding may sound appealing and, indeed, has been used productively in many instances, there are inherent problems. First, gambling through state-run lotteries appears to attract a disproportionate number of low-income people who often have little schooling. Many disagree with the concept of a lottery system for this reason (Brimley & Garfield, 2004). Second, although lottery funding is initially viewed as extra money to supplement other, more stable sources, over time having this easy source of funds often leads to the reduction of more stable funding. In other words, a state's attitude may be "We have all this lottery money so we don't need to give schools as much from the state budget." This is risky business, from both state and local standpoints, considering the uncertainty of a lottery's ability to provide money consistently for schools.

In tough economic times, difficult budgetary decisions must be made at all levels. This often proves especially difficult at the state level. When money is tight, some services and programs must be cut. Because education is such a large part of a state's overall budget, the decision to withdraw funding from schools is both public and painful. In 2010 most states faced shortfalls, including California, where some citizens have gone from passive disapproval to aggressive action. More than 60 individual students and their families, 9 school districts from throughout the state, the California School Boards Association, California State PTA, and the Association of California School Administrators filed a lawsuit against the state based on their view that the current educational finance system is unconstitutional. Through *Robles-Wong* v. *State of California,* the plaintiffs are asking that California's finance system, specifically its funding policies for education, be changed. They are asking that the state determine the cost to adequately fund public education to meet both the state's own program requirements and the needs of the students. The state would then have to develop and implement a new finance system consistent with California constitutional requirements.

Figure 11.11 provides two editorial opinions published in the Santa Rosa *Press Democrat* that reflect the situation in communities all across California. Following the two pieces is this chapter's ***Letter to the Editor*** written by a citizen in response to the first opinion piece.

LOCAL FUNDING. The source of local funding for schools is primarily **property taxes**. Values of property are determined, and a small percentage of the assessed amount (usually less than 1%) is collected annually and used for local services. Most goes to schools (Brimley & Garfield, 2004). On the surface, using property taxes to finance education seems reasonable. After all, everyone benefits from an educated citizenry.

Figure 11.11 Editorial opinions

Published: Wednesday, May 26, 2010
The Press Democrat, Santa Rosa, CA

Written by Frank Pugh

I'm a local school board member and also the president of the California School Boards Association. In this last capacity, I assisted our organization in filing the historic *Robles-Wong* v. *California* lawsuit against the state of California last week. It has been reported by at least one national newspaper reporter that this lawsuit could be on par with *Brown* v. *Board of Education* for the potential to affect the future of education funding in the state of California.

In short, we argue that California's broken school finance system is unconstitutional. We also believe that California's school finance system is unsound, unstable, insufficient, and erratic. This current system is not aligned with required educational programs or with student needs.

As a result, our students are being denied the opportunity to master the educational programs that the state requires. Education is a fundamental right of every child in California, and our state constitution requires a school system that prepares students to become informed citizens and productive members of society.

The formulas that this state relies upon to fund education date back to the early 1950s. The formulas do not take into account, for example, the costs to implement demanding standards, the requirements of No Child Left Behind, special education, the California High School Exit Exam, the diversity of the children we serve and the avalanche of unfunded mandates required from our state Legislature.

The facts are clear about the staffing ratios in California schools. California is 49th among all states in student-to-teacher ratios. We are 45th in instructional aides. We are 46th in district officials and administrators. We are 48th in total school staff. We are 49th in guidance counselors. We are 50th in librarians.

California spends $2,131 less per pupil than the national average, ranking the state 44th in the country. From a different perspective, California spends less per pupil than each of the largest 10 states in the nation—almost $6,000 less per pupil than New York.

With school funding not being a priority in our state, is it any wonder why we are not as successful as we should be in student achievement? Because of the lack of interest on the part of our lawmakers in solving the school finance problem, we were left with no choice but to file a lawsuit against the state of California.

Published: Wednesday, June 6, 2010
The Press Democrat, Santa Rosa, CA

Editorial Opinion

By practically any measure, financial support for public education in California is discouraging. So is student achievement.

According to statistics compiled from various sources by the *New York Times*, the Golden State is tied for 47th in the nation in fourth-grade reading and tied for 46th in the nation in eighth-grade math.

With districts eliminating school days and increasing class sizes because of budget cuts, California's rankings probably will get even worse, though there isn't much farther to go in this race to the bottom.

So it was hardly surprising when a group of students, parents and school officials filed a lawsuit challenging the state's method of funding education for California's 6 million public school students.

If schools expect a larger share, or a dedicated source of revenue for education, they must accept greater accountability, including data-based evaluation of the performance of teachers, principals, schools and entire districts, as well as open enrollment and other forms of parental choice.

Better resources must be matched by better achievement.

However, as illustrated in Figure 11.12, many people believe an alternative method of funding public education should be imposed. In 1978 California was the first state to put a limit on how high property taxes could go. California's Proposition 13 was a model for other states. Now almost all states impose what is called a **tax cap** on local property taxes, or an upper limit to taxation.

Governing and Financing Public Schools in the United States

Letter to the Editor

This letter appeared in the Santa Rosa, California, newspaper, *The Press Democrat*. It was written in response to an opinion piece published the week before. The author is expressing frustration over state funding for education.

JUNE 5, 2010 SCHOOL LAWSUIT

[Frank] Pugh has taken action in a situation that has been neglected for so long—the survival of our schools, as we have known them. We have seen the governor make and break promises about funds coming to our schools; they never come. As Pugh so rightly puts it: "Our state constitution requires a school system that prepares students to become informed citizens and productive members of society." I have watched this requirement be ignored, and our students often leave school unprepared to function in our communities, earn a living, and, more important, ready to be informed citizens, as we so vitally need in these rapidly changing times.

Bravo to Pugh for assisting in his role as president of the California School Boards Association in taking action by filing "the historic Robles-Wong v. California lawsuit against the state of California."

Penny Wolfsohn
Santa Rosa

Source: The Press Democrat / Santa Rosa, California.

Now it's your turn. Write a letter to the editor from the perspective of a future teacher expressing your views about funding and education, specifically the situation in California. You may comment on any, or all, of the writer's expressed opinions. The following questions may help you frame your thinking but should not limit or determine what you write.

1. Ms. Wolfsohn obviously agrees with Mr. Pugh's perceptions concerning California state funding for education. She lays at least some blame on Governor Arnold Schwarzenegger. Do you think she is literally talking about the actions of one person?

2. While Mr. Pugh and the author of the editorial that follows agree that funding is a problem, the editorial brings to light specific achievement difficulties. Do you think funding and academic success are necessarily linked? If so, how? If not, why not?

3. Ms. Wolfsohn wrote her letter before the second editorial opinion appeared in *The Press Democrat*. What would you add to her point concerning funding that might make her case stronger in the eyes of a wider audience who may or may not agree that funding and academic success go hand in hand?

4. The second author ends his piece suggesting some specific steps schools should take. Now that you know more about accountability and school choice, do you agree with his suggestions? If so, why? If not, why not?

Write your letter in understandable terminology, remembering that readers of newspaper Letters to the Editor are citizens who may have limited knowledge of school practices and policies.

IMPACT OF RELIANCE ON PROPERTY TAXES. Let's consider what reliance on property taxes for almost half of public school funding might mean for different communities. A district composed of middle-to-upper socioeconomic suburban neighborhoods with prospering retail stores and a couple of thriving industries will likely generate a healthy amount of money with a relatively low percentage of the assessed property value. In this case people who own homes and businesses pay what might be considered reasonable taxes on their property and appear to have adequate funding for schools. Now think about a district in a very rural area, with a lot of land, but few homes, with families who drive out of the area for jobs or who work in the few businesses located in the district. In this case, home and business owners may have to pay a much larger percentage of the assessed value of their property to support schools. There may simply not be enough property value to generate adequate funding. Finally, consider a densely populated urban area, with many people who are renters in high-rise buildings and often living on government subsidies such as welfare. An area such as this may have large numbers of children and few home owners. In some urban areas, business and industry provide an adequate tax base, but in others the base is very low, resulting in inadequate school funding.

We moved into this home in 1968. We made the last of our monthly mortgage payments the same year we both retired. Our pensions were supposed to give us enough income to stay right here for as long as our health allows. But year after year the value of the house goes up, with all the new stores and shopping centers popping up in the area. Our property taxes have doubled. If they go much higher, we may have to move. We raised our kids, and now they're raising their own. I'm all for good schools, but not if we lose our home.

Patrick Watson/PH College

I have a good job that allows my wife, who used to be a third grade teacher, to homeschool our two kids. We live in an upscale neighborhood and are very happy with our lives. But what we're not happy about is the way our property taxes are skyrocketing. I believe in public education, but we can afford to homeschool while the kids are young, and then they'll go to our church's private 6–12 school. Why should I have to pay exorbitant property taxes for schools I'll never use?

Shutterstock

I don't have kids and never plan to. I like my life as it is, with good friends and a job that calls for me to travel to interesting places. I bought a great downtown loft apartment with payments I can afford. However, now that this area of downtown is being revitalized, the value of my place is on the rise, along with escalating property taxes. I understand that most of this money goes for public schools. Well, the school a few blocks away sure doesn't look like much of my money, or anyone else's, is being spent there. If that school represents how this school district is spending my money, I'll vote for any decrease of the spending cap.

Getty Images–Stockbyte, Royalty Free

Relying on property taxes to provide a substantial portion of support for public education can create a funding gap that further exacerbates socioeconomic differences. And, as we have discussed, where there are socioeconomic gaps, there are almost certainly achievement gaps. In states with tax caps, it may not be possible for communities to raise the percentage of the tax on assessed property value, even when most people believe it should be done to support their schools. They are stuck with the limit, despite what may be unfair and nonproductive funding. If you hear or see an expression such as "Drop the cap, end the gap," you'll now better understand the meaning of this slogan. Read more about the funding gap in Figure 11.13. With all the problems inherent in using property taxes as the primary source of local funding, alternatives are often sought.

LOCAL FUNDING ALTERNATIVES. Some communities are attempting to support public education through an increase in sales tax. For instance, when sales tax is raised from 6% to 7%, an extra penny is collected for every dollar spent on taxable goods. This translates into a sizable amount of money. For a district, such an increase could mean less dependency on property taxes as the source of local funding.

Another way school districts acquire funds is to borrow money through what is called a **bond referendum,** an amount of money stipulated for specific projects. When using a bond referendum, the school board asks voters in their district to approve the borrowing of the money (the bond) that will be repaid over a period of time. Bond referendums can be for hundreds of millions of dollars. In some states, boards are not required to ask voters for permission to borrow money for schools. The request may need only city or county council approval.

PRIVATE DONATIONS. In addition to federal, state, and local funding, many districts and individual schools receive private gifts of either money or goods. These gifts rarely account for more than 3% of the total amount of school funding (Brimley & Garfield, 2004). Individuals and foundations may contribute to a particular program or project and have a

Figure 11.13 The funding gap

"Closing the achievement gap is a familiar theme these days. But lurking behind the achievement gap is another contentious issue: funding. Excellence in education doesn't come without a price tag." This statement by Amy Azzam, associate editor of *Educational Leadership*, begins her 2005 special report on *The Funding Gap 2004*, a study conducted by the Education Trust.

The study used the financial data from the U.S. Census from each of the more than 14,000 school districts. The focus of the study was on funding disparities by state between high-poverty and low-poverty districts, as well as between high-minority and low minority districts. The results revealed that more than half the states provide less money to high poverty districts than to low poverty districts. This translates into less money for high-minority areas since there tends to be a higher concentration of minorities in high poverty areas.

The disparities become even more glaring when we consider the fact that it costs more for high-poverty districts to meet the same standards as low-poverty districts, by some estimates as much as 40% more. Education Trust found that with this cost adjustment, 36 states provide an average of $1,348 per students less for high-poverty versus low-poverty districts. Some states have disparities as high as $2,500 per student.

Given the study results, Education Trust recommends that states:

- reduce reliance on local property taxes
- spend extra money to help low-income children
- do away with funding gaps among individual schools within districts

Azzam closes her report by stating "Closing the achievement gap starts with closing the funding gap. Only by providing the necessary resources can states help ensure quality education for all students."

Source: Azzam, A. M. (2005). The funding gap. *Educational Leadership, 62*(5), 93.

significant impact on that particular segment of school life. However, states, districts, and schools should be cautious about considering private gifts when planning budgets. These sources are often onetime donations or may prove to be unstable.

How Are Funds for Education Spent?

Just as with the ability to generate money varies greatly from state to state and district to district, the amount each state spends on public education varies as well. Rather than totals per state, the number that is most meaningful is the amount of money spent per pupil.

EXPENDITURE PER PUPIL

The average amount of money spent from federal, state, and local sources on an individual student is called the **expenditure per pupil**. A comparison of expenditures per pupil by state is found in Figure 11.14. Keep in mind as you look at this figure that the cost of living, and consequently the cost of education, varies from state to state and region to region. Does almost three times the learning occur in Washington, D.C., where expenditures per pupil are over $20,000, as in Arizona, where per pupil spending is about $6,300? The answer, of course, is *no*. Look back at Figure 11.13, which points out that children of poverty require 40% more spending. Spending more to educate students who need extra services to succeed in school is being responsive to differences that often relate to race, socioeconomic status, and levels of disabilities. There are so many variables to consider, including issues such as the percentage of teachers who are experts in their teaching fields, state-of-the-art or dilapidated facilities, and large or small class size. They all cost money.

The national average expenditure per pupil has continually increased. Everything required to fund education becomes more expensive, as with any large enterprise. When gas prices rise, so does the cost of transportation. When construction costs rise, so does the cost of building new schools. The more diversified student populations become, the more expensive it is to hire personnel to meet their needs. It is understandable that public education is

Figure 11.14 Average expenditures per pupil by state, 2009

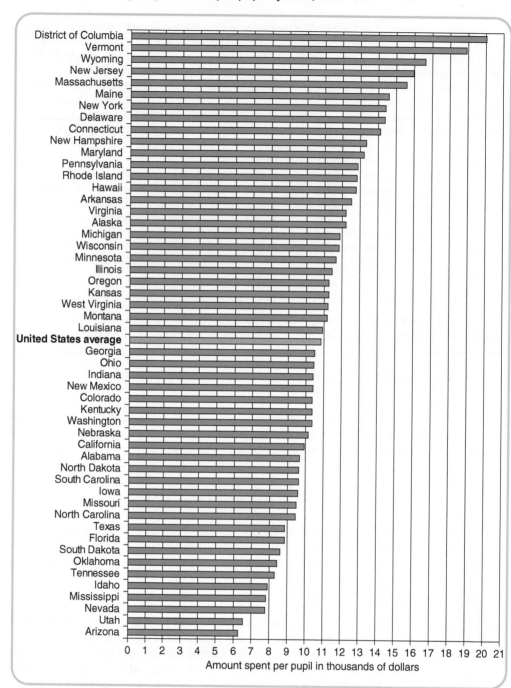

Source: National Education Association. (2009). *Rankings of the states 2008 and estimates of school statistics 2009.* Retrieved June 18, 2010, from http://www.nea.org/assets/docs/09rankings.pdf

Points of Reflection 11.5

What is your view of the connection between spending on education and student achievement? What do you base your opinions on?

criticized for increased spending when there appears to be little progress in terms of test scores. But it is a complicated issue as schools continue to struggle with the connection between spending and levels of learning.

This chapter's *In the News* feature is a story of how private funds and public schools can work together to achieve success, at least cautious success at this point in the tale. The story focuses on the Village Academy in Delray Beach, Florida, and pulls together many of the concepts discussed so far in this book including the achievement gap, segregation and integration, community involvement in schools, class size, and high expectations.

Governing and Financing Public Schools in the United States

In the News abcNEWS

The Power of the Neighborhood School

Village Academy is the first new school to be built in Delray Beach, Florida, in 30 years. Before its establishment many of Delray's children (mostly poor, mostly minority) took long bus rides to get to schools attended primarily by white children from mostly middle- to upper-class families. In this ABC video you see Village Academy as a K–2 school in the beginning. By 2007 it was a K–8 school, with plans to add a grade a year through 12th grade. Village Academy changed not only the length of the bus ride but also the attitudes of an entire community.

To view this video, go to the In the News section of Chapter 11 on MyEducationLab for this text and watch the clip *The Power of the Neighborhood School.* Then respond to these items.

1. In the video you hear that the school has many extras provided through private funding from a philanthropist.

Why is this private/public school partnership having the positive results you see at Village Academy?

2. In the video you hear the Village Academy founder say that he has replaced diversity as a goal with the development of the power of community. What does he mean by this?

3. What elements of the Village Academy qualify it as a full-service school?

4. Given what you know about the dropout epidemic in the United States, what are some plausible reasons for the high dropout rate of minority students bused to other areas from Delray Beach?

ALLOCATION OF EDUCATION FUNDING

With any large endeavor there are administrative and other costs that affect, either directly or indirectly, the cause or people served. So it is with education. It would be wonderful if 90% of an education budget could go directly into the classroom to pay teachers, buy books and supplies, and provide the latest technology. But as you saw earlier in this chapter, support for the work of individual teachers in their classrooms requires (at least as the education system is currently configured) people in district and state positions. Some of the current programs with the greatest impact require national level support as well.

Figure 11.15 shows the average expenses of a school district. Considering there are more than 15,000 school districts, labeling only about 10% of the spending as "Other support services" isn't bad. The allocation of more than 60% directly to instruction is impressive, with most spent on teacher salaries. The rest buys books, classroom supplies, technology, and so on.

- *General administration* includes district-level administrators.

- *Student transportation* mainly involves school buses. The buses must be purchased, maintained, and filled with gas, and drivers must be paid.

- *Instructional staff support* includes curriculum and instruction specialists, teacher training, and teacher assistants.

- *Student support services* include school psychologists, nurses, behavior specialists, home liaisons, and others who work with students with needs, special and otherwise (not including special education teachers).

- *School administration* refers to principals and assistant principals and funds needed to support their positions. Notice that over twice as much is spent at the school level versus the district level.

- *Operation and maintenance* includes anything related to facilities—building repair, custodial staff, lights, water, heat, air-conditioning, and grounds.

Figure 11.15 How funds are spent at the district level

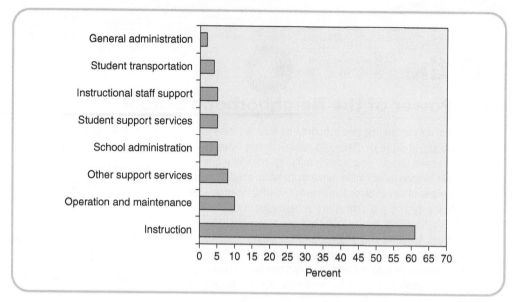

Source: U.S. Census Bureau. (2009). Public education finances. Washington, DC: Author.

CONCLUDING THOUGHTS

The only way teachers can hope to understand and possibly influence the more political aspects of education in the United States—basically what happens outside the individual classroom—is, first of all, to be informed. It's actually very interesting to learn about the support systems that help us do what we do in the classroom. You can be engaged by keeping up with education-related current events at all levels and informed by reading education journals and books. The second step to affecting the bigger picture of education is to have the will to be involved, to step outside the classroom doors and advocate for children in the larger arena of the community, the district, the state, and the nation.

After reading the *Chapter in Review,* read about Chris, Brenda, and Tim as they advocate for an after-school arts program at Rees Elementary. Then respond to items in this chapter's *Developing Professional Competence*.

Chapter in Review

How does the federal government influence public education in the United States?

- The president, the U.S. Congress, and the federal court system endorse specific programs and make and enforce laws that impact schools.
- The U.S. Department of Education initiates programs and mandates the compliance of states using federal money as leverage.

What is the state's role in public education?

- Each state has its own unique governance system.
- State governors, legislatures, and court systems all impact the functioning of education within the state.

- A state board of education is a volunteer policy-making body that has oversight responsibilities.
- A state department of education functions under the leadership of a state superintendent and many administrators who work to support schools and teachers.

How do school districts function?

- A school district is made up of schools defined by geographic boundaries.
- District school boards set policies that affect the operation of schools.
- A district superintendent is the chief executive officer of a school district and may have a staff with specified duties.

What is the management structure of individual schools?

- The principal oversees every aspect of a school and answers to the district for all that occurs.
- Assistant principals and teacher leaders play important roles in school management.

What other entities impact the governance of public schools in the United States?

- Parents and families have the potential to positively impact student success in school.
- Businesses have a vested interest in effective schools that prepare their employees and consumers. Business-school partnerships benefit both.
- Universities and teacher education faculty prepare teachers and impact education.
- Special interest groups are composed of concerned citizens who work for the benefit of specific causes within schools.

How are public schools financed?

- On average, state and local funding share about 92% of the funding burden equally, with federal funds accounting for most of the rest.
- Federal funds are either earmarked for specific purposes in the form of categorical grants or given for states to use at their discretion in the form of block grants.
- State funds are generated primarily through sales taxes and income taxes.
- Most local funds usually come from property taxes, a controversial source.
- Private donations provide boosts to specific programs and efforts but account for a very small percentage of total school funding.

How are funds for education spent?

- The amount spent on each student, the expenditure per pupil, varies greatly from state to state.
- Over half of the money spent on public education goes for expenses related to classroom instruction. The rest is spent on support services, including administration, facilities, and transportation.

Developing Professional Competence

Visit the Developing Professional Competence section on Chapter 11 of the MyEducationLab for this text to answer the following questions and begin your preparation for licensure exams.

The arts emphasis at Rees Elementary School is more extensive than in most elementary schools. Both fine arts and performance arts are part of the everyday world of Rees students. They learn about art and do art during the school day, with evidence of this on display throughout the school. But as their student population begins to shift, and the teachers become aware of more and more students going home to empty houses and remaining there for several hours before their parents get home from long days at work, Chris, Brenda, and Tim decide it's time to take art beyond the 3 P.M. afternoon dismissal bell. To do this will take time and money.

Chris Roberts has a good idea about what's involved in working through the public school governance system, thanks to his experiences with the initiation of multiage classrooms. He has volunteered to take on the task of finding support for the idea of Afternoon Arts and finding funding to make it happen. He understands the meaning and value of these two pertinent standards:

INTASC Principle 10, Knowledge

The teacher understands schools as organizations within the larger community context and understands the operations of the relevant aspects of the system(s) within which s/he works.

NBPTS

Accomplished teachers can evaluate school progress and the allocation of school resources in light of their understanding of state and local educational objectives.

Think through this scenario and answer the following multiple-choice questions:

1. What challenges do you anticipate that may stem from the fact that Rees Elementary is in Utah?
   a. Utah is a rural state and incorporating the arts may be difficult.

b. Utah's per pupil expenditure is comparatively quite low.

c. There may be resistance among the new families in the Rees attendance zone.

d. There are few models of arts programs.

2. In what order would Chris want to present the Afternoon Arts program to individuals and groups to gain approval and possible funding?

a. principal, district arts director, community businesses, families.

b. families, principal, district arts director, state curriculum director.

c. principal, community businesses, families, district arts director.

d. principal, district arts director, state curriculum director, families.

3. Rees has a state arts grant, but this funding will be withdrawn next year, given the tough economic times. Which of the following would *not* be a possible source of funding for Afternoon Arts?

a. community businesses contributing to the program

b. district funding designated for at-risk students

c. federal categorical grant

d. federal block grant

Now it's time for you to respond to two short essay items involving the scenario. In your responses, be sure to address all the dilemmas and questions posed in each item. Your responses should each be between one half and one double-spaced page.

4. Refer to item 2. In one well-developed sentence for each, describe the kind of support Chris might expect from the people/groups in the response choices.

5. The teachers who believe in the potential of Afternoon Arts will likely want to be part of the program. Should they be paid for the 3 hours a day required, or should the intrinsic value of the program and what it may mean to kids who need it be enough reward for their efforts? Justify your response.

Where DO I Stand NOW?

In the beginning of the chapter you responded to 40 items, indicating your level of agreement with each concerning who and/or what agency should be in charge of which aspects of school. Now that you have read the chapter, completed exercises related to the content, engaged in class discussions and so on, complete the following items in your course notebook.

1. What is one aspect of how the federal government interacts with public education that you think is viable and why? What is one aspect of how the federal government interacts with public education that you do *not* agree with and why?

2. From what you now know about sources of funding for public schools, with which aspect do you agree most (examples: federal percentage and use; state percentage and where it comes from; local funding through property taxes; other)?

3. Look back at *Where Do I Stand?* and determine one item on which your opinion varies by least 2 points from what you now know to be reality. Have you changed your opinion? If so, why? If not, why not?

MyEducationLab

The MyEducationLab for this course can help you solidify your comprehension of Chapter 11 concepts.

• Explore the classrooms of the teachers and students you've met in this chapter in the Teaching in Focus section.

• Prepare for licensure exams as you deepen your understanding of chapter concepts in the Developing Professional Competence section.

• Gauge and further develop your understanding of chapter concepts by taking the quizzes and examining the enrichment materials on the Chapter 11 Study Plan.

• Visit Topic 5, "Governance and Finance," to watch ABC videos, explore Assignments and Activities, and practice essential teaching skills with the Building Teaching Skills and Dispositions unit.

References

Azzam, A. M. (2005). The funding gap. *Educational Leadership, 62*(5), 93.

Biddle, B., & Berliner, D. (2002). Unequal school funding in the United States. *Educational Leadership, 59*(8), 48-59.

Brimley, V., & Garfield, R. (2004). *Financing education* (9th ed.). Boston: Allyn & Bacon.

Council of Chief State School Officers. (2006). *Chief state school officers method of selection.* Retrieved June 20, 2005, from http://www.ccsso.org/chief_state_school_officers/method_of_selection/index.cfm

Hess, F. M. (2002). *School boards at the dawn of the 21st century: Conditions and challenges of district governance.* Arlington, VA: National School Boards Association. Retrieved June 10, 2007, from http://www.nsba.org/site/docs/1200/1143.pdf

Hess, F. M. (2010). Weighing the case for school boards. *Phi Delta Kappan, 91*(6), 15-19.

Lambert, L. (2003). *Leadership capacity for lasting school improvement.* Alexandria, VA: Association for Supervision and Curriculum Development.

Mizell, H. (2010). School boards should focus on learning for all. *Phi Delta Kappan, 91*(6), 20-23.

National Association of State Boards of Education. (2005). *State education governance at-a-glance.* Retrieved June 20, 2006, from http://www.nasbe.org/Educational_Issues/Governance/Governance_chart.pdf

National Education Association [NEA]. (2009). *Rankings of the states 2008 and estimates of school statistics 2009.* Retrieved June 18, 2010, from http://www.nea.org/assets/docs/09rankings.pdf

National Governors Association [NGA]. (2010). NGA center for best practices. Retrieved June 20, 2010, from http://www.nga.org/portal/ site/nga/menuitem.8274ad9c70a7bd616adcbeeb501010a0/?vgnextoid=e9e8fbc137400010VgnVCM100000 1a01010aRCRD

North American Association of State and Provincial Lotteries. (2010). *Member lotteries.* Retrieved June 18, 2010, from http://www.naspl.org

Nylander, A. (2007). National school board survey. Retrieved June 23, 2010, from http://www.oldham.kyschools.us/files/reports/National_Surveys/National%20School%20Board%20Survey%202007%20Final%20Results_pdf.pdf

Sergiovani, T. J. (2001). *The principalship: A reflective practice perspective* (4th ed.). Boston: Allyn & Bacon.

Snider, J. H. (June 2010). It's the public's data: Democratizing school board records. *Education Week.* Retrieved from http://www.edweek.org/login.html?source=http://www.edweek.org/ew/articles/2010/06/16/ 35snider.h29.html&destination=http://www.edweek.org/ew/articles/2010/06/16/35snider.h29.html&levelId=2100

White House. (2010). *Education.* Retrieved June 17, 2010, from http://www.whitehouse.gov/issues/education

U.S. Census Bureau. (2009). *Public education finances 2007.* Retrieved June 17, 2010, from http://www2.census.gov/govs/school/07f33pub.pdf

U.S. Department of Education. (2001[A1]). *Statistics of state school systems: Revenues and expenditures for public elementary and secondary education.* Washington, DC: U.S. Department of Education, National Center for Education Statistics. Retrieved August 2, 2006, from http://www.nces.ed.gov.

U.S. Department of Education. (2006). *The federal role in education.* Retrieved July 27, 2006, from www.ed.gov/about/overview/fed/role.html

U.S. Department of Education. (2009). Characteristics of public, private, and Bureau of Indian Education elementary and secondary school principals in the United States. Retrieved June 18, 2010, from http://nces.ed.gov/pubs2009/2009323/tables.asp

Index

Page references followed by "f" indicate illustrated figures or photographs; followed by "t" indicates a table.